Doing Business in Today's Hong Kong

A review of what makes Hong Kong work

BY MEMBERS OF AMCHAM, HONG KONG

Published in association with
The American Chamber of Commerce
in Hong Kong

HONG KONG
OXFORD UNIVERSITY PRESS
OXFORD   NEW YORK
1988

Oxford University Press

Oxford   New York   Toronto
Petaling Jaya   Singapore   Hong Kong   Tokyo
Delhi   Bombay   Calcutta   Madras   Karachi
Nairobi   Dar es Salaam   Cape Town
Melbourne   Auckland

and associated companies in
Berlin   Ibadan

First edition published by AmCham Publications 1976
Second edition published by South China Morning Post Ltd in
conjunction with The American Chamber of Commerce in Hong Kong 1980
This edition first published by Oxford University Press in association with
the Publications Department of The American Chamber
of Commerce in Hong Kong 1988
Published in the United States
by Oxford University Press, Inc., New York

ISBN 0 19 584296 0

British Library
Cataloguing-in-publication Data
available

Library of Congress
Cataloging-in-publication Data
available

Printed in Hong Kong by Nordica Printing Co.
Published by Oxford University Press, Warwick House, Hong Kong

Contents

Appendices

Illustrations

Figures

Maps

Preface

Doing Business in Today's Hong Kong was first published by the American Chamber of Commerce in 1976. An updated edition followed a few years later, and the title has proved to be a valuable and established reference for both new-comers and old-timers in the local and regional business community.

In view of the dynamic nature of Hong Kong, we have decided to once again update this useful publication. We are indebted to members and others who have contributed to the project, and are also delighted that an agreement has been reached with Oxford University Press to co-publish the new edition.

We hope *Doing Business in Today's Hong Kong, Edition III,* will help businessmen both in Hong Kong and overseas to better understand the opportunities of doing business in the world's foremost free and fair trade city market.

Paul M. F. Cheng
President
The American Chamber of Commerce in Hong Kong

Foreword

Hong Kong remains a superb place to do business. Its attractions include totally free markets, a modern global communications system, major banking facilities, an extensive transportation network, and skilled English-speaking personnel. It is both an important market for American goods and services, and an excellent base of operations for business with the People's Republic of China and other East Asian nations. More and more American companies are establishing a presence in Hong Kong.

It is said that Hong Kong is one of the easiest places in the world for foreign businesses to establish themselves. While it is true that foreign companies can quickly begin operations in Hong Kong, a basic knowledge of Hong Kong and its groundrules improves firms' capabilities and prospects.

Doing Business in Today's Hong Kong, prepared by the American Chamber of Commerce in Hong Kong, is an important source of such knowledge. Newcomers to Hong Kong and veterans alike will profit from the information presented. I am confident that this book will assist you in your efforts to do business in Hong Kong and enable you to contribute to and profit from this unique international center of business and finance.

Donald M. Anderson
United States Consul General
Hong Kong

Acknowledgements

The American Chamber of Commerce in Hong Kong
Executive Director: Ralph Spencer

Executive Committee
President: Paul M F Cheng
First Vice President: Richard Johannessen Jr
Vice Presidents: William W Flanz; Joseph F Movizzo; Henry Steiner; Edward W Tilling
Treasurer: Edward Onderko
Governors: William T Alumkal; Peter F Barrett; William A Best Jr; Alex Blum; Michael Clancy; Robert K Giss; Henrietta Ho; John T Kamm; Jeffrey A. Marks; Jeffrey S Muir; Clark T Randt Jr; Glen C Rasmussen; Raylene B Thompson
Ex-Officio Governor : Ira D Kaye

Doing Business In Today's Hong Kong Subcommittee
Sean G Spence (Chairman)
E Barton
R Hinshaw
Ted Powell

Publications Department
Publications Manager: Fred S Armentrout
Publications Assistant: Katherine Kong
Publications Secretary: Phoebe Fan
Computer Assistance: Steven Townsend
Contributing Editors: Kenneth Barrett, Barry Parr
Illustrations and Map Updating: Unity Design Studio
Cover Design: Henry Steiner
Cover Slide: Courtesy of Hong Kong Tourist Association
Industrial Map: Courtesy of Jones Lang Wootton
MTR Map: Courtesy of Mass Transit Railway Corporation
Land-use Map: Reprint Permission of Hong Kong Government
Three-dimensional Maps of Hong Kong: Reprint Permission of Topomedia International

Introduction

by Sean G. Spence

The contribution of American companies to Hong Kong's development as an important powerhouse of commerce in Asia can be measured in many ways. One is the sheer monetary value of US investment here. Another is the liveliness of The American Chamber of Commerce in Hong Kong. Membership of AmCham has grown significantly in the last few years, not least because membership is open to non-American companies, and it has been an exciting forum for bringing Hong Kong's ever growing international business community closer together.

It is therefore understandable that businessmen setting up for the first time in Hong Kong, or arriving to take up new posts here, as well as those who have been active here for a long time but who are always interested in exploring new ideas, should look to the Chamber's publications for an insight into what makes Hong Kong tick. When the Business Expansion Committee of AmCham was asked to produce a new edition of this publication, it was soon evident that merely addressing the facts of doing business in Hong Kong would only partially satisfy readers' needs. The authors of this edition have therefore attempted to focus on the issues which face businessmen. What is the special chemistry that makes Hong Kong such an important meeting place for the economic powers of the world? How is Hong Kong developing its role in the broad spectrum of industries in which it participates? What do the answers to these questions mean for the newly arrived businessman who may be equipped only with a suitcase and some good ideas? Within the confines of this publication we have not attempted to give a comprehensive answer to these and all the other questions which are bound to arise. However, we do hope that this book will help its readers to ask the right questions and know what to do with the answers.

As a work which distills the thoughts and enthusiasms of a wide range of members of the Chamber, it is almost impossible to give full acknowledgement to all who have helped in its production. The authors themselves especially deserve our thanks for producing their manuscripts while somehow carrying on with their demanding jobs and for patiently and enthusiastically responding to 'suggestions'. In addition, many others made contributions which helped influence the direction of the book, among whom special thanks are due to: Bob Wilson; Barry Parr; Richard Golombek; Roger Hinshaw; Ed Barton; Tom Goetz; Ted Powell; Mark Blacker; Mary Faith Higgins; Peter Barrett; Fred Fredricks; and Henry Steiner.

Even during the preparation of the final drafts, major changes were taking place in Hong Kong—in its evolving relationship with the PRC, in the extent of Japanese and European investment here, in the relationship between Hong Kong and its major market, the US, in Hong Kong's relationship with its neighbors to the north and south in Asia, and in the emergence of new industries. The speed of these changes and the challenge of keeping pace with them are part of the fun of doing business here. We hope this book in some small way helps its readers to participate, with profit, in this exciting community.

Sean G. Spence was chairman of an AmCham subcommittee charged with the production of this book. He is an Associate with Russell Reynolds Associates Inc.

Chapter 1

Backdrop

by Thomas D. Gorman

Overview

* Hong Kong is a city of change, a master of survival against great odds.
* Hard-headed yet superstitious, sophisticated yet easily panicked, rooted in China yet Western-oriented: business in Hong Kong can be paradoxical.
* Hong Kong's history is relevant to its present and future.
* China is playing an increasingly crucial role in Hong Kong's economic life — and vice versa.
* Hong Kong people temper their pride of being Chinese with a distaste for Chinese politics.

Hong Kong's ultra-dynamic environment is a catalyst for change, and a continual challenge to its people's ingenious ability to adapt and respond to it. Few cities in history have had the challenge, or the privilege, of such dramatic change in so short a time span.

Books, like this one, which offer guidelines on doing business in a particular market must concentrate not only on current and projected market conditions, but also those changing economic, social and political factors that have such a strong impact on the business environment. Given the rapid and fundamental changes in Hong Kong since the 1950s, as well as the future reversion of the territory to Chinese sovereignty, it is .essential to acquire some historical perspective before we can come to an understanding of business in Hong Kong. Failure to consider the paradox, the contradictions, and the underlying currents and crosscurrents at play in Hong Kong's development into an international trade center would be a serious omission in business planning.

A typical visitor's perspective on Hong Kong is not unlike the view from a speeding roller coaster: focusing beyond the next turn or looking backward is all the more challenging because the immediate present is so gripping.

Looking Backward

Strange as it may seem today, for the quarter century preceding the mid-1970s, the view from Hong Kong to North America or Europe seemed clearer, and in some respects nearer, than the view to China. Up until that time, North American and European markets were far more important to Hong Kong than the Chinese market, and in Hong Kong, it has traditionally been the market which commands the most attention.

Until the early 1950s, when the United Nations enacted its embargo on trade in strategic goods with China during the Korean War, Hong Kong was primarily a trading and trans-shipment point for China trade. The embargo, coupled with an influx of industrialists leaving China as the new PRC government made life difficult for capitalists, spurred the birth of Hong Kong's light manufacturing base. Wave after wave of immigrants from China fueled the manufacturing sector's supply of cheap, productive labor, and almost four decades of export-led growth followed.

A generation later, Hong Kong's laissez-faire environment and geographical position had attracted international financial institutions and deal-making enough to catapult it into leadership as a world financial center, behind London and New York. Reinvigoration of China's foreign trade in the late 1970s contributed to the rebirth and diversification of the entrepot business and the service sector in Hong Kong. By the mid-1980s the service sector was taking up slack from manufacturing in share of work force employed.

Such rapid growth brought prosperity, higher wage rates, and the demand to move up-market to compete in overseas markets for traditional domestic manufactures, such as garments, textiles, consumer electronics, plastic products, toys, watches, photographic and optical products, telecommunications, light machine tools, etc.

Foreign investment and international business presence in Hong Kong grew steadily, and the skyline developed a profile that would be the envy of city fathers anywhere in the world. Milton Friedman and others hailed Hong Kong as the bastion of unshackled free enterprise.

Side by side with the sophistication of world class commercial and communication facilities, however, is juxtaposed a fairly superstitious set of attitudes that prevail in traditional business circles. Even some of the most hard-headed business executives place great stock in the influence of geomancy, or *fung shui*, in determining, among other things, the most auspicious timing for business deals, the most appropriate location for new office facilities, and interior design schemes that maximize a manager's lucky tendencies.

China Questions

1997

Following the death in 1976 of Chairman Mao, and the tremendous changes brought by Deng Xiaoping's open door policy, beginning in 1978-79, the economic integration of Hong Kong and China has led to an expanded degree of mutual awareness in a relatively short period of time. For China, this process has been concurrent with increased economic involvement in world markets generally. In Hong Kong the process has had special political significance and sensitivity, as people prepare for the coming transition from colonial status to a Special Administrative Region of the People's Republic of China on July 1, 1997.

Hong Kong in the 1980s has been dominated by developments relating to the Sino-British agreement on the future of Hong Kong. From 1982-84, the territory had a severe case of jitters while the Sino-British talks were held, initially in an environment of visible acrimony. Likewise, international business was anxious to see whether steps would be taken to maintain Hong Kong's uniquely favorable investment and trade climate.

The outcome of the Sino-British negotiations, as embodied in the Joint Declaration, has met with a positive reception by international business, and a cautiously positive reception by the local populace, acutely conscious of the fact that the only alternative to the Joint Declaration as presented was no declaration at all.

Local public opinion in Hong Kong toward the future political status of the territory rests on a kind of seesaw, with one end weighted by the pride of being Chinese, and the other end weighted by a distrust of Chinese communism. The achievements of the colonial administration over the past 140 years are obvious and account for much—some would say most—of Hong Kong's success in developing into a world trade center with a prosperous economy and stable social environment. However, the roots of Hong Kong's historical status as a colony are tangled in among a century or more of Western exploitation of China's internal weaknesses.

Although most international investors may not dwell on it, the average Hong Kong adult is aware that Hong Kong owes its beginnings as a British colony to the Opium War, fought because of China's impatience with growing supplies of opium being brought in and sold by British and other Western merchants.

Hong Kong Island was ceded in perpetuity to the British by the Treaty of Nanking, signed in 1842 after China's loss in the Opium War of 1839. Kowloon Peninsula and Stonecutters Island were ceded in perpetuity by the Convention of Peking in 1860. In 1898, the Second Convention of Peking gave Britain a 99-year lease on the New Territories, a 365-square-mile area between Kowloon and the Chinese border, including 235 offshore islands. The lease of the largest portion of Hong Kong's territory, the New Territories, occurred close to, and in a few cases actually during, the lifetimes of

Hong Kong's nonagenarians and some of the more aged Chinese leaders.

The People's Republic of China, founded in 1949, did not recognize treaties that were, from their viewpoint, signed at gunpoint with an illegitimate regime. One of China's early actions upon joining the United Nations was to write to the United Nations committee handling decolonization matters, suggesting that Hong Kong and Macau be removed from the list of remaining colonies. Ambassador Huang Hua wrote: 'They are Chinese territories which have been under the occupation of the British and Portuguese authorities, respectively. The solution to this question falls entirely within the sphere of Chinese sovereignty and does not belong to the category which is usually called "colony". ' The Chinese request was accepted, and the media in Hong Kong gradually began referring to Hong Kong as 'the territory' rather than 'the colony'. China had already given a clear public sign that she viewed Hong Kong as a special exception to the rules, a situation she was willing to tolerate in a fairly practical way for an unstated period of time, as long as her ultimate sovereignty was respected.

Opening Doors

A generation of isolationism and extreme xenophobia ended soon after Chairman Mao's death with the consolidation of power by Deng Xiaoping. The new regime gave priority to accelerating China's foreign trade, and to the encouragement of foreign investment to bring in new technology, management skills and capital. Hong Kong was ideally positioned to assist, with its well-oiled facilities, its efficient work force, and its international ties in finance, culture and language.   Chinese corporations eagerly expanded and diversified their investments in capitalist Hong Kong, in manufacturing, real estate, retail business, shipping, publishing, insurance, financial services, tourism, and other industries. Chinese banks became an aggressive force in retail banking in Hong Kong, and a Chinese investment company launched foreign currency-denominated bond issues. Various Chinese provinces opened trade offices in Hong Kong.

Hong Kong's trade performance tracked the rapid growth of China's import and export trade, and Hong Kong provided something on the order of 60 percent of total foreign investment in China, much of it concentrated in nearby Special Economic Zones. The greater number of PRC Chinese corporations in Hong Kong—hundreds in the mid-1980s compared to a dozen or so 10 years earlier—helped attract foreign companies to set up shop in Hong Kong as a convenient China trade staging point.

In addition to the soaring import, export, and re-export business for Hong Kong after the 1970s, China emerged for the first time as a major new market for Hong Kong's domestic manufactured goods, including microcomputers, electronic components, telecommunications equipment and consumer electronic products. This helped insulate Hong Kong from the woes of its neighbors, like Singapore, faced with sluggish demand and growing protectionism in key overseas markets during the mid-1980s.

During the mid-1970s, China traders were a rare breed of individual in Hong Kong. Before China's door opened, trade contacts were largely restricted to the twice-yearly Canton Trade Fair, and business opportunities were very limited by today's standards. The fastest route to Beijing from Hong Kong took more than 24 hours, and the process of obtaining a visa was slow and cumbersome.

By the mid-1980s, most Hong Kong business people were China traders in one way or another. Transport links between Hong Kong and China—road, rail, air, sea—exploded in number and volume of freight and passengers carried. Despite early fears that the Special Economic Zones would compete with Hong Kong, one positive result was that they offered Hong Kong manufacturers access to cheaper land and labor for less sophisticated manufacturing and assembly sub-contracting.

In 1979, with China's door firmly opened, Chinese leader Deng Xiaoping stated that the three primary goals of China during the 1980s were to modernize the economy, to reunify the nation (a reference to Taiwan, Hong Kong and Macau), and to combat hegemony (a reference to the rivalry between the United States and the Soviet Union). All three had direct or indirect bearing on the question of Hong Kong's future.

It was also in 1979 when the then-governor of Hong Kong, Sir Murray Maclehose, was invited to visit Beijing, the first visit of a Hong Kong governor. Sir Murray discussed the question of Hong Kong's future with Deng Xiaoping, and although the contents of the discussion have not been made public, it is widely believed Deng stated China's unequivocal position that China did not recognize the three treaties and looked upon Hong Kong as part of China. Sir Murray reported, on his return, Deng's message to investors to 'put their hearts at ease.'

Preludes to Agreement

By 1982, with the expiration of the lease on the New Territories only 15 years away, pressure grew in Hong Kong for some reassurances about the future. In September, 1982, British Prime Minister Margaret Thatcher visited Beijing, and raised the question of Hong Kong with Premier Zhao Ziyang as well as Mr Deng. The discussions appeared to a somewhat cynical Hong Kong public to be less than cordial, prompting an immediate drop in the Hang Seng Index and the Hong Kong dollar's value. To make matters worse, the Hong Kong press seized upon Mrs Thatcher's stumbling on the steps of the Great Hall of the People, from which she emerged with her contingent after the discussion with Premier Zhao. Unhurt, her final posture in the slip had nonetheless resembled a kowtow in the direction of the late Chairman Mao Tse-tung's mausoleum.

Flexibility, responsiveness to changing trends, adaptability, and resilience in the face of adverse circumstances: these are a few of the descriptive accolades Hong Kong people have earned in recent decades, and some of the factors cited for the territory's outstanding economic success. Despite the previous tests to which these qualities had been subjected, the run-up to 1997 proved to be the greatest test of all.

From the time of Mrs Thatcher's visit until the signing of the Joint Declaration in December 1984, Hong Kong was bothered by uncertainty over its future. The period was marked by limited but worrying outbreaks of social unrest, including a public protest against cost increases (in particular, for electricity) as the Hong Kong dollar declined in value, and a taxi strike that triggered riots and resulted in 130 arrests. The worst point was September 1983, when the Hong Kong dollar plummetted to 9.5 against the American dollar following the fourth round of Sino-British talks, which were perceived to be tense and strained. As the Hang Seng Index dropped a cool 65 points to 785, the panic buying of rice and toilet paper left some supermarket shelves empty.

The crisis gripped the business community, and came at a time when serious woes in Hong Kong's once booming property market were already causing bankruptcies and threatening the viability of some major local companies. Hong Kong's trade partners lost confidence in the local unit and insisted on prices being quoted in other currencies.

Reversing his earlier position that no measures were required or indeed possible to shore up the battered currency, Hong Kong's then-financial secretary, Sir John Bremridge, hastily returned from overseas and announced that the Hong Kong dollar would be pegged to the US dollar at the rate of HK$7.80 to US$1. He also abolished the 10 percent withholding tax on Hong Kong dollar deposits, putting them on an equal tax footing with foreign currency deposits.

Within a few days, the Hong Kong dollar stabilized in the range of 8.37, and soon gravitated near to the pegged value. The speed with which the remedial measures worked seemed incredible. The effect was like a fever being broken. Nonetheless, the media reaction underlined what a hapless position the Hong Kong government occupied in the 1997 scenario, as the press flung accusations at the British of using the currency crisis to enhance their negotiating stance, only stepping in at the last possible moment to save the dollar.

Although details of the Sino-British talks remain confidential, there is widespread speculation that the notable warming in atmosphere between the fourth round, preceding the September crisis, and the fifth round, which began October 18, was a result of Britain's clear signal to China that she would yield on the fundamental and emotionally charged issue of Hong Kong's sovereignty.

It was only after the fifth round of talks that the phrase 'useful and constructive' came to be used by official spokesmen to describe the just concluded talks. 'Useful and constructive' came to be a familiar refrain, eventually becoming synonymous in Hong Kong with diplomatic doublespeak.

But if one fever had been broken, Hong Kong was not yet fully cured.

Another steep drop in the Hang Seng Index was caused by the announcement in March 1984 that one of Hong Kong's oldest and biggest British trading firms, Jardine Matheson and Company—the model for *Noble House* in James Clavell's novels—was moving its corporate holding company to Bermuda. Despite the company's public assurances that this was only a legal move, involving no departure of people or assets, a skeptical public tended to see it as a case of 'cut and run' when the going gets rough. Pun-loving Cantonese newspapermen also had a go at the Cantonese pronunciation of the late governor Sir Edward Youde's Chinese name, which rhymed with 'ready to leave.' With no direct role in discussing their future, Hong Kong people understandably felt awash in powerful historical currents which would determine their own and their children's future.

Perhaps the ultimate sign of panicky behavior came in May 1984, when a run occurred, not on a bank, but on a cake shop. In Hong Kong it is customary for wedding guests to receive cakes, and for convenience these are often distributed in the form of gift certificates. People who attend many weddings accumulate a number of these coupons over a period of time. So, when a rumor about the financial viability of Hong Kong's leading cake shop swept through the market, thousands of people descended upon the 47 branches of the cake shop chain to cash in their coupons, in fear that the value might be lost. An incredible effort was mounted by the still viable cake shop company, which made good on all the coupons within a two-day period. Some people were seen leaving the shops with 10 or more cakes.

Ironically, international interest in freewheeling capitalist Hong Kong was whetted by the unprecedented level of publicity about it in overseas press reports during the period of Hong Kong's highest anxiety. Most of the international publicity, while identifying the uncertainties about the long-term future, was positive. On the tourist front, a surge of arrivals was due at least in part to the overseas perception that those who wanted to see the real Hong Kong should do so post-haste.

Partly as a result of publicity, but mostly because of economic factors, American investment in manufacturing in Hong Kong continued to grow throughout the uncertain 1982-84 period. After a brief lag during the same time, Japanese investment also picked up, spurred even more briskly in 1986 by the record strength of the yen, with Japanese companies seeking less expensive manufacturing sources.

Most wealthier Hong Kong people long ago acquired foreign passports as a means of providing a safety valve in the event of future need, and for traveling convenience in the meantime. Others who can afford them will likely endeavor to do the same. Some American and other foreign corporations have provided overseas assignments as a benefit to key staff to assist them in acquiring foreign passports. Many of the younger professional people who have opted for an overseas posting still prefer to return to Hong Kong once their stay in the foreign country has satisfied the minimum residence requirement. Returning to Hong Kong with a foreign passport, they feel they have the best of both worlds.

The Future

The period since the Joint Declaration was signed has proven that most Hong Kong people are willing to give the situation a try. Hong Kong's close trade links with China have also helped fuel a solid business recovery in the trading sector, and economics traditionally speak louder than politics in Hong Kong. Indeed, the Hang Seng Index lately soared through the 3,500 barrier.

Foreign investors, especially from the United States and Japan, seem bullish on the future of Hong Kong as a lower cost manufacturing and service base for China and Southeast Asian markets. Others have also shown interest. In 1986, for instance, a Swedish Chamber of Commerce was established in Hong Kong to cater to the needs of the 60 or more Swedish companies with operations in Hong Kong. The Canadians and British have also stepped up investment in the territory, and a British Chamber of Commerce was formed in 1987.

Protectionism in general, and especially in Hong Kong's leading export market, the United States, looms on the horizon as a threat to continued export-led growth. Hong Kong government lobbying efforts have been stepped up, but it may be that domestic American economic performance will be the most important determinant in how far protectionism is carried. Hong Kong's legendary speed and flexibility in gearing up to new market conditions will be continuously put to the test by protectionist moves in key markets. China's application to join GATT is a good sign, since her non-participation could have left Hong Kong without a big brother to go to bat for it in that important organization after 1997.

Despite its hallowed tradition of 'positive non-intervention' in business, the Hong Kong government in the mid-1980s was giving mixed signals as to the degree it was willing to step further into the realm of business. The government's rescue of several ailing banks, rising levels of taxation, and especially new tax reforms aimed at eliminating tax avoidance, raised concerns in the business community as to whether the new position was 'probable non-intervention.' In fairness, the situation is still a very favorable one for business in Hong Kong vis-a-vis the pro-business attitude of government, as well as the tax and regulatory environments.

One common observation among foreign business visitors, especially from English-speaking countries, concerns the advantage of having widespread English language ability in Hong Kong. Educators now debate the relative roles that English and Chinese should play in Hong Kong schools, and it is likely that Chinese— Cantonese as well as Mandarin—will increase in importance in the waning years of colonial administration. At the same time, concern has been expressed that Hong Kong should not lose its notable advantage in English skills, which are essential to maintain its competitive position as an international trade center.

At this writing, intense debates about the future political structure in Hong Kong are underway, coinciding with the work of the Basic Law Drafting Committee, appointed by China to draft the legislative framework to be promulgated in 1990 for the Special Administrative Region government to administer from July 1, 1997. In 1985, the first indirect elections to Hong Kong's Legislative Council whetted the appetite of some local politicians for more direct electoral participation by the people. Other conservative voices believe this to be premature and unacceptable to China. So the debate continues, and will continue to do so as 1997 approaches.

Given the traditional disinterest of Hong Kong people in political activism and public issues, many were surprised to see more than one million signatures collected in opposition to the Daya Bay nuclear power plant, currently under construction close to Hong Kong's border, in China. Although the unprecedented public outcry in Hong Kong will not forestall the project, it may signal the development of a greater sense of common public interest among Hong Kong people, and more active interest in issues affecting local society.

The outcome of the talks between China and Portugal on the timetable for Macau's reversion to Chinese administration has also borne fruit. In early 1987 it was announced that Macau's Portuguese administration will revert to Chinese rule a few days before the end of the present century, outlasting the British departure from Hong Kong by two years. Like Hong Kong, Macau will then be administered as a Special Administrative Region. The future of Hong Kong depends in large measure on China, coupled with, of course, the Hong Kong people. Even die-hard cynics in Hong Kong will admit that the dramatic reforms which have taken place in China since 1976 argue in favor of a Chinese leadership well-disposed to keeping Hong Kong on a stable and prosperous track.

For their part, Hong Kong Chinese people have acquired, in a short period of time, a much greater awareness of the situation in China. Even those who distrust the Chinese communists for historical and ideological reasons are increasingly pleased to see an economically and militarily strong China take her proper place in the world community and adjust her style of economic management toward a more market-oriented direction.

In the meantime, the important point is that, in Hong Kong, it's business as usual.

Thomas D. Gorman is President of
China Consultants International
(HK) Ltd.

Chapter 2

Legal Groundrules

by Mary Faith Higgins
Claudio de Bedin & Roy I. Delbyck

Overview

* Government controls or disclosure requirements on businesses are minimal.
* Financial statements need not be filed if a US company is a wholly-owned subsidiary of another company.
* Shelf companies may be purchased within a matter of days.
* No minimal capitalization requirements for a private company.
* Six-month visa normally granted to intending residents with employment.
* Holders of dependent visas ie spouses and children are allowed to accept employment with no special permissions.
* Minimal red tape in the granting of registration for workplaces.
* No compulsory union membership.
* Copyright laws essentially follow those of the United Kingdom, with Hong Kong a party to the Paris Convention.

Hong Kong is in business to do business. Government intervention through regulatory controls or disclosure requirements remains at a minimum despite the increasing complexity and sophistication of the territory's economic base. It is therefore not surprising that Hong Kong has no anti-trust laws. The tax bite is low: currently a maximum 18 percent for companies and 16.5 percent for individuals. Capital can be freely imported or exported and profits and dividends can be freely converted and remitted overseas.

Setting Up in Hong Kong

Overseas companies setting up in Hong Kong generally either register the overseas company with the local authorities (the presence resulting from such registration is commonly referred to as a 'branch office') or form a locally incorporated subsidiary, which, unlike the branch office, is legally distinct from the overseas company. Other permissable methods of carrying on business are partnerships and sole proprietorships. Before choosing any form of presence, the tax implications from both a Hong Kong and overseas perspective should be carefully considered.

Branch Office

Registration of Overseas Companies

Within one month of establishing a place of business in Hong

Kong, overseas companies opting for a branch office presence are required to submit various documents and forms to the Hong Kong Companies Registry. These documents include the company's articles of incorporation, bylaws, financial statements and information about its secretary and directors. Registration is somewhat more complicated if the company is not incorporated in an English-speaking jurisdiction, in which case an English translation of these documents will also be required together with various certifications by and about the translator.

The Companies Registry will also require a list of one or more persons resident in Hong Kong (it is quite common for the company to appoint a law or accounting firm or secretarial company for this purpose) who are authorized to accept, on behalf of the company, service of process and any notices required to be served on the company. Furthermore, the company will need to submit the addresses of its principal place of business in Hong Kong and of its principal place of business (if any) and registered office (or its equivalent) in the place of its incorporation.

Financial Statements

All documents filed with the Companies Registry are of public record, although relief from financial exposure does exist.

Financial statements need not be filed if a company would have qualified as a 'private company' if incorporated in Hong Kong. The Registrar of Companies generally grants an exemption to US companies from the requirement to file financial statements if the company in question is:

i) a wholly-owned subsidiary of another company or does not have more than 25 shareholders and has never had since the last day of its financial year or the date of its incorporation (whichever applies) more than 25 shareholders;

ii) not required by the law of its place of incorporation to publish its accounts or deliver copies of its accounts to any person in whose office they may be inspected as of right by members of the public; and

iii) there are no provisions in the company's constitution, articles or by-laws for the creation or issue of bearer shares or share warrants and its shares are not transferable by delivery.

Various documents will be required to be lodged with the Companies Registry to establish this exemption initially and on an ongoing basis. The exemption does not relieve the company from having to file financial statements with other government departments (eg, tax returns with the Inland Revenue Department), keep proper books of accounts and appoint auditors.

Time Frame and Other Matters

Typically, two to four months will pass from the time the first documents are submitted to the Companies Registry until a Certificate of Registration is issued. The time frame, however, differs significantly from company to company depending on the completeness of the documents initially submitted and on any complications which may arise. The government fees for maintaining and updating the registration are minimal. And, unlike a subsidiary, a branch office may generally fold its tent and leave Hong Kong without lengthy and expensive legal procedures. Branch offices can be closed by a simple filing.

Subsidiaries

An overseas company opting for a subsidiary, rather than a branch office, presence in Hong Kong generally will form a Hong Kong private company. (A Hong Kong public company is very rarely utilized as the subsidiary entity.) A private company is a company whose Articles of Association:

  i) restrict the right to transfer its shares;
 ii) limit the number of its shareholders to 50 (excluding present employees and former employees whose shareholdings continue after employment); and
iii) prohibits any invitation to the public to subscribe for any shares or debentures of the company.

Limited liability attaches to the shareholders of a private company by the inclusion of provisions to that effect in the Memorandum of Association.

Purchase of an Off-the-shelf Private Company

Rather than specially incorporating a subsidiary, the overseas parent often acquires the subsidiary by the purchase, from an accounting or law firm or secretarial company, of a ''shelf company'', ie an already incorporated private company. The information required and documents to be signed to transfer the ownership of the shelf company to the parent are involved, and in the usual case, one to two weeks may be needed. It is, however, possible to complete the process in two days. This contrasts with the far longer period required to incorporate a subsidiary or to register an overseas company.

Although the shelf company will usually have been dormant since incorporation it is essential to ensure that it is not purchased subject to existing liabilities. While there usually is a choice of shelf company names, these names are often undesirable. The newly acquired company's name can, however, be changed on application to the Companies Registry provided the desired name is not the same as, or confusingly similar to, a name already registered. It usually takes three to four weeks for the Companies Registry to approve a change of name.

Registered Office

A private company must have a registered office in Hong Kong to which all communications and notices are usually addressed. The registered office is also the place where the company is required to keep its statutory books and records. The registered office need not, however, be the place where the company carries on business.

Directors, Shareholders and Secretary

Private companies are required by law to have a secretary and at least two shareholders and two directors. Directors need not own shares in the company. Individuals and companies (subject to certain limitations where a company acts as a director) may act as secretary, directors and shareholders. To satisfy the requirement of two shareholders, the overseas parent will often appoint a nominee to hold one share in trust for it. Directors and shareholders need not be resident in Hong Kong.

Unlike directors and shareholders, the secretary, however, must, if an individual be resident in Hong Kong and, if a company, must have its registered office or place of business in Hong Kong. The secretary is often a service company provided by a law or accounting firm or secretarial company, who will also provide, if required, nominee shareholders and directors and the registered office. The CEO of a Hong Kong company is usually a managing director. The offices of president and vice-president are generally not used.

Capital Structure

There is no minimum capitalization requirement for a private company. The share capital of the company may at the time of incorporation, be denominated in any currency. Stamp Duty is payable at the rate of 0.6 percent on the authorized share capital, which may generally be increased by the shareholders at a future date. Typically, shelf companies are incorporated with a minimal authorized capital (eg HK$1,000 divided into 1,000 shares of HK$1 each) which can then be increased after the shelf company is acquired by the overseas parent. A new company can, of course, be incorporated with a larger authorized capital.

Corporate Purposes

The objects (ie corporate purposes) clauses of the Memorandum of Association of shelf companies must be checked to ensure that they are sufficiently broad to authorize the proposed activities of the subsidiary. If not, these clauses may be amended to refer specifically to all the activities in which the subsidiary intends to engage. Alternatively, if a new company were incorporated, these clauses could be tailored to the company's requirements.

Other Matters

The subsidiary is required (as is the branch office) to maintain proper books of accounts and appoint independent auditors. Although there is no requirement for private companies to file, as a matter of public record, financial statements with the Companies Registry, the Inland Revenue Department will generally require that audited financial statements accompany the subsidiary's tax return.

All Hong Kong companies are required to hold an annual general meeting of their shareholders in each calendar year although the first shareholders' meeting can be held within 18 months from the date of incorporation. No more than 15 months must elapse between the dates of any two consecutive shareholders' meetings. The Registrar of Companies may, however, in certain circumstances extend this period.

As mentioned above, folding the tent of a subsidiary is considerably more complicated and costly than closing a branch office and will usually require liquidation of the subsidiary.

Business Registration

Branch offices, subsidiaries and any other entity or person carrying on any form of trade, commerce, craftmanship, profession, calling or other activity for the purpose of gain are required to apply annually to the Inland Revenue Department for a Business Registration Certificate. Application must initially be made within one month from the commencement of business in Hong Kong by completing the appropriate form and paying the prescribed fee (currently HK$600 per annum for both a branch office and a subsidiary) to the Hong Kong government. While shelf companies will usually 'come equipped' with an existing Business Registration Certificate, it is important to check whether they do have this certificate.

If the Hong Kong presence has more than one address at which it carries on business, a Business Registration Certificate must be applied for in respect of each address. The certificate must be displayed at the address to which it relates. Any changes in the registration particulars (eg, a change from a shelf company name to a desired name) must be notified to the Inland Revenue Department within one month from the date of the change. If the Hong Kong presence carries on business under a trade name, a separate certificate must be obtained under the trade name.

Name Approval

Prior to actually proceeding with the incorporation of a subsidiary, changing the name of a shelf company, or the registration of an overseas company (ie, branch office), it is advisable to apply to the Companies Registry in writing as to whether the proposed name is available. The application must be accompanied by the prescribed fee for each proposed name. If the Companies Registry is satisfied that the proposed name is not the same as, or confusingly similar to a name already reserved or registered, then the proposed name or names may be reserved for a period of three months (and renewed for successive three-month periods) from the date of application. The amount of time required in order to obtain name approval varies but on average is about three to six weeks. Failure to reserve a name prior to submission of documents to incorporate a subsidiary or to register a branch office will lead to delays as the Companies Registry will not proceed until the name has been approved. If a proposed name is rejected by the Companies Registry, the applicant typically will submit other names for approval.

Immigration and Identity Cards

Assignment of Expatriate Personnel and their Families

Prior to assignment to Hong Kong expatriate staff should obtain an employment visa by application to the Consulate, High Commission or Visa Office of the United Kingdom in the country of the expatriate's residence. The Immigration Department is not enamored of expatriates arriving in Hong Kong on tourist visas and thereafter applying for an employment visa. British citizens, holders of a United Kingdom passport issued in the United Kingdom and certain persons having a close connection to Hong Kong by birth or residence do not require employment visas before taking up employment in Hong Kong.

Typically, the branch office or subsidiary will sponsor the expatriate and undertake to the Immigration Department to repatriate him or her at the cessation of employment in Hong Kong. Before issuing the employment visa, the Immigration Department requires various documents from the employer and the employee which will generally include copies of the Business Registration Certificate, the Certificate of Incorporation (if a subsidiary) or Certificate of Registration (if a branch office), the expatriate's diplomas and resume, financial information concerning the employer, a statement as to why the position cannot be filled by a local hire and an outline of the compensation package. Since a period of at least two months is required for completion of this paperwork, the application should be filed well in advance of proposed departure dates.

A visa authorizing a one-entry stay of six months is normally issued first to intending residents. Applications for extensions and for multiple re-entry visas can be made at the head office of the Immigration Department in Kowloon or at any of its 10 branches on Hong Kong Island, in Kowloon or the New Territories.

Dependents, which under the present policy are usually regarded as being the wife and children of the holder of an employment visa, will apply for a dependent's visa for Hong Kong. This is generally granted on the production of the marriage and birth certificates. Further, the holders of dependent visas are allowed to accept employment without additional paperwork or permission from the authorities.

Tourist Visas

The following visa restrictions apply to visitors to Hong Kong:

United Kingdom citizens may enter Hong Kong for stays of up to six months without a visa.

Visitors holding the following passports may enter Hong Kong for visa-free stays of up to three months:

Andorra	Italy	Austria
Liechtenstein	Belgium	Luxembourg

Brazil	Monaco	Netherlands
Chile	Norway	Colombia
Portugal	Denmark	San Marino
Ecuador	Spain	Eire
Sweden	Israel	Switzerland
British	Turkey	
Commonwealth		
Citizens		

Visitors holding the following passports may enter Hong Kong for visa-free stays of up to one month:

Bolivia	Mexico	Costa Rica
Nepal	Nicaragua	El Salvador
Pakistan	Finland	Panama
Paraguay	Greece	Peru
Guatemala	Tunisia	Honduras
Iceland	Uruguay	Venezuela
Dominican	West Germany	United States
Republic		

Thai passport holders may remain in Hong Kong for up to 14 days without a visa and nationals of US Trust Territories and all countries other than those listed below are granted stays of up to seven days without the need for further formalities.

Holders of the following passports and all stateless persons always require a visa regardless of their length of stay in Hong Kong:

Albania	Libya	Afghanistan
Mongolia	Argentina	North Korea
Cambodia	People's Republic	Romania
Czechoslovakia	of China	Cuba
South Yemen	East Germany	Soviet Union
Hungary	Taiwan	Iran
Vatican States	Laos	Vietnam

Visitors are required to hold onward or return tickets and to have adequate funds to cover their expenses in Hong Kong without accepting employment.

Because the policies of the Immigration Department may change from time to time, the above information should be confirmed before coming to Hong Kong.

Identity Cards

Under the Registration of Persons Ordinance, virtually anyone over the age of 11 who enters and intends to stay in Hong Kong for more than 180 days must apply for a Hong Kong Identity Card. Identity Cards can be obtained by applying at one of the four Registration of Persons offices in the Territory. An adult must apply for an Adult Identity Card within 30 days of becoming a Hong Kong resident or reaching 18, and an application for a Juvenile Identity Card should be made on behalf of persons between the ages of 11-17 within 30 days of his or her becoming a resident or reaching age 11. There is no charge for the issuing of an Identity Card.

Workplaces

In Hong Kong the proprietor of a registrable workplace (which would include factories, mines, quarries and places in which 'dangerous' or 'scheduled' trades are performed) must, before the first occasion on which any industrial process is commenced or before any industrial operation is carried on there, apply to the Commissioner of Labor for a certificate of registration or for a provisional registration. These will not be granted to workplaces in a new non-industrial building, except in certain circumstances when the ground floor of a new non-industrial building may be issued with a provisional registration.

Labor Department inspectors will visit all premises applying for registration and will suggest alterations and modifications to ensure the health and safety of workers. Particular attention is paid to the provision of adequate lighting, floor space, fresh air, lavatories and drinking water for employees. Other government agencies, typically the Fire Services Department, will at some stage either be involved or be required to give their consent that the laws and regulations relating to their sphere of interest have been complied with.

Companies planning to rent industrial space should contact the Labor Department in advance to avoid becoming occupants of a workplace that may be unregistrable. In addition to its authority to refuse to issue a registration, the Commissioner of Labor can also cancel an existing registration. Further, magistrates are empowered to order the closing of premises at which dangerous conditions and practices exist and the proprietors of such workplaces and other specified persons may be subject to various fines and other penalties.

Although strict compliance with the various laws relating to industrial premises are required, the Hong Kong goverment does not impose as much "red tape" as is apparent in many other countries. The time needed to obtain the required certificates and approvals to start a factory or manufacturing process will depend upon the particular characteristics of each application.

Employment Regulations

There are a number of ordinances that affect the employment of individuals in Hong Kong and the rights and duties as between employer and employee.

The Employment Ordinance, in general, regulates the relationship between an employer and employee in respect of employment contracts (either written or oral) providing for a salary of up to and including a specified monthly amount. The ordinance deals with a variety of matters including maternity protection, rest days, payments of wages, severance pay, sickness allowance, holiday and annual leave payments, employment agencies, etc.

Contracts which exceed the specified monthly amount fall outside of the Employment Ordinance and are generally only construed in accordance with the contractual relationship that exists between an employer and employee. In view of the fact that disputes may arise, it is advisable to ensure that employees, in all cases, have a written employment contract.

There is no compulsory union membership in Hong Kong. Nevertheless, pursuant to the Employment Ordinance, employers are now obliged to allow workers to be members of trade unions and to allow them the right at any appropriate time to take part in trade union activities.

Additionally, there is legislation in Hong Kong relating to employees' compensation. This has general application excepting, however, persons employed casually, out-workers or any members of the employer's family. The legislation provides a "code" for injury compensation and the mode of calculation for such payments. The liability to pay compensation is not, however, absolute, particularly if an employee was negligent and as a result contributed to the accident. An important point to note is that employers must arrange for compulsory insurance to cover themselves against possible claims.

Trade Marks

Hong Kong's law governing trade marks, design registration, patents and copyright follow essentially the law of the United Kingdom.

The proprietor of a trade mark can apply to the Trade Marks Registry for registration of a mark he is using or proposes to use in Hong Kong. If the Registry is satisfied that the mark is inherently registrable as a trade mark, they will permit the mark to proceed to registration in Part A of the Register; this will essentially give the applicant absolute protection for his mark.

If the Registry considers that a trade mark is not registrable in Part A of the Register, where, for example, the mark is descriptive of the goods or is a surname or a geographical name, the mark may nevertheless proceed to registration in Part B of the Register if the Registrar is of the opinion that the proposed mark is capable of distinguishing goods with which the proprietor is connected. Part B registration would not prevent a third party from continuing to use an identical or similar mark if he could demonstrate that its use is not likely to deceive the public. In all other respects, Part B and Part A registrations are equally effective.

Because Hong Kong is a party to the Paris Convention, a person who has previously applied for registration of a trade mark in a Convention country can obtain priority of registration of the same trade mark in Hong Kong (ie, the Hong Kong registration will be backdated to the date of the prior application), provided that application is made in Hong Kong within six months of such prior application. The Convention gives priority of registration only: it does not guarantee registration. The various use classes under which trade marks are registered are the same in each country which adheres to the Paris Convention.

Responsibility for policing the use of a trade mark is essentially that of the trade mark owner. There are, however, companies in Hong Kong who specialise in monitoring trade mark transgressions in Southeast Asia.

The United Kingdom Designs (Protection) Ordinance automatically extends to Hong Kong the benefits of a design registration obtained under the Registration Design Act 1949 of the United Kingdom. The registered design holder is not required to register his United Kingdom design registration in Hong Kong.

Patents

With regard to patents, Hong Kong grants no original patents although it does have a Patent Registry. An applicant must first obtain a patent from the United Kingdom Registry before registering it under the Hong Kong Registration of Patents Ordinance. The Hong Kong registration is in effect a certified copy of the United Kingdom patent to which is attached a Hong Kong Certificate. There is no examination procedure in Hong Kong and the granting of a Hong Kong certificate is virtually a formality.

Copyright

Copyright protection is available without the necessity of registration with any government body. The subject matter of copyright includes all original literary, dramatic, musical and artistic works.

It is available in Hong Kong to persons and companies in countries who are signatories to a variety of international copyright treaties. There are also complicated provisions relating to nationality, residence and domicile of the creator of a work which essentially requires the creator, if not a British subject, to be domiciled or resident in Hong Kong at the time the work was published. Works published overseas are only protected in Hong Kong if Hong Kong is a party to a copyright convention with the country of first publication.

Mary Faith Higgins is a Resident Partner
of Graham and James.
Claudio de Bedin is a Solicitor of
Robertson, Double & Boase.
Roy I. Delbyck is an Attorney of
Baker & McKenzie.

Chapter 3

Finance

by Steve K. Baker

'Perhaps the best example is Hong Kong ... Government plays an important role that is limited primarily to our four duties interpreted rather narrowly. It forces law and order, provides a means for formulating the rules of conduct, adjudicates disputes, facilitates transportation and communication, and supervises the issuance of currency.'

Milton and Rose Friedman
Free to Choose

Overview

* No control on foreign exchange and capital flows.
* Minimal government debt in a marketable form.
* Favorable tax environment.
* Minimal government intervention on banking.
* Absence of a central bank.
* A three-tier financial system: licensed banks, licensed DTCs and registered DTCs.
* Presence of international financial institutions.
* Local banking regulations focus on preventive measures.
* Low transaction cost—no withholding tax, reserve requirement and deposit insurance.
* Electronic banking services well established.
* Developing capital and futures markets.
* Growing importance as a financial gateway to China.

The economic success of Hong Kong over the past three decades has been based on a system of free enterprise. As an open economy with excellent telecommunication facilities and, most importantly, a highly productive and intelligent workforce, Hong Kong has flourished.

Starting as an entrepot in the pre-World War II period, it became a major manufacturing and export centre in the 1960s. In the 1970s, it has grown into a mature service economy.

Classical economic theory describes economic diversification as passing through three stages—agricultural, manufacturing, and services—and often equates levels of development with the stage to which an economy has evolved. In the real world, economies seldom fall so neatly into any such classification. Nevertheless, statistics do indicate that almost all of the advanced industrial countries and the more advanced developing nations have moved toward a service economy with more than half of their overall economic output being contributed by the services sector.

The extent of financial development in Hong Kong can be gauged from the money supply-to-GDP ratio which provides some indication of 'financial deepening'. In 1986, Hong Kong's M2/GDP ratio reached 1.78, significantly higher than that of all other Asian economies. This high financial ratio, moreover, was accompanied by a rising level of per capita income.

Hong Kong has clearly emerged as one of the most important financial centers in Asia. It is catching up on the world leaders in foreign exchange trading and has greatly improved the scope and sophistication of its money market activities. In terms of the size of its external asset holdings, it ranked 9th in the world at the end of 1986 with outstandings of US$155 billion.

Public Finance

Hong Kong is perhaps unique in a world of market economies. It pursues an economic policy of limited government intervention and has refrained from subsidizing any economic activities. This policy has led to a substantial increase in economic output. Hong Kong's real per capita GDP at US$4,565 in 1986 was the fourth largest in Asia after Australia, Japan, and Singapore in that order. The Hong Kong government's budget policy follows the cyclically balanced budget approach which suggests that budget deficits during recessions should be made up by surpluses in times of prosperity so that the budget is balanced over the business cycle. The government expects that this approach will prevent the occurrence of a secular growth in the public debt.

For seven consecutive years, fiscal 1976 through fiscal 1982, there was a string of budget surpluses virtually every year. Over this period, total revenue grew at an average rate of 31 percent a year, higher than the 22 percent GDP average growth during the same period.

However, revenues of land sales have slipped sharply ever since fiscal 1982 due to saturated market conditions. In addition, the slowdown of worldwide economic activities led to reduced growth in Hong Kong's gross domestic product. The result was that the budget swung into deficit in the financial year 1982/83.

Government accounts remained in the red for three consecutive years ending fiscal 1985. As a result of the revenue shortfall, the accumulated fiscal budget surpluses were reduced by a total of HK$7,052 million during the matching period to about HK$15,520 million as of April 1, 1985. In consequence, the ratio of total consolidated public expenditures to GDP also dropped steadily to the 16 percent level in fiscal 1985.

Government accounts turned back to a favorable position in the financial year of 1985-86, recording a budget surplus of HK$1,443 million. It was followed by a handsome surplus of HK$3,942 million in fiscal 1987. The projected budget surplus for fiscal 1988 is HK$1,768 million.

Taxes in Hong Kong are levied under the Inland Revenue Ordinance and are charged mainly on earnings and profits originating in Hong Kong, not on income arising from abroad. In addition, Hong Kong, unlike most countries, does not levy taxes on royalties, dividends, sales or capital gains. The low overall rates of taxation have historically been one of the fundamental tenets ensuring the continued strength of the economy.

The current outstanding public debt of the Hong Kong government is about HK$240 per capita and the debt service ratio is much less than one percent. The items making up Hong Kong's public debt include a HK$1 billion Hong Kong Government Bond issue and four long-term loans in various currencies from the Asian Development Bank for the finance of self-liquidating public works projects.

Government Finance (HK$m)

Fiscal year ending Mar 31	Revenue	Expenditure	Surplus/deficit	Accumulate fiscal surplus
1973–74	5,241	5,169	72	2,700
1974–75	5,875	6,255	−380	2,320
1975–76	6,520	6,032	488	2,808
1976–77	7,494	6,591	903	3,711
1977–78	10,233	8,997	1,236	4,947
1978–79	12,557	11,090	1,467	6,414
1979–80	16,796	13,872	2,924	9,338
1980–81	30,290	23,593	6,697	16,035
1981–82	34,313	27,778	6,535	22,570
1982–83	31,098	34,598	−3,500	19,070
1983–84	30,400	33,393	−2,993	16,077
1984–85	36,343*	36,902	−559	15,518
1985–86	41,241	39,798	1,443	16,961
1986–87	43,870	39,928	3,942	20,903
1987–88 est	46,177	44,409	1,768	22,671

Note: *Included a HK$1,005 million government bonds financing.

Source: Hong Kong Monthly Digest of Statistics, various issues. The 1987–88 Budget Speech.

Banking

Exchange Fund and Money Supply

Prior to 1845, uncoined silver was circulated in Hong Kong as legal tender. From that year onwards, the Oriental Bank, the Hongkong and Shanghai Bank and the parents of the present Standard Chartered Bank and the Mercantile Bank started to issue their own bank notes and although not legal tender, these became customary means of payment.

An ordinance of 1895 restricted the issue of bank notes to specifically authorized banks, namely the above three, excluding the Oriental Bank which had by then become defunct.

When China abandoned the silver standard in 1935, Hong Kong followed suit. The government set up an Exchange Fund to which note-issuing banks were obliged to surrender all silver previously held by them against their note issues, in exchange for non-interest bearing certificates of indebtedness. The stated purpose of the fund was to regulate the exchange value of the currency of Hong Kong. In practice, it is also responsible for the daily management of the external reserves of the Hong Kong government.

The Exchange Fund is now managed by a committee which comprises the Financial Secretary as chairman, the chief executives of the Hongkong and Shanghai Banking Corporation (HKSBC) and the Standard Chartered Bank, and the Secretary for Monetary Affairs Branch. Two additional members were appointed to the committee in late April, 1986, with their terms of office running from May 1, 1986 until September 30, 1988.

It has been disclosed that the bulk of the Exchange Fund is held in assets which are denominated in foreign hard currencies. Assets other than bank deposits are mostly in highly liquid forms including bonds, notes and treasury bills. In early 1982, the fund transacted its business through 87 banking, safe custody and security accounts located in 13 countries. These included five accounts with central banks and 16 with various financial institutions. In a speech addressed to Legislative Council in April 1986, the Financial Secretary disclosed that the fund "contains the major part of Hong Kong's visible reserves—say HK$19 billion—plus the note and coin backing—say another HK$19 billion".

As with most modern nations, the basic components of the money supply in Hong Kong are currency and deposit liabilities. Since January 1978, banknotes have been issued in Hong Kong by two private commercial banks — the HKSBC and the Standard Chartered Bank. On October 17, 1983, the government abandoned the official float policy and announced a policy of pegging the Hong Kong dollar at HK$7.8 per US dollar. In response to the new exchange rate policy, the note-issuing mechanism between the government and the note-issuing banks has also changed. Henceforth, the Certificates of Indebtedness, which are issued by the Exchange Fund to the note-issuing banks to be held as cover for their note issues, will be issued and redeemed only against payment in US dollars, at the fixed exchange rate of US$1 = HK$7.80.

These Certificates of Indebtedness, therefore, provide the legal backing for the notes issued by the banks—apart from their small fiduciary issues which are limited to a total of HK$95 million which are backed by securities issued or guaranteed by the British or Hong Kong governments.

Coins of five dollars, two dollars, one dollar, 50 cents, 20 cents, 10 cents, five cents and notes of one cent denomination are issued by the Exchange Fund using the Hongkong and Shanghai Banking Corporation as its agent.

At the end of 1986, Hong Kong's money supply, M1, M2, and M3 stood at HK$56,094 million, HK$518,131 million and HK$594,085 million, respectively. In the absence of any exchange control, the key determinants of the growth of the money supply in Hong Kong will continue to be the demand for credit and the net acquisition of foreign currency assets by the financial institutions in the local financial marketplace.

The Growth of the Banking Sector

The process of financial development in Hong Kong has been more of a gradual evolution, a spontaneous response to the challenges its growing economy created. Prior to 1970, the banking sector remained largely local in its scope of operations. Then rapid economic expansion and concomitant overseas investments during the 1970s induced a sharp increase in the demand for banking services. However, the process of financial development continued to be hindered by the complete moratorium imposed by the Hong Kong government on the issuance of new bank licences.

It was not until 1978 that Hong Kong began to move in the direction of financial liberalization. One major positive step was the lifting of the moratorium on bank licensing in March 1978. The policy has remained in effect until now.

Liberalization has enabled a number of reputable foreign financial institutions to enter the Hong Kong banking system. In terms of regional distribution, 79 foreign banks from 15 countries were granted new bank licences during the period March 1978 to December 1986. The lifting of the moratorium has effectively reduced the monopoly of existing banks by reducing population per bank, increasing the elasticity of loan demand and consequently resulting in an improvement in social welfare.

As of December 31, 1986, there were 151 licensed banks in Hong Kong with a bank branch network of 1,537 offices. Of these, 35 were local banks with the remaining 116 coming from 22 foreign countries. In addition, there were 38 licensed deposit-taking companies, 254 registered deposit-taking companies and 134 bank representative offices operating in Hong Kong at the end of December 1986.

Benefitting from the government's liberal economic policies, the banking system has shown a rapid growth over the past five years in terms of total assets, loans, and deposits. The total assets of the Hong Kong banking system rose by an average compounded growth rate of 28 percent a year to reach HK$2,150 billion at the end of 1986. Total loans and customer deposits grew by an average rate of 14 percent and 28 percent a year, with outstandings reaching HK$501 billion and HK$563 billion, respectively.

Banking Concentration

Total banking concentration is high in the Hong Kong market. One indicator is the number of new branches. During the period 1981-1986 the number of new banking offices increased by 391 to 1,537. About one-third of the 391 new bank branches were opened by the five largest locally incorporated banks, each of which has total assets in excess of HK$10 billion.

In terms of market share, the 31 locally incorporated banks together accounted for an estimated 36 percent of the total assets of the Hong Kong banking sector in 1985 and absorbed some 60 percent of total customer deposits. The Bank of China group (nine China incorporated banks with four locally incorporated banks which have maintained close relationship with them) claimed a 27 percent share in total bank assets and a 26 percent share in customer deposits. Foreign banks accounted for the remaining shares of 37 percent in total bank assets and 14 percent in total customer deposits.

Sources and Uses of Funds

Locally incorporated banks in Hong Kong obtain a high proportion of their funds from traditional deposits. Other sources of funds include call and short-term borrowing in the interbank market, retained earnings, and issues of capital stock. On the other hand, foreign banks in Hong Kong depend crucially on offshore funding from the Euro and Asian currency markets as the Hong Kong Banking Ordinance permits the inclusion of overseas accounts in the assessment of liquidity. Nevertheless, most foreign banks continue to rely on the local interbank market for short-term loanable funds.

On the liability side, the major liability item of all commercial banks and DTCs was 'amount due to banks abroad'. This category accounted for more than 45 percent of the total liabilities of the banking system. The second largest liability item was 'customer deposits' for banks and 'amount due to domestic banks' for DTCs. During the past five years, the DTC sector has lost much ground to the commercial banks in the competition for customer deposits. Nevertheless, it is interesting to note that a large proportion of money market transactions still involve back-to-back arrangements among banks and their wholly-owned DTC subsidiaries.

On the asset side, the largest asset item for the banking sector was 'amount due from banks abroad' at year-end 1986. It was followed by the category 'loans and advances' which constituted some 23 percent of the total assets. For the DTCs sector, the two largest asset items were 'loans and advances' and 'amount due from banks abroad', accounting for 24 percent and 26 percent of the total assets, respectively.

Due to the fact that almost all foreign banks in Hong Kong have small local deposit bases, customer deposits usually account for less than 10 percent of total liabilities. As a matter of fact, they are the frequent borrowers in the interbank market.

The Interbank Market

Interest rates in Hong Kong have generally moved in tandem with international money rates but, sometimes, with a considerable time lag. Because of the absence of a central bank in Hong Kong, interest rates for savings deposits and fixed deposits with a maturity of 15 months less one day are determined by the committee of the Hong Kong Association of Banks (HKAB). The HKAB does not make any rules on interest rates charged on loans and advances. The prime rate in Hong Kong is practically determined by the two note-issuing banks, the HKSBC and the Standard Chartered Bank. Although other licensed banks in Hong Kong are not bound to observe the prime rate adjustments, they normally take it as the 'base rate' for pricing their loans to best clients.

In the United States, banks are interconnected by the market for federal funds, which is really the domestic interbank market. In Hong Kong, the interbank market has been one of the major sources of short-term funds for most banks. It allows the cash-hungry banks to manage their daily liquidity positions.

Interbank rates in the Hong Kong financial marketplace tend to fluctuate in line with prime rate movements, with a spread of 50 to 100 basis points below the latter. In practice, interbank funds are generally considered as an unstable source of funds, because rate adjustments in the past shows that such actions are influenced by the elite few rather than by the pure forces of supply and demand.

The tenor of interbank funds ranges from overnight to six-month but money is commonly dealt in at call and for maturities not exceeding three months. The Hongkong and Shanghai Bank group and the PRC banks are the major suppliers of Hong Kong dollar funds in the interbank market.

In the five-year period ending 1986, the gross size of the Hong Kong dollar interbank market increased by some HK$43 billion to HK$70 billion. The gross size of foreign currency interbank fundings during the same period increased by seven-fold to HK$143 billion equivalent at the end of 1986.

Since the second half of 1979 there has been a significant shift in the maturities of interbank borrowings. The size of 24-hour call interbank borrowing reduced sharply, whereas there was a growing demand for interbank funds with longer maturities, noticeably in one-month and three-month. This development trend in interbank transactions is likely to reduce significantly the seasonal liquidity strain on the local banking system.

Interbank Market in Hong Kong

	Gross size of interbank market			Interbank rate Average %			Prime Rate Ave. %
Period end	HK Dollar	Foreign currency	Total	Over-night	1-Month	3-Month	
1980	16933	9852	26785	11.41	13.41	13.37	13.63
1981	26721	18977	45698	15.65	17.04	16.92	17.49
1982	36411	26069	62481	12.51	12.78	12.84	14.19
1983	41543	43289	84833	10.48	11.04	11.18	12.31
1984	52343	60820	113164	10.57	10.75	11.15	12.51
1985	57680	70338	128019	6.28	6.41	6.86	8.18
1986	70248	143414	213662	5.84	5.81	5.97	7.06

Source: *Hong Kong Monthly Digest of Statistics*, Economic Department, Citibank, N.A. Hong Kong

The Payment Mechanism

Hong Kong's payment clearing system is administered by the Hongkong and Shanghai Banking Corporation and applies only to Hong Kong dollars. It is paper-based. For auto-pay instructions, the clearing is done by the exchange of tapes amongst the banks at 10:00 am. For cheques, the settlement made for Hong Kong dollar treasury transactions, the clearing is done at 6:00 p.m. In both cases, the settlement is done the following day at 10.15 a.m. There are more than 150 banks in Hong Kong but only 10 are clearing house settlement banks.

An on-line real-time Clearing House Automated Transfer System (CHATS) came into use in February 1984. At the time of writing, there are more than 50 member banks in CHATS which can exchange transactions up to 4:30 pm with final settlement the following day at 10:15 a.m. The potential of CHATS is great. It helps reduce physical handling of cheques, thereby lowering the expense of clearing them. In the near future, banks in Hong Kong will be able to provide an automated interface. Instructions given to member banks of CHATS through SWIFT, telex, electronic banking connection, will be automatically passed on to the clearing house.

On the retail market, banks in Hong Kong began to provide electronic payment service to customers with the introduction of the automated teller machines (ATMs) in the second half of the 1970s.

At present, a majority of the major licensed banks in Hong Kong have installed automated teller machines either within their branch offices or in discrete locations. They now collectively operate more than 1,500 ATMs in the local financial marketplace.

The application of an electronic funds transfer system for point-of-sale transactions became effective in June 1985 with the introduction of the "Easy Pay System", organised by Electronic Payment Services Co (HK) Ltd which is owned by 29 banks in Hong Kong with the HKSBC, Hang Seng Bank, Standard Chartered Bank, Bank of China, Bank of East Asia, and Citibank as board of directors.

The system enables automated teller machine (ATM) card holders to debit their bank accounts directly at merchants' premises and pay the retail bills for goods purchased or services received. No cash is involved in the entire process.

All major ATM card issuing banks have linked up to the system. Presently, there are 134 merchant outlets with around 300 EPS terminals. The Electronic Payment Services Co (HK) Ltd plans to expand the EPS network by installing 700 more EPS terminals in merchant shops in the near future.

Bank Financing

Bank loans are the principal source of financing for Hong Kong business. Offered for both short-and long-term needs, repayment term varies from on demand to one year. Term loans can be obtained with either fixed rates of interest or floating rates, which are generally determined as a specific percentage above the Hong Kong Interbank Offered Rate (HIBOR) or Hong Kong Dollar Prime Rate. Fixed rate loans are rarely offered for periods of longer than five years. Loans negotiated with floating rates can be obtained from one to eight years or longer, .depending on purpose and repayment ability.

Analysis of Bank Loans and Advances for use in Hong Kong (HK$m)

	Dec 83	Dec 84	Dec 85	Dec 86
Manufacturing	16,210	16,940	17,962	23,479
Building and construction	37,194	39,332	33,813	31,265
Wholesale and retail	23,165	26,024	28,221	32,601
Property purchase	14,571	17,001	22,280	32,335
Transport & transport equipment	13,811	13,985	13,818	12,483
Financial concerns	13,973	13,377	15,844	19,302
Public utilities	2,684	4,135	4,407	4,304
Others	40,265	45,437	55,664	72,433
Total loans and advances for use in Hong Kong	161,873	176,231	192,009	228,202

Source: Hong Kong Monthly Digest of Statistics.

Banks in Hong Kong compete fiercely for prime loan business. Because of the territory's law allowing free movement of capital into and out of Hong Kong, foreign banks and deposit-taking companies are able to compete on an equal basis with domestic institutions.

At the end of 1986, the outstanding bank loans and advances for domestic use amounted to HK$228 billion, up 19 percent over the year-earlier total. Bank lending to building and construction and for property purchases accounted for about 27 percent of the year-end 1986 outstanding; the comparable proportion in 1975 was about 10 percent. To a certain extent, the substantial real estate portfolio highlighted the large size and increased complexity of the development projects in the markets and the growing sophistication of the Hong Kong banking system to meet with the changing financial needs of customers.

With the presence of 150 licensed banks and some 300 finance companies in Hong Kong, there is never a shortage of financing opportunities for both domestic and multinational businesses operating in Hong Kong. The common form of bank facilities available in the local financial marketplace include the following:

Trade Financing and Services

Bankers Acceptances

A draft or bill of exchange drawn on and accepted by a bank to provide current financing for merchandise trade transactions. The bank's acceptance indicates an irrevocable promise to pay the draft or bill at maturity. The acceptance itself, when eligible under the Federal Reserve Bank's criteria, can be bought and sold short-term at discount as a money market instrument in the acceptance market.

Collection

A draft drawn on and accepted by a bank to finance a bill for collection arising from a transaction involving the import or export of merchandise. A correspondent drawing such a draft on the bank must provide shipment details and assurance of no other acceptance financing in effect on the same merchandise.

Pre-export

A draft drawn on and accepted by a bank for a correspondent's customer who has a firm contract of sale and requires funding in advance of his merchandise being shipped to buyers.

Commercial Credit (Import/Export)

A letter of credit in which the drawings usually require the beneficiary to submit shipping documents related to merchandise trade transactions specified in the credit. Can be revocable or irrevocable. Irrevocable credits may be either straight or negotiation-type credit.

Shipping Guarantee

An instrument issued by a bank, usually to a common carrier, on behalf of the customer to allow the customer to take delivery of merchandise in lieu of shipping documents in accordance with the instrument's stipulated terms and conditions.

Lending Facilities

Advance in Current Account

Short-term overdraft loan extended by a bank to a correspondent to fulfill short-term working capital-type funding requirements.

Short-term Loan

Line of credit A bank's obligation to extend short-term credit to a correspondent, subject to periodic review, amendment or cancellation at any time.

Revolving credit Formal commitment allowing a correspondent to borrow short-term and repay bank loans at will on revolving basis under specific terms and conditions.

Placement

Short-term placement of fund by a bank with other financial institutions as an inter-bank money market tool.

Long-term Loan

Formal commitment with a final maturity in excess of one year, in which a correspondent repays the lender according to a formal agreement.

Asset-based Lending

Ship

Term lending with first preferred ship mortgage as primary security.

Real Estate

Term lending with first preferred real estate mortgage as primary security.

Other Asset-based Lending

Term lending with merchandise mortgaged or assets pledged to a bank (other than marketable securities) as primary security.

Lease Financing

Equipment Finance

Finance customer's purchase of equipment on a term basis.

Ownership of equipment rests with the customer but mortgaged to the bank during tenor of the facility.

Hire Purchase

A bank rents the equipment to the customer on a term basis with pre-agreement that customer purchases the equipment at end of tenor.

Equipment Lease

Finance customer's purchase of equipment on a term basis through leasing arrangement with customer's undertaking to purchase the equipment at end of lease period, usually at nominal price.

Other Lease Financing

Variation of lease financing other than equipment finance, hire purchase and equipment lease above.

Apart from the traditional banking facilities described above, some banks in Hong Kong also offer a variety of electonic banking services tailored to meet the particular requirements of local business.

Through an electronic banking terminal located in his own office, the customer can access the banking system for balance and account detail reporting, initiate funds transfer instructions, open letters of credit (LCs), and monitor the current money market situation. State of art technology is employed also to permit automatic balance reporting using the telephone. In addition, direct communication links between clients and the New York system permits on-line US$ funds transfers and cash management.

Another example of electronic banking services is the cross-border electronic LC: a banking innovation particularly suited for

Asian countries. A client domiciled in another country, instead of using a local bank to open an LC and involving many different banks in both the buyer's and the seller's countries during the process, can now deal directly with a bank in the seller's country from their own EB terminal. By reducing the number of bank links in the chain, electronic LCs provide savings in money and time, plus they reduce the chance of communication errors.

To meet the special financing needs of multinational business, some banks, mainly foreign-based, offer multi-currency financial services to customers. These special international financing and/or exposure management transactions include currency swaps, parallel loans, back-to-back loans, simulated currency loans, and intercompany forward contracts, among many others.

Regulatory Environment

The Three-tier System

The structure of Hong Kong's financial system is fairly simple and is composed principally of three types of active financial institutions: licensed banks; licensed deposit-taking companies; and registered DTCs.

Licensed Banks

To qualify for a banking licence, a locally-incorporated licensed bank must have a minimum paid-up capital of HK$100 million. No additional capital requirement is needed for the opening of new bank branches. For the foreign incorporated banks in Hong Kong, the capital requirement is measured against the financial statement of their parent companies.

Licensed banks are the only financial institutions authorized to operate checking and savings accounts. Banks may accept deposits of any size and maturity from the public but are restricted in the interest rates they can offer by the interest rate rules of the Hong Kong Association of banks (HKAB).

Deposits of greater than HK$500,000 with terms of maturity of less than three months, however, have no restrictions on the interest rates that can be offered.

A foreign bank which wishes to transact banking business in Hong Kong shall apply to the Governor in Council, through the Commissioner of Banking, for a bank licence.

The present criteria for banking licence applications include the following:

i) The parent banking organization should have total assets, less contra items, of at least US$14 billion or equivalent.

ii) It is incorporated in a country the monetary authorities of which exercise effective prudential supervision and have no objection to the establishment of a branch in Hong Kong.

iii) Some acceptable form of reciprocity is available to Hong Kong banks.

Each new licence so granted is subject to limitation on branching.

The criteria set for a locally incorporated institution that wishes to apply for a bank licence include a minimum public deposit of HK$1,750 million and total assets, less contra items, of HK$2,500. The right of granting final approval to any application goes to the Governor-in-Council.

Licensed Deposit-taking Companies

A licensed deposit-taking company must have a minimum issued share capital of HK$100 million and paid-up capital of HK$75 million. Licensed DTCs have no restrictions on the interest rates they can offer, nor are there any limits on the terms of maturity they can accept on deposits; they are prohibited, however, from accepting deposits of amounts less than HK$500,000. In general, these companies are often affiliates of foreign companies that tend to specialize in project finance, syndicated loans, underwriting, corporate advice, investment services and other related finance services.

Application to become a licensed DTC shall apply to the Financial Secretary, through the Commissioner of Banking. The applicant company should have substantial assets, net of contra items on its book in Hong Kong and have actively traded as a deposit-taking company for at least three years before the date of application, among other qualitative criteria.

Registered Deposit-taking Companies

A registered deposit-taking company must have a minimum paid-up capital of HK$10 million and may only accept deposits of not less than HK$100,000 with a maturity period of not less than three months. There are no restrictions on interest rates that can be offered. Registered DTCs are mainly smaller finance companies that specialize in services such as stock market finance, hire purchases, and mortgages.

In March 1981, the government announced a suspension of any

application for registration as a deposit-taking company. The moratorium remains in force at the time of writing, with exemption under two considerations:

i) More than 50 percent of the applicant's voting capital is held by a bank which is recognized as such in the country or place in which it is incorporated; and

ii) Such bank is adequately supervised by the prudential supervisory authorities of that country or place.

In Hong Kong, licensed banks are encouraged to build up published reserves out of published profits and to build up their own inner reserves (generally not permitted elsewhere). The minimum paid-up capital plus reserve requirement for a domestic bank is HK$200 million. Again, the reserve requirement does not apply to foreign incorporated banks in Hong Kong. The minimum paid-up share capital plus published reserves is HK$150 million for a licensed DTC and HK$20 million for a registered DTC.

Hong Kong Association of Banks

The Association (formerly known as the Exchange Banks' Association) was incorporated on January 12, 1981 under the Hong Kong Association of Banks Ordinance. The objectives are to make rules from time to time for the conduct of the business of banking, to act as an advisory body to its members, and to provide the clearing facilities to member banks. Unlike the banking associations in most countries which are largely voluntary bodies with no legal empowerment, the HKAB is a statutory body and every licensed bank in Hong Kong is required to be a member of the Association and to observe the rules agreed upon at the committee.

The HKAB consists of three major bodies — the committee, the consultative council, and the disciplinary committee.

The committee consists of three continuing or permanent members and nine elected members. The three continuing members are the Hongkong and Shanghai Banking Corporation, the Standard Chartered Bank, and the Bank of China. Of the nine elected members, four will come from the locally incorporated banks against five to be elected among foreign incorporated banks in Hong Kong. The chairmanship of the HKAB committee shall be rotated biennially between the HKSBC and the Standard Chartered Bank. Upon obtaining the approval of the Financial Secretary, the committee has the right to make rules on matters relating to the following:

i) The setting of maximum rates of interest in respect of Hong

Kong dollar denominated customer deposits and specified instruments;

ii) The conduct of foreign exchange business and the setting of brokerage and minimum commissions in lieu of exchange;

iii) The setting of minimum charge/commissions for securities and safe keeping, custody business, issuance of guarantees or other documents, and of any other banking services;

v) The prohibition of members from transacting any specified type of business or using any particular type.

The consultative council of the HKAB is to advise the committee on any matter relating to the business of banking. At present, it is made up of three continuing members and 21 elected members. The elected members are required by statute to be geographically representative. The ordinance stipulates that the chairman and vice-chairman of the committee shall ex officio be the chairman and vice-chairman of the consultative council.

The disciplinary committee consists of four members—two continuing members, one locally incorporated bank, and one foreign incorporated bank. The chairman shall be one among these four member banks. The function is to ensure that the fellow members of the HKAB conduct their business in compliance with the rules set by the committee. A breach of any rule can be subject to severe penalties.

Licensed banks in Hong Kong (excluding the three unincorporated banks) are broadly classified into two categories under the interest rate rules of HKAB. Banks under category II are allowed to quote an interest rate of 50 basis points above the basic rate on money held at 24-hour call or notice, seven-day call or notice, and on deposits fixed for a period of one week or longer.

However, the interest rate on savings accounts is common to all licensed banks in Hong Kong. At present, the PRC bank group members and some locally incorporated banks are classified into category II under the interest rate regulations of the HKAB.

The 1986 Banking Ordinance

The Banking Bill 1986 which was passed into law on May 28 that year, is made up of 22 parts, and combines the two existing ordinances governing banks and DTCs. The provisions include:

Roles and Powers of the Commissioner of Banking The powers of the Commissioner of Banking are greatly expanded beyond his traditional supervisory functions. He is empowered with discretionary rights to interfere with the administrative decisions of an authorised institution (a bank or a DTC) in terms of key personnel appointments, voting power of the controller at general meeting, and business decision for the sale or disposal of a business by amalgamation, or through mergers and acquisitions. The commissioner may, after consultation with the authorised institution, appoint another external auditor to act with the auditor appointed by an authorised institution to examine the books of the company. In addition, the commissioner may from time to time issue guidelines, specifying business practices which should not be engaged in by all authorised institutions or by a single party.

The ordinance also provides appeal to the Financial Secretary or the Governor-in-Council with respect to the exercise of the discretionary powers by the banking commissioner. The commissioner is also requested to provide an annual report to the Governor-in-Council on the working of the ordinance and the activities of his office during that year.

Capital Adequacy Ratio The ordinance stipulates that an authorized institution (a bank/DTC) incorporated in Hong Kong will have to maintain a statutory minimum of five percent capital adequacy ratio. The commissioner has the right to increase this ratio for a particular institution up to eight percent for a bank and up to 10 percent for a deposit-taking company.

The capital adequacy ratio is calculated, based on Hong Kong dollar value, by multiplying each of the five predetermined categories of assets by respective applied risk weights to produce an adjusted total of risk assets which is then divided into the institution's modified capital base.

Any institution required to comply with a higher ratio than five percent may appeal to the Financial Secretary against the variation. A contravention of the ratio is not in itself an offence but it is an offence to fail to report the contravention to the commissioner, or not to take remedial action required by the commissioner for the institution to comply with the ratio.

A transition period of about two years after the enforcement of the ordinance is allowed for authorised institutions to adjust their capital base to the proposed requirement.

Liquidity Ratio The ordinance also stipulates that all authorized institutions in Hong Kong shall maintain a liquidity ratio of not less than 25 percent in each calendar month. The liquidity measurement tries to match liquefiable assets against all liabilities maturing or callable within one month. A contravention of the ratio is not in itself an offence, but failure to report the contravention, or not to carry out remedial action required by the commissioner, is an of-

. The liquidity ratio requirement will apply to all authorized
utions in Hong Kong.

ie Financial Secretary has the right to change the statutory
liquidity ratio for all authorised institutions. The banking commissioner, if in his opinion considers the situation as proper, may
increase or decrease the liquidity ratio for a particular authorised
institution. Unlike the capital-to-risk asset ratio, no upper limit is
set for the liquidity ratio.

The ordinance further stipulates that no authorised institution
should, without the approval of the banking commissioner, cause
the sum of all charges over its assets (less contra items) in Hong Kong
to exceed five percent of the sum total of the value of those assets.

Financial Markets

Capital Market

Commercial banks play a significant role in the development of the
capital market in Hong Kong. The spectrum of capital market instruments available in the Hong Kong financial marketplace is expanding rapidly.

The wave of innovation on the capital market is, to a certain extent, motivated by the growing trend of securitization in other
financial markets. Securitization is a revolutionary process in bank
financing, transforming bank loans into debt instruments. It is expected that securitization will create new business markets for
financial institutions as well as innovative fund-raising opportunities for governments, cooperation and individual investors. The
beauty of securitization is that it enhances liquidity of the asset
holdings of investors while expanding the possibilities for reducing
borrowing costs for the borrowers.

At present, the major types of capital market instruments
available in the Hong Kong market include certificates of deposit,
commercial papers, promissory notes and bonds. However, the
market for these instruments is essentially a primary market and
secondary market trading remains insignificant.

Negotiable Certificates of Deposit

A negotiable certificate of deposit, often called an NCD, is essentially a receipt issued by a commercial bank given in exchange for a
deposit of money, with the promise of the issuer (mainly commercial banks) to pay back the holder of receipt on a specified date. The
negotiability of the instrument implies that it can be traded in a

secondary market before maturity. NCDs in Hong Kong are issued either with a fixed rate or on a floating rate basis. Fixed-rate CDs have become most popular since early 1985 when a downtrend in interest rates was anticipated. In the nine years ending 1985, more than 150 NCDs were issued in the financial marketplace, absorbing a total capital of HK$21 billion equivalent. Denominations of the NCDs commonly run as low as $50,000, but the majority are written for amounts above $250,000. The maturities run from one year to five years, with most NCDs maturing within three years. Interest rates of most NCDs are competitive with one-month Hong Kong interbank offered rate.

Commercial Paper

Commercial paper is a form of financing developed in the United States. The debt instrument is widely used in Europe and North America but limited to the largest corporations in Hong Kong. The commercial paper market in Hong Kong is currently estimated at HK$10 billion and is growing rapidly.

It is composed of short-term, unsecured negotiable notes sold in the money market by investment banks. These notes can have maturities ranging from 30 to 270 days, though most range from 45 to 180 days.

Commercial paper in Hong Kong is usually placed through an agent who solicits bids on the paper from a tender panel composed of a number of investment banks selected by the agent. The panel bids on the paper by sealed ballot at a rate set in relation to the HIBOR, as determined by a group of so-called reference banks. Notes are awarded to the lowest bidders until all the notes are sold or a maximum, previously agreed, rate of interest has been reached. If the latter is the case, then a group of underwriters purchases the remaining notes.

After the initial tender offer, a secondary market develops as the banks resell their holdings. The ultimate owners of the paper usually are institutional investors and other companies looking for short-term investments at attractive rates. Since the unsecured commercial paper carries a slightly higher risk than other forms of investment it offers correspondingly higher rates of return. Because of the relatively small size of the Hong Kong commercial paper market, secondary trading is limited.

Promissory Notes

Promissory notes are direct obligations of a corporation. In May 1982, Cheung Kong (Holdings) Ltd launched an unsecured US$200 million Euronote facility. It is issued through a series of three-or six-month US dollar bearer notes, over a period of five years, with the interest rate carrying a coupon of 0.25 per cent over the Singapore interbank offered rate (SIBOR).

In September 1983, Securities Pacific Corporation came up with another US$100 million short-term notes facility. The facility is available in three- or six-month notes on a revolving basis for up to seven years.

Bonds

Corporate bonds, the main form of debt financing in more developed capital markets, are rarely used in Hong Kong.

Throughout 1985, only three bond issues were launched in the market, raising a total capital of HK$1.5 billion. Development of a local bond market is hampered by the absence of any need for government debt securities. By consistently adhering to fiscal policies mandating a balanced budget, the Hong Kong government has avoided substantial borrowing. The few offerings of government debt that have occured have been so small that no secondary market has developed.

Nowadays, the distinction between the money and capital markets has become increasingly blurred by funds constantly being rolled over from one market to the other. A unique example of this development is the launch of the first Hong Kong dollar-denominated money-market fund by an investment banker in June 1986. We can expect a great number of these money-market funds (MMFs) coming on stream in the short run.

Investors can invest in the funds for as little as HK$50,000 and enjoy greater diversification of investments than they would possibly obtain by themselves. In addition, the MMFs provide the average investors with the money market rates and a higher degree of liquidity. In sum, it seems that the MMFs will become a useful alternative to the savings and fixed-term deposits for those concerned with maximizing their profits by converting their temporary surplus cash into liquid interest-bearing instruments.

Foreign Exchange Market

Supporting and accompanying the development of Hong Kong's banking business is the rapid expansion of the foreign exchange market in Hong Kong.

There are no official statistics for the volume of the Hong Kong foreign exchange market. Market estimates, however, indicate an average daily turnover of around US$25 billion in forex trading in all currencies. This is equivalent to some six percent of the daily turnover of the world foreign exchange market.

Hong Kong is a spot-oriented market. Currencies actively traded are US$/DM, US$/Yen, US$/HK$, US$/STG, US$/SFR, and US$/A$. Dollar-Deutschemark transactions take up about 40 percent of the daily turnover, with dollar-yen transactions accounting for another 30 percent of the market. Apart from US$/HK$, there is no active forward trading due to the lack of commercial base and/or lack of interest from market participants. The US$/HK$ forward market, even with good commercial business, is sometimes thin because of the volatility of the HK$ interest rates. At present, about one quarter of the total forex transactions in Hong Kong are handled by the members of the Foreign Exchange Brokers Association.

Hong Kong now has a very sophisticated foreign exchange market, bank customers can choose between foreign exchange options, currency swaps, and long-dated forward contracts in Hong Kong dollars with maturities of up to five years, among others.

Foreign exchange options give the buyer the right, but not the obligation, to buy and sell currencies at a given rate for a particular period of time. Currency swaps allow the user to hedge a long-term foreign exchange risk or obtain below-market financing by exchanging their foreign-currency liabilities for those of another.

In addition to foreign exchange transactions, loans, and deposits are offered in a variety of currencies. Banks in Hong Kong also provide interest rate risk management products to customers. These products include: forward interest rate, which guarantees a future interest rate; ceiling rate, which provides rate protection in a rising rate environment; collar rate, which sets parameters for both high and low-end interest rates; floor rate, which guarantees a minimum return on a US dollar deposit or CD portfolio should interest rates fall; and the interest rate swap, an agreement to exchange the basis of interest rates on loans or deposits.

√ Stock Market

The Hong Kong stock market provides a source of new capital funds for corporations. It is also a popular area for local speculators. As a result, the market is both large and extremely volatile and trading in equity securities is predominantly a secondary market.

Throughout most of its history the Hong Kong exchange was

actually four separate exchanges: the Far East, the Kam Ngan, the Hong Kong, and the Kowloon. On April 2, 1986, the stock market entered into a new era with the opening of the unified exchange, the Stock Exchange of Hong Kong, at Exchange Square complex in Central. Trading on the exchange is broker to broker and virtually all transactions are being handled by automated dealing systems.

According to the Securities (Amendment) Ordinance 1985, members of the unified exchange will have to comply with certain capital requirements. Individual members must put up a minimum capital of HK$1 million (US$128,000), while corporate members must put up HK$5 million (US$641,000). Partnerships require the amount prescribed for an individual or corporation for each dealing partner. In each category, 10 percent of the capital requirement must be in cash.

There are now about 320 stocks listed, although only around 30 shares are actively traded on the market. The total market capitalization of the Hong Kong stock market at the end of July 1987 was about US$75 billion, lower than the comparable figures of US$1,711 billion for Japan, US$1,710 billion for the US, and US$180 billion for Australia, but was ahead of the US$26 billion market capitalization for Singapore and US$28 billion for Taiwan.

The Stock Exchange of Hong Kong publishes its own index of stock prices—the Hong Kong Index. This comprises 45 leading stocks which collectively represent some 87 percent of the total market turnover, and about 85 percent of the total capitalization.

Both the Hong Kong Index and the Hang Seng Index, which is based on the daily market values of 33 leading stocks selected on the basis of their capitalization, will continue to be quoted in the market.

Selling common stock has the advantages of not binding a company to fixed interest payments and of increasing a company's debt capacity to the extent that the additional shares improve its debt service ratio.

The two main methods for the flotation of new companies are public offers and private placements. According to the Exchange Listing Rules of the Stock Exchange of Hong Kong Ltd, applicants for new listing should have an initial aggregate market capitalization of at least HK$50 million and a minimum of 25 percent of the company's paid-up share capital must be offered to the public. To qualify for a placement, the applicant should have a market capitalization of not less than HK$20 million and a minimum of 25 percent of the company's issued share capital must be made available for placing.

An offering of common stock is usually handled by investment bankers who act as managers and co-managers and offer the shares to the public. A group of underwriting banks and brokers backs the issue and guarantees a minimum price for the stock.

Hang Seng Index Futures

The history of the stock index futures market is very young. It was not until 1982 that trading in stock index futures contracts made its debut in the United States. In Hong Kong, a financial futures working party was formed by the Hong Kong Commodity Exchange in January 1982 to make recommendations to the government about the introduction of trading in stock index futures in Hong Kong. In May 1985, the government agreed to the establishment of the Hong Kong Futures Exchange to assume responsibility for the trading of all futures contracts. The first financial futures contract being introduced is the Hang Seng Index futures contract based on the performance of the Hong Kong stock market.

The Hang Seng Index futures contract started trading on May 6, 1986, adding further breadth and sophistication to the Hong Kong financial system.

A stock index futures contract represents an obligation to deliver at settlement date an amount of cash equal to a fixed value (HK$50 in the case of the Hang Seng Index futures contract) multiplied by the difference between the stock index value at the close of the last trading day of the contract and the price at which the future contract is originally entered into.

On the other hand, an investor always has the option of determining his actual profit or loss any time prior to the expiry of the contract by reversing his position in the futures exchange market. However, in this case his actual profit or loss will depend on the price of the Hang Seng Index prevailing at that time.

In order to ensure that participants in the futures market can discharge their contractural obligations satisfactorily, an initial margin of HK$10,000 of investor equity is required before any contract can be established. This margin deposit is not a down payment nor is there any loan granted in connection with the contract traded. It is simply 'good faith' money against fluctuation in the price of the futures.

Floating profit and loss associated with a particular contract position will be computed at the daily closing and will be offset against the client's margin position. This floating balance will be available for creating further contracts and if there is floating loss which result in the margin deposit falling below the minimum margin requirement, the client will be requested to make a further deposit in the next trading day in order to make up for the short fall.

Commodities Markets

In May 1985, the former Hong Kong Commodity Exchange was restructured to become the Hong Kong Futures Exchange, and assumed the sole right to conduct trading in financial futures and in futures contracts for sugar, soyabeans and gold. Gold futures were introduced in 1980. The commodity exchange is relatively small by international standards but recent moves to allow it to broaden its membership and trade in financial futures contracts may allow it to grow substantially in coming years. In 1986 the exchange reported that trading in sugar totalled 273,800 lots of 112,000lb each, trading in soyabeans totalled 330,524 lots of 30,000 kilograms each, and trading in gold totalled 6,366 lots, each of 100 troy ounces.

Gold and Silver Markets

Gold is traded actively on both local and international markets. The Chinese Gold and Silver Exchange Society operates the third-largest market in gold bullion in the world. Gold traded at the society is 99 percent fine, measured in taels and sold in Hong Kong dollars. Prices on the exchange are generally equivalent to those quoted in Zurich, London and New York. Membership of the society is closed at 193 firms. The international market, known locally as the loco-London market, trades bullion of 99.5 percent fine gold, measured in troy ounces and sold in US dollars.

International bullion traders and major banking institutions are the largest traders in this market. Delivery of gold purchased at the loco-London market is made in London. There was no trading in silver from 1935 to 1978 and the newly-instituted market is still small.

Insurance Market

The same conditions that have made Hong Kong an attractive place for financial institutions have drawn a large number of insurance companies to the territory.

Insurance business in Hong Kong is mainly divided into four regulated classes, namely, life, fire, marine and motor vehicles (third-party risk) business in addition to other types of smaller business such as medical insurance. Hong Kong has 287 insurance companies, 129 of them local, about one-third of the remainder from Great Britain and the majority of the rest distributed between the United States, Japan, Switzerland, and other developed countries.

Insurance companies are regulated by the comprehensive Insurance Companies Ordinance of 1983. The law is modelled on the United Kingdom Insurance Companies Act. The Insurance Ordinance limits the insurance business to companies that can demonstrate a minimum capitalization of HK$5 million (HK$10 million for companies that plan to undertake both long-term insurance and insurance required by statute). Insurance companies must also maintain a solvency margin requirement of HK$2 million to HK$6 million depending on the kind of insurance offered. Finally, companies seeking to offer insurance must satisfy the Registrar General (appointed Insurance Authority for purposes of enforcing the Ordinance) that their directors and controllers are qualified to run an insurance company.

Banking in the Future

Financial systems in Asia, as throughout the world, are moving in the direction of liberalization and internationalization. New York, the primary financial center, has set the example for others with establishment of international banking facilities (IBFs) in 1981. Japan, Taiwan, Australia, Switzerland, the UK, and France have taken tangible steps towards reducing financial industry restrictions. Thus, financial industry demarcations in the world in general are breaking down. This development trend will help to promote integration of national capital markets, consequently encouraging financial flows on a regional basis.

As a backdrop to this development, the government should ensure that Hong Kong has a sound financial system to facilitate the flow of funds between lenders and borrowers via a fair price mechanism. Any price mechanism which attempts to create a protected market for the elite few is likely to dampen Hong Kong's competitive edge on the international front. It may also generate additional burdens on the regulatory authorities as funds will shift into the unregulated markets.

Therefore, one major development in the Hong Kong banking system we may expect to see in the future is related to the regulatory environment. Although banking authorities will continue to focus on the safety and integrity of the domestic banking system, we will see great efforts to be made in breaking down those artificial barriers which attempt to disguise market reality.

At the same time, the Hong Kong banking system will move rapidly towards international financial integration. Indicative of this trend is the active foreign exchange market in Hong Kong and the growing maturity of domestic money and capital markets.

Financial innovation involves new product introduction and technology. New products might include futures and option trading in interest rates, foreign exchange futures, financial indexes, money market funds, just to cite a few. More will evolve as competition and the market become freer. In terms of technology, electronic delivery will change the fundamental nature of the product line. Those institutions which offer the quickest and most effective control over data will come out on top. The key challenge here to ensure success is the need for managed flexibility in relation to specific corporate treasury needs.

In the future, the Hong Kong banking sector will be involved more substantially in the financing of China's modernization plans. This can range from traditional correspondent banking services to the provision of investment consultancy services and information delivery. As Hong Kong moves closer to 1997, the influence of China on Hong Kong's economy will further increase.

Changes in the financial sector will naturally reflect the political changes. But overall, the outlook for Hong Kong as a financial center remains excellent.

Steven K. Baker is Division
Executive, East Asia Division,
Citicorp/Citibank.

Chapter 4

Taxation

by James M. Yager & David H. Southwood

In the intricate world of international taxation, it is refreshing to encounter the relatively uncomplicated Hong Kong system which imposes comparatively low rates of taxation.

The system was first introduced in Hong Kong in 1947 and was based on the same principles used by many of the Commonwealth countries. The original system has remained substantially unaltered.

Liability to income tax in Hong Kong is generally not dependent on the residence of the taxpayer. Rather, Hong Kong uses a territorial basis of levying tax, where liability is limited to income derived from sources within Hong Kong. Income derived from sources outside the territory is generally not assessed.

Multinational corporations are naturally attracted by this, which is why many of them use Hong Kong as their regional headquarters. By operating through a Hong Kong subsidiary they may be able to indefinitely defer their income from home country tax while incurring low Hong Kong taxation. Properly structuring the income to be from sources outside Hong Kong may result in no Hong Kong tax and a deferral of home country tax.

Individuals too find Hong Kong an ideal place to work. Subject to qualification tests and limitations, they can exclude their foreign earned income from home taxation while incurring low Hong Kong taxes. As with a commercial operation, if part of their earned income is derived from sources outside both Hong Kong and the home country, that income may totally escape taxation.

Four Separate Hong Kong Income Taxes

There is no total income tax in Hong Kong. There are instead four separate and distinct taxes on income:

  i) Profits Tax, assessed on profits arising from business carried on in Hong Kong;
 ii) Salaries Tax, assessed on income arising from any office, employment or pension in Hong Kong;
iii) Interest Tax, assessed on the recipient of interest earned from Hong Kong sources;
 iv) Property Tax, assessed on the owner of land and buildings situated in Hong Kong.

As a general principle each of the taxes is assessed separately and a person may have assessments in respect of all four taxes.

There are exceptions to the general rule, applicable to both individuals and corporations. Individuals can in certain circumstances apply for personal assessment when income from all four sources is combined and assessed together. Corporations carrying on business in Hong Kong are generally exempt from Property Tax and Interest Tax and have their total income assessed to Profits Tax.

Any source of income which does not fall within one of the four specific taxes is not subject to tax at all.

Profits Tax

Scope of the Tax

Individuals, corporations, bodies of persons and partnerships are liable to the charge in respect of assessable profits arising in or derived from Hong Kong.

Specifically, the law provides that profits earned by a person will be assessed to Profits Tax if:

i) the person is carrying on a trade, profession or business in Hong Kong; and

ii) is deriving a source of assessable profits in Hong Kong from that trade, profession or business, other than profits from the sale of capital assets.

It is important to appreciate that both conditions must be satisfied before liability to Profits Tax can arise.

Rate of Tax

Tax is assessed on the profit adjusted for tax purposes at the rate of 18 percent in the case of corporations and 16.5 percent for other non-corporate persons for tax years ending after March 31 1987.

Source of Profits

As a general rule, the source of profits is 'where in substance the operations which give rise to the profit took place', after having identified each step in the series of transactions involved in a particular trade or business. This principle is commonly applied to profit derived from the sale of goods and to commission income received where the person acts as an agent for a non-resident principal. There is no distinction in the scope of the charge between residents and non-residents.

Sale of Goods

Goods may be sold by a person who has done nothing more than purchase them from another party (eg sale of goods purchased from a wholesaler). On the other hand, the seller may have manufactured the goods from raw materials or may have purchased goods in a semi-finished condition and have used labour and materials in bringing the goods to a completed state.

Where the essence of the business is a whole series of operations then the place where one operation is performed does not necessarily determine the locality from which the whole profit is derived. Where a merchant is concerned merely with the purchase and resale of goods, however, the place where the contract of sale is concluded will frequently be the determining factor in deciding where the resultant profits are to be located.

Nonetheless, the courts in Hong Kong have held that the place where the contract of sale is concluded cannot be viewed in isolation and other factors, for example, the place where the contract of purchase of the goods is concluded and the place where pre- and post-contract negotiations and services take place, may also be relevant.

In particular, the place of conclusion of the contract of sale is a very material factor in the determination of the source of a merchanting profit, and care should be taken to ensure that this is outside Hong Kong if the profits are not to be subject to Hong Kong Profits Tax.

Although the Inland Revenue Department is known to have accepted that the conclusion of a contract outside Hong Kong by an employee is contributory evidence of an offshore source, there is stronger legal support for the exclusion of profits where the contractual arrangements are made by a 'permanent establishment' outside Hong Kong. In this context, a permanent establishment need not be a full branch elsewhere, but can be as a single agent, perhaps an employee, resident in another country, with a general authority to negotiate and conclude contracts of sale.

Other factors which the Inland Revenue Department will consider in determining source relate to the physical locality of the goods sold. Goods sold ex-stock maintained in Hong Kong, or which originate in, come to, or pass through Hong Kong will frequently be taken to be indicative of a Hong Kong source where the negotiation and conclusion of the contract of sale cannot be shown to be the crucial factor which is the essence of the business.

Commission Income

In determining source of commission income, a general division may be drawn between 'passive' and 'active' income.

Passive income refers to income derived under an obligation, ie from a contract of sale concluded between two independent parties, as opposed to income derived from the performance of some activity. In the former the source of the income will be dependent on the situs of the contractual obligation that gave rise to the income, whereas the latter will be determined by reference to the place where the activities were performed.

The Inland Revenue Department has published a Statement of Practice entitled Hong Kong Profits Tax—Locality of Profits, which identifies the following source of commission income as falling outside of the scope of Profits Tax:

* Income earned by a Hong Kong company holding a 'Far East Area' sales representation from the sale of group profits from:
  i) Actively soliciting orders ex-Hong Kong, on behalf of its principals; either by sending sales representatives overseas for the purpose; or by employing sub-agents overseas.
  ii) Factually doing nothing whatsover, either itself or through sub-agents.
* The receipt of 'infringement commission' for sales ex-Hong Kong in respect of which the Hong Kong company does nothing.
* Sales commissions received in respect of sales made by third parties but paid to the Hong Kong company under a directive from the parent company.
* Receipt of service fees for the provision of manufacturing know-how supplied by the parent company where the Hong Kong company has no proprietal rights over the know-how provided.
* Income derived from the supply of goods from stock maintained in Hong Kong in respect of sales negotiated and concluded by non-resident associated companies.

Deemed Trading Receipts

Certain types of income are deemed to be subject to Profits Tax whether or not an actual trade or business is being conducted in Hong Kong. These types of income are generally derived from the use of tangible or intangible property in Hong Kong, eg plant hire, patent or trade mark royalties.

Income Excluded

The following income is excluded from the charge to Profits Tax:
  i) a dividend from a corporation chargeable to Profits Tax;
 ii) profits or income of a capital nature;
iii) interest paid or payable on;
    a) a tax reserve certificate;

b) a government bond issued under the Loans (Government Bonds) Ordinance;

c) any profit on sale of a government bond;

* Interest income or profits from disposal of securities accruing to an authorized unit trust.

Statutory Deductions

Generally an expense will qualify as an allowable deduction in the computation of the assessable profits if it has been incurred for the purposes of earning profits chargeable to tax.

Certain types of deductions are treated specially as follows:

Depreciation

Favorable depreciation allowances are available for investment in certain types of buildings and equipment.

An allowance for depreciation is permitted for taxpayers who incur capital expenditures on specified assets used for the purposes of a trade, business, or profession, the profits from which are chargeable to Profits Tax. The allowances fall into one of three categories:

i) industrial building allowance;

ii) commercial rebuilding allowance;

iii) initial and annual allowances on plant and machinery.

The allowance takes the form of an initial allowance (except for commercial rebuilding allowance), given in the year of assessment in which the capital expenditure is incurred, and an annual allowance for each year of assessment during which the asset is used, including the year of acquisition, until such time as tax relief has been given for the qualifying cost of the asset.

Nature of allowance	Initial Allowance	Annual allowance
Industrial building	20%	4%
Commercial rebuilding	—	0.75%
Plant and machinery of residual value, depending upon type	55%, 10%	20%, 30%

Industrial buildings include any part of a building or a structure used for a factory, mill, transport, manufacturing, storage, farming, scientific research, communication, and for producing water, gas or electricity.

Any non-industrial building or structure used in a trade, business or profession in Hong Kong qualifies for the commercial rebuilding allowance of 0.75 percent of the capital expenditure.

Plant and machinery receives a favorable 55 percent initial allowance and an annual allowance depending upon its working life. Annual rate of depreciation for typical depreciable items are as follows:

Air conditioning plant	10%
Aircraft	30%
Electronic data processing equipment	30%
Electronics manufacturing machinery and plant	30%
Furniture (excluding soft furnishing)	20%
Lifts and escalators	10%
Motor vehicles	30%
Plastic manufacturing machinery and plant including moulds	30%
Textile and clothing manufacturing machinery and plant	30%

Losses

Losses incurred may be carried forward indefinitely (but not back) for application against any assessable profits of any trade of the same company. However, new anti-avoidance provisions can limit the utilization of losses when there is a change of ownership.

Interest

The deduction of interest is limited to interest paid on money borrowed:
 i) from a person subject either to the Profits Tax or interest tax on that interest;
 ii) from a financial institution, provided the loan is not secured or guaranteed by a deposit which yields income not subject to Hong Kong tax; or
 iii) wholly and exclusively to finance machinery, plant or trading stock used in the production of assessable profits, provided the lender is not an associate of the borrower.

Special rules apply for financial institutions, public utility companies, publicly quoted debentures and commercial paper.

Anti-avoidance Legislation

In the past few years there has been a trend by the Hong Kong government to introduce an anti-avoidance legislation with potential for more sweeping provision to deal with both specific and general schemes which the government sees as against the spirit of Hong Kong's relatively simple legislation. These are aimed primarily at tax driven schemes, ie where the tax advantage is the primary reason for the transaction.

Returns

The incorporation of a company or the registration of a branch in Hong Kong normally will result in the Inland Revenue Department issuing Profits Tax return forms on April 1 of each year, requesting that they be completed and furnished to the department within one month of the date of issue.

The commissioner will subsequently issue a notice of assessment stating the amount assessed, the tax charged and the due dates of payment. The assessment notice will usually include provisional tax for the current year, normally computed on an amount equal to the amount assessed for the preceding year; and will also require payment of the balance of final tax for the preceding year (calculated on the difference between the provisional tax paid for the preceding year and the total asset assessed for that year).

Salaries Tax

The Charge on Earnings

Salaries Tax is charged on an individual in respect of his income arising in or derived from Hong Kong from any office or employment or profit and also on any income derived from services rendered in Hong Kong.

As tax is imposed on a territorial basis, the concept of residence has little or no relevance to the charge to Salaries Tax. Both residents and non-residents are subject to Salaries Tax if they have Hong Kong source income from employment. The source is determined by a two-stage test.

Fundamental Location of Employment

Under Hong Kong tax law it is firstly important to distinguish whether an employment (not income) will be considered to have its source in or outside Hong Kong.

i) If an employment is fundamentally sourced in Hong Kong the taxpayer will have a liability to Salaries Tax on all remuneration received, even if some of the duties are performed outside Hong Kong.

ii) If an employment is fundamentally sourced outside Hong Kong, the liability to Salaries Tax is limited to tax on remuneration for services performed in Hong Kong. In this case the source of income is then important and a tax payer would normally be entitled to apportion his income from duties in Hong Kong on the basis of days spent inside and outside the territory, with the income for non-Hong Kong days being exempt from tax.

In either case, if duties are only performed in Hong Kong during visits here amounting to 60 days or less in a tax year, no liability will arise. The Inland Revenue Department will not normally recognize as "visits", periods of less than 60 days spent in Hong Kong where the individual is based in Hong Kong and or has a place of residence here.

The question of source of employment has been a contentious one in recent years and professional advice should be sought if an employee performs duties outside Hong Kong.

Definition of Remuneration

Having decided whether, and to what extent, remuneration arises in Hong Kong, a further important factor is what constitutes taxable remuneration. Remuneration is defined as including any wages, salary, leave pay, fees, commission, bonus, gratuity, perquisite or allowance.

Tax Charge

The tax charged is the lowest of:

i) the standard rate of 16.5 percent of net assessable income less approved charitable donations; or

ii) net assessable income less approved charitable donations and personal allowances charged at progressive rates as follows for the year of assessment 1987/88 (year ended March 31, 1988):

increase			Per cent Tax	HK$
First	HK$10,000	@	5	500
Next	HK$10,000	@	10	1,000
Next	HK$20,000	@	15	3,000
Next	HK$20,000	@	20	4,000
Balance		@	25	

Personal Allowances

The personal allowances for 1987/88 are as follows:

Personal allowances	HK$
Personal (single)	29,000
(married)	60,000
Additional (single)	5,000
(married)	10,000
Child: 1st	11,000
2nd	8,000
3rd	3,000
4th-6th (each)	2,000
7th-9th (each)	1,000
Depentent parent (each)	9,000
Additional dependent parent (where parent resides with taxpayer) (each)	3,000

It should be noted that a taxpayer will receive the full allowance (if eligible) against his income whether he is in Hong Kong for part or all of a year of assessment, ie there is no pro-rating of the allowances.

Net Assessable Income—Deduction of Expenses

In order to arrive at net assessable income, deductions from assessable income may be made for certain expenses (other than items of a domestic, private or capital nature) which have been wholly, exclusively and necessarily incurred in the production of assessable income and for depreciation allowances. However, the criteria for allowing such deductions are very strict and in practice there are few eligible deductions.

If an employee or his wife makes contributions to approved charities and those contributions amount to at least HK$100 in the year of assessment, these may be deducted provided they do not exceed 10 percent of assessable income after deducting allowable expenses and depreciation allowances.

Taxation of Benefits

The definition of income for Salaries Tax purposes includes 'perquisites', ie non-cash benefits, and allowances if provided as a reward for services. Allowances and benefits provided in a tax efficient manner may result in significantly reduced taxation.

Only three benefits are specifically mentioned in the Inland Revenue Ordinance.

Housing Benefits

This covers the cost of rent, rates and management charges (not utilities).

The provision to the employee of rent-free or subsidized rental accommodation by the employer may result in a very low assessable benefit. If the accommodation is provided as a 'rental reimbursement' (as defined) then the employee is normally treated as having an assessable benefit as follows:

1 room 4% of other assessable income
2 rooms 8% of other assessable income
Flat/house 10% of other assessable income

Care has been taken to ensure that the housing benefit is taxed as above rather than as a housing allowance, in which case the total cost to the employer is assessed on the employee.

Leave Passage Allowances

The value of any leave passage allowance or airfares granted to an employee is exempt from Salaries Tax, provided that it is expended for that purpose. There is no limit to the amount or frequency of such tax-free benefits, the only qualification is that they are actually expended for the given purpose.

Share Option Schemes

Any gain realized by the exercise, assignment or release of an option to acquire shares is taxable if the option was granted to an individual because of his employment or office. It should be noted that it is the exercise rather than the granting of the option which is the tax 'trigger'.

Other Benefits

In the absence of specific provisions in the tax statutes in respect of other benefits it is necessary to resort to case law. The important rules are:
  i) cash allowances are taxable;
 ii) non-cash benefits (benefits-in-kind) may be taxed at their face value if they are 'cash equivalents' eg gift vouchers or luncheon

vouchers; goods taken in kind eg clothing, are assessed at their 'second-hand' value;

iii) the assumption by the employer of a liability that an employee has contracted for himself, represents an assessable benefit;

iv) for a benefit-in-kind to be exempt from Salaries Tax, it is essential that the particular service provided on the employee's behalf be contracted for and paid for by the employer.

Filing Requirements

Both employees and employers have duties in the filing of information with the Inland Revenue Department.

General

There is no statutory requirement for an employer to bear any tax in the case of a default made by his employee. Provided an employer has fully complied with his obligatory responsibilities in submitting proper returns etc, he will not be subject to any fines or penalties. However, once an employer has given notice that an employee is to depart from Hong Kong, he must retain any monies due to the employee for one month from that date and may be required by the Inland Revenue Department to meet the employee's tax obligations out of such monies.

Employer's Obligations

The employer has to file returns notifying the Inland Revenue Department of the commencement and cessation of employment of employees. In addition the employer has to file an annual return giving the income and personal details of all employees employed in the year. There are no provisions requiring the regular deduction of tax from salaries.

Employee's Obligations

The employee has a corresponding obligation to inform the Inland Revenue Department of his commencement and cessation of employment, and to file a Salaries Tax return in respect of each tax year. The return covers both spouses' income. There are no provisions for separate taxation of husband and wife, although, by election, they can be separately assessed, with each party bearing his/her own share of the total tax bill, pro-rated to their respective incomes.

Penalties

There are no interest charges for late filings but penalties may be levied where without reasonable excuse there has been default in submitting the necessary returns within the specified period.

Basis of Assessment and Payment of Tax

In May each year the taxpayer is required to lodge a tax return showing actual income, derived by him in the preceding year ending March 31. The Inland Revenue Department will issue an assessment based on the return which sets out the final liability for each year, giving credit for Provisional Tax paid, and also a demand for Provisional Tax for the current year. Payments are normally made in January and April.

Tax Effective Considerations

It is possible to effect Salaries Tax savings by properly structuring an employee's compensation and benefits package prior to arrival in Hong Kong, or before finalizing employment details. Although it is never too late to undertake this exercise, it is advisable to consult a tax advisor prior to finalizing compensation details.

Interest Tax

Interest Tax is basically a withholding tax applied at the standard rate of 16.5 percent on interest and annuity income (either paid or credited) arising in or derived from Hong Kong.

Successive amendments to the Inland Revenue Ordinance have narrowed the scope of the tax in order to apply to only a limited number of occasions. Notable exemptions include interest paid on Hong Kong government debt, deposits with financial institutions and interest paid to corporations carrying on a trade or business in Hong Kong.

Property Tax

Property Tax is an income tax assessed on the owner of land or buildings situated in Hong Kong from which he derives rental income. Owners of all separately rated units of property are liable to Property Tax, although certain areas in the New Territories are not chargeable until brought within the scope of the tax by the governor. Corporations are exempt from Property Tax and pay Profits Tax instead.

The tax is payable by the owner of property. If a person who is not an owner sub-lets a property, he is liable to Profits Tax but not Property Tax.

The tax is charged at the standard rate of 16.5 percent on the net assessable value, which is 80 percent of rent receivable less any rates paid by the owner of the property.

Sundry Matters on Taxation of Income

Personal Assessment

Although Hong Kong has a schedular system with four taxes on income, it is possible for an individual to elect for Personal Assessment which brings together all sources of income into a single assessment which may, on occasion, be advantageous. In order to make an election you must be either a permanent or temporary resident of Hong Kong. This is one of the few occasions where the concept of residence has any significance in Hong Kong tax law.

Taxation of Dividends

Hong Kong does not tax dividend income.

Capital Gains Tax

There is no capital gains tax in Hong Kong, nor any other form of tax on capital gains. However, the Inland Revenue Department may seek to subject to Profits Tax the repeated realization of gains through the regular buying and selling of assets on the grounds that such transactions constitute a trade in those assets.

Social Security

There is no contributory system of social security in Hong Kong.

Double Taxation

Hong Kong does not have a double taxation treaty with any country; nor does it allow a foreign tax credit for taxes paid to another jurisdiction except for Commonwealth income tax relief. Hong Kong gives this relief where Commonwealth income tax has been paid on the same income. For this purpose Commonwealth income tax means a tax imposed by a qualifying Commonwealth country.

A recent proposal would enable salaries tax payers to exclude from salaries tax any income for services rendered in another jurisdiction if the tax payer is chargeable to, and has paid, tax in that jurisdiction.

Duties and Taxes not Measured by Income

Doing business in Hong Kong may result in exposure to duties and taxation which are not measured by income.

Estate Duty

Estate Duty is levied on the principal value of property situated in Hong Kong passing on the death of an individual. It is levied on a geographical basis, and the important factor is that a liability arises because of the location of property (including deemed property) in Hong Kong rather than the residence of the deceased at the time of death.

Although there is no lifetime gift tax as such in Hong Kong, gifts made during the lifetime of the deceased may still attach to his estate for Estate Duty purposes if the gifts are made within a certain time of death or if made with reservations as to title.

Estate duty is levied at rates of tax ranging from six percent on estates valued at HK$2 million to 18 percent on estates with chargeable property in excess of HK$5 million.

Stamp Duty

The Hong Kong Stamp Duty Ordinance provides that the execution of certain documents are subject to Stamp Duty. The duty is levied on the following instruments:
  i) Leases, agreements or contracts for sale or conveyances of immovable property in Hong Kong.
 ii) Contract note or transfer of Hong Kong stock.
iii) Issuance in bearer form of stock, loan capital and units in a unit trust that may only invest in loan capital.

Certain documents are subject to a fixed Stamp Duty while other documents are subject to duty based on a percentage of the value of the transaction.

Other Taxes

Various other taxes are imposed which generally do not materially affect the average person living in Hong Kong. These include:

Rates

A charge of six percent of the rateable value of the property is levied on the occupation of property in Hong Kong. Rates will not impact a tenant of rented property who pays his monthly charge inclusive of rates as those will then be paid by the landlord.

Import and Excise Duties

Hong Kong is generally a free port. However, the following items are subject to import duties: liquor, tobacco, hydrocarbon oils and methyl alcohol. Exceptions apply for small quantities brought into Hong Kong by individual travellers.

Airport Tax

A departure tax is assessed on all passengers leaving Hong Kong by air.

Hotel Tax

Five percent is the amount currently added to accounts for hotel accommodation.

James M. Yager is an Associate with
Peat Marwick Mitchell and Co.
David H. Southwood is Director of
Peat Marwick Mitchell and Co.

Chapter 5

Hong Kong's Global Trade Profile

by Sharon Freeman Horton

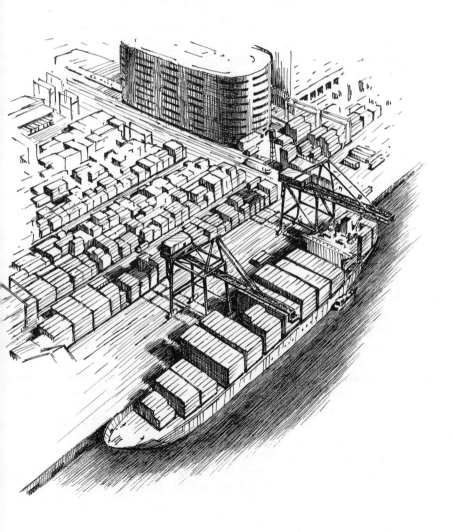

Overview

* The value of Hong Kong's visible imports and exports is almost double that of its GDP.
* The US, China and Japan are the three largest trading partners.
* Total value of Hong Kong's imports rose by 19 percent in 1986 over the previous year.
* China is growing in importance, becoming a 'domestic' market.
* Will the Hong Kong government play a future role in orchestrating industrial development?
* Increase in re-exports show entrepot spirit still thriving.

In the first half of this century, Hong Kong was not much different from many cities in China. The territory was wealthier than some of the major cities there, but not markedly so. Compared with Shanghai, China's leading business manufacturing and educational center, Hong Kong was primarily an entrepot and appendage of the British Empire.

Hong Kong's fortunes begin to change when, after the revolution in China, the territory came to inherit much of the managerial expertise and capital which sought refuge here. This infusion of talent helped to provide the resources necessary for industrialization.

A United Nations trade embargo against China helped the demise of entrepot trade in the early 1950s, and this, taken together with the fact that Hong Kong's internal market was always small, provided the impetus for the territory to develop a policy of export-oriented industrialism.

Successful development of an export-led economy was made possible in part by the administrative structure and its laissez-faire governance. By virtue of its British administration, Hong Kong enjoyed the advantages of Commonwealth preference which enabled its products to be more competitive in overseas markets and which also helped to stabilise its currency.

Throughout the territory's development, the policy of the government has been to allow external economic conditions to influence the economy at all levels. It is under these circumstances that the economy has had the greatest flexibility and resilience to respond to the vagaries of the industrialization process.

The question is, where does Hong Kong go from here. There is a consensus that the territory, and other Newly Industrializing Countries (NICs), must undergo another phase of economic transformation if they are to create another period of rapid economic expansion. Attendant with this are questions of how to launch a new industrial revolution and what role the government should play in the future to help create the conditions for growth.

In order to understand Hong Kong's future direction, it is important to understand where it has been.

Economically, the growth of the past twenty years has been much faster than that of Western industrialized countries. Its growth has also outpaced that of many Asian countries and has found recent counterparts in places like South Korea, Taiwan and Singapore.

The engine of economic growth and development in Hong Kong has always been trade. In the past three decades, Hong Kong's total trade has increased more than 34-fold. In fact, the value of its visible imports and exports is almost twice the size of its GDP.

While the trade statistics are impressive, it is important to note that Hong Kong is still very much dependent on trade to survive. Because almost all of its foodstuffs and raw materials have to be imported, it must earn the revenue with which to purchase these inputs. This comes from exports. Moreover, because the production process through which exports are created is characterized primarily as assembling in nature, Hong Kong has to export in great volumes to earn its 'value added' income.

Presently China, Japan and the USA are the three largest trading partners of Hong Kong. The way the system works is that Hong Kong earns its revenue from the US and other Western countries by exporting low grade manufactured goods. This revenue is in turn mostly spent on food and raw materials from China, and for machinery, equipment and consumer goods from Japan.

Hong Kong's trade statistics for 1986 reflect this pattern as follows (expressed in HK$ millions):

	Exports	Imports	Re-exports
USA	64,219	23,198	22,362
China	18,022	81,633	40,894
Japan	6,212	56,398	6,676
West Germany	11,003	8,041	2,688

Imports

Among the questions that are important when considering Hong Kong's imports are:
* Will they increase, decrease, or maintain current levels?
* Will they differ in composition or be replaced by
    domestically produced goods?

* Will the sources of supply likely change in the future?

Addressing the issue of demand for imports, because Hong Kong's imports comprise chiefly of foodstuffs, raw materials, machinery and fuel—most of which are not available in the territory—it can be said that the demand for imports is not particularly changeable.

One caveat, however, is that if export earnings continue to rise, it is likely that consumption of both local and foreign goods will also rise. Should this occur, it would be likely also that the relative share of imports of capital and consumer goods would also increase.

One factor which restricts the growth of imports is price. Generally speaking, in a world of rising prices, the costs of imports will tend to rise more rapidly than the value of Hong Kong's exports; the territory is thus vulnerable to imported inflation. This can only be offset by an increase in prices for exports.

The price and availability of supply from alternative sources therefore has to be considered. The present composition of Hong Kong's imports from its three top suppliers at present is:

Supplier and end-use category	HK$ million 1986
China	
All merchandise imports	81,633
Consumer goods	37,738
Raw materials and semi-manufactures	28,630
Foodstuffs	10,210
Capital goods	3,553
Fuels	1,502
Japan	
All merchandise imports	56,398
Raw materials and semi-manufactures	27,765
Capital goods	13,991
Consumer goods	12,938
Foodstuffs	1,702
United States of America	
All merchandise imports	23,198
Raw materials and semi-manufactures	7,402
Capital goods	7,160
Consumer goods	5,306
Foodstuffs	3,116

This pattern of importation has been fairly consistent over time. The total value of all Hong Kong's imports increased by 19 percent in 1986 over 1985. The actual prices of these imports increased by five percent in this period, and they increased in previous periods from the same sources.

It is difficult to pinpoint the exact price which would cause a substitution of supply. It is clear, however, that import prices will be likely to continue to rise. Increases were recorded for capital goods (+ 16 percent), consumer goods (+ nine percent) and raw materials and semi-manufactures (+ three percent); foodstuffs prices didn't significantly change from 1985 but fuel prices decreased significantly. In value terms, consumer goods increased (+ 28 percent); raw materials and semi-manufactures (+ 23 percent); foodstuffs (+ 13 percent); capital goods (+ nine percent) and fuels (−20 percent).

The most significant components of Hong Kong's imports are raw materials and semi-manufactures which constitute 43 percent of the value of 1986 imports. The major items in these categories are: all fabrics (17 percent); and thermionic cathode valves and tubes, diodes, transistors and electrical microcircuits (10 percent). These items are inextricably linked with Hong Kong's exports, as inputs to the manufacturing process.

As long as Hong Kong is in this particular export trade sector, then it is expected that a similar pattern of imports will prevail.

Exports

The question is, whether Hong Kong can realign itself to compete in a much more competitive world for its exports market. In becoming one of the top twenty exporting nations, Hong Kong essentially mobilized its abundant supply of cheap labor to respond to the demand of Western nations for cheap manufactured goods.

In having the competitive advantage of a cheap and ample labor supply, the need to infuse large amounts of money in capital equipment was obviated. Thus, at this juncture in its development, Hong Kong finds itself at a comparative disadvantage with some of its Asian competitors such as Japan, which has a much more broad base of technical know-how and equipment.

Hong Kong's economy is now at a crossroads. Since the late 1960s, exports of light manufactured products such as textiles and electronics have been facing increasing competition from other NICs. Moreover, while many of Hong Kong's competitors are attempting to diversify their manufacturing base, Hong Kong's progress toward this goal has been slower.

Today, as in the past, exports are highly concentrated with a few markets and items:

Rank	Country	Value of Exports	Total % of Exports	% Share by Item
1	USA	64,219	42	41 (apparel)
2	CHINA	18,022	12	16 (fabric)
3	WEST· GERMANY	11,003	7	57 (apparel)
4	UK	9,918	6	49 (apparel)
5	JAPAN	6,212	4	38 (apparel)

Five countries thus represent almost three quarters of Hong Kong's export markets. If Canada is included (three percent), the figure is almost 75 percent. Within these countries, apparel or textiles is the single largest import. This is also the case for China although its imports from Hong Kong are a little more diversified.

In quantitative terms, the more highly concentrated a country's exports are, the greater is its 'coefficient of concentration'. Hong Kong's is around the 50 mark on a scale of 1 to 100. The greater the value of concentration, the greater the instability of the economy. As compared with other developing countries, however, Hong Kong's coefficient is slightly lower.

Despite its concentration, there has been export growth in 1986, at a rate of value of only one percent lower than import growth at 18 percent and 19 percent respectively. The principal commodities exported in 1986 were:

	Per cent
Clothing	34
Watches and clocks	7
Textile fabrics	6
Toys and dolls	5

In respect to textiles and clothing, Hong Kong, Taiwan and South Korea all have maintained their market share and are equally facing new trade restrictions. With toys and games, both Taiwan and South Korea are capturing an increasing market share, especially in the USA.

Regarding photographic equipment, optical goods, watches and clocks, Hong Kong is also facing increasing competition from Taiwan and South Korea, although its products have slightly increased their market share.

To focus on Hong Kong's number one export market, the USA in 1986 represented a significant share, with exports valued at US$9.4 billion and ranking third in volume and value behind Taiwan and Korea.

To further highlight the role that Hong Kong and East Asian NICs have in US trade:

* Between 1985 and 1986, the overall US trade deficit with the East Asian NICs (Hong Kong, Singapore, South Korea and Taiwan) increased by US$5.8 billion to US$30.8 billion.

* US imports from the NICs grew 17 percent in 1986 to US$49.1 billion from the 1985 level of US$41.9 billion. Arrivals from Korea and Taiwan gained substantially. Purchases of passenger cars from Korea, newly introduced to the US market, alone rose from US$6.3 million in 1985 to US$851.4 million in 1986. Imports of footwear, sweaters, and ADP equipment also gained strongly.

* US imports from Hong Kong grew 11 percent, a rate slower than that from NICs overall.

While there is no question the United States is by far Hong Kong's most important export market, China is also gaining in importance. In fact, a vital determinant of Hong Kong's future trade growth will be its relationship with the PRC.

Reforms in China and the opening door have forged stronger and expanding economic links between the two. As a result, Hong Kong is now much more an economic part of China than at any time in recent history. This is largely because the territory has developed an industrialized economy, supported by a modern economic infrastructure, a competitive manufacturing sector, a global financial and commercial network and a skilled managerial and industrial workforce; all on China's doorstep.

For Hong Kong, China now promises to be something the territory has never had—a large 'domestic' market. This is proving to be especially valuable now that Hong Kong is striving to diversify its exports away from its enormous dependence on the US market.

Rapidly increasing trade is more evidence of the growing Hong Kong-China connection. In recent years, economic reform in China has begun to redefine the character of the traditional trading pattern. After the Korean war, Hong Kong continued to import a substantial quantity of goods from China (mostly food), but had virtually no exports, and Beijing accumulated huge trade surpluses. Since the PRC opened up its market, Hong Kong has become a major supplier to the mainland, both in its role as a manufacturer and as an entrepot.

The principal divisions of Hong Kong's export trade with China include (HK$ million):

	1984	1985	1986
Textile yarn, fabrics, made-up articles and related products	2,028	2,123	3,652
Miscellaneous manufactured articles (mainly baby carriages, toys, games and sporting goods)	1,500	2,062	2,720
Telecommunications and sound recording and reproducing apparatus and equipment	2,050	2,309	2,418
Photographic apparatus, equipment and supplies and optical goods; watches and clocks	469	886	1,104
Electrical machinery, apparatus and appliances, and electrical parts thereof	680	1,048	1,033
Total	11,283	15,189	18,022

In 1985, when Hong Kong experienced a six percent overall decline in exports, China was a bright spot, consuming a 35 percent increase over 1984. The question is to what extent setbacks in Western markets can be offset by increasing sales to China. If China tightens its imports then it is expected that exports from Hong Kong, which are not semi-manufactures related to sub-contracted processing or joint ventures, could also be reduced.

All this admittedly raises more questions than it answers.

One could say that the findings through examination of the export trade statistics fall into two camps, that which we do know and that which is left to speculation. What we know is that:

* Hong Kong is presently the world's largest exporter of garments and textile fabrics, toys and watches and certain electrical gadgets.
* Hong Kong's export volumes of most principal commodities rose in 1986, as did the prices for most of these commodities.
* In volume terms, Hong Kong's exports to its top five markets increased, as did their associated prices.
* Hong Kong's exports are fairly concentrated sectorally and geographically to certain markets, with the China market growing in importance.

What we don't know is:
* How Hong Kong will face increasing competition from other NICs for export markets in the future.

* How Hong Kong will fare under increasing protectionist pressures, especially from the USA.
* How the structure of governance in the future will lend itself to continued growth and development for Hong Kong.

The answers to these questions hold the future of Hong Kong trade.

Challenging the Competition

Hong Kong came to be what it is today through its intelligent and industrious labor force. Indeed, it is the territory's most important economic resource, but it is in need of training. Statistics however show there has been an improvement in education that is likely to continue.

There has also been government support in recent years to promote technical training, and a new department devoted especially to technical training was created in 1982.

Just how far the government should go to promote industrial restructuring is the question of the moment. By comparison, the governments of South Korea and Singapore took a particularly proactive role in orchestrating private business development. In theory this is in opposition to the foundations on which Hong Kong was based and through which it has prospered.

Thus far, there have been two phases of structural change in economic growth. The first occurred in the 1960s and ushered in the manufacturing boom. The second occurred in the 1970s and established Hong Kong as a financial center. The question now is whether there should be a third industrial revolution which would place Hong Kong in a position to compete with countries such as Japan in supplying more sophisticated, more technically advanced products. Should this be the direction for the future, it will require a great deal of government support.

Trade Barriers

Britain was the first to impose trade restrictions on Hong Kong back in the 1950s. Presently, the heat is coming from the USA to impose restrictions on imports of textile yarns and clothing. This started in 1959 and resulted in tariff quotas in 1961. Since that time many EEC nations have also instituted barriers.

The present trade restriction is usually effected in such a way that Hong Kong agrees to restrain her export of textiles and clothing within certain limits in one year to a specified nation. At present, the territory has bilateral agreements with the US, the EEC, Austria, Canada, Sweden, Finland and Switzerland. These are, in turn, based on the guidelines presented by the Multi-Fibre Arrangement (or MFA), which is conducted by GATT (General Agreement on Trade and Tariffs).

Though GATT aims to promote free trade, exceptions are taken into consideration. From the late 1950s, competition was particularly felt in trade in textile products and this gave rise to growing pressure from the textile industries of the developed countries (ie importing nations) for measures to limit 'disruption' allegedly caused by relatively low-priced imports from developing nations; and for 'breathing space' to allow for gradual adjustment. This led to trade restrictions in textile products.

In the early 1960s, first the Short Term and then the Long Term Cotton Agreement came into being to regulate international trade in cotton textile products. In 1973, the Long Term Cotton Arrangement was replaced by the MFA, a more comprehensive instrument, covering more than cotton textiles; and it has been revised and extended twice in 1977 and 1981 each after four years' interval. MFA indicated the guidelines for the developed importing countries to apply selective restraints in respect of particular textile products from particular sources. It also provides for annual growth allowance, swing, carryover, and carryforward.

However, since 1978, a clause regarding 'reasonable departures' has been added. Under this clause, if any importing nation is confronted with pressing 'import problems', it can demand for deviation from those measures proposed by the MFA. Obviously, it leads inevitably to the misuse of the provision by developed importing countries as a license to disregard the terms of the MFA and to extract highly restrictive bilateral agreements from exporting countries.

For three years, since the invention of 'reasonable departures', there is evidence of a proliferation of bilateral agreements having features at variance with the MFA. These include agreements where restraint limits are expressed in terms of price instead of in quantities of merchandise; agreement with provisions for far less than the MFA minima in respect of swing, carryover and carryforward; agreements providing for export restraint on those items not indicated in the MFA; and agreements containing cutbacks in quota. In consequence, like other exporting nations, Hong Kong also suffers.

Governance

The British lease on the New Territories, which consists of over

90 percent of Hong Kong's land area, will expire on June 30, 1997. China and the United Kingdom held negotiations on the future of Hong Kong for over two years before they initialed a joint declaration on September 26, 1984. The Joint Declaration was signed by representatives of the two governments on December 19, 1984. It went into force after an exchange of ratification instruments on May 27, 1985. The two countries agreed that China will resume sovereignty over Hong Kong on July 1, 1997 when Hong Kong will become a Special Administrative Region (SAR) of China.

The agreement stipulates that Hong Kong's present social and economic systems will be preserved for 50 years, until 2047. It will remain a free port and a separate customs territory, and continue to run its own finances independently. The central government of China will not levy taxes in the SAR. The SAR will conduct its own external relations by concluding agreements with other countries in the fields of economy, culture, trade, finance, shipping, tourism and sports. It will also issue its own travel documents. The conduct of foreign affairs and defense will be the responsibility of the central government of China, as it is currently the responsibility of the UK. The currency will remain freely convertible.

In assessing the probability that this lofty goal of special administration can be achieved, it is important to understand what Hong Kong means to China.

Through Hong Kong, China has easy access to what every developing country needs—foreign funds for investment and development activities. Hong Kong is one of the world's largest banking centers, with 140 full-branch foreign banks, another 143 foreign bank representatives and 280 deposit-taking companies. In addition, there is a large, local banking community—dominated by the Hongkong and Shanghai Bank—actively involved in China business.

These financial intermediaries—especially Beijing's own Bank of China group with thirteen 'sister' banks—have been instrumental in assisting Beijing with many of its specialized capital needs. Through Hong Kong's banking system, China has been able to obtain syndicated loans, float bond issues and finance for its foreign trade activities.

Hong Kong has also been China's most important source of direct foreign investment. It is estimated that over the past five years since 1979, Hong Kong has accounted for 60 percent of all investment in China and 70 percent of all joint venture projects. The territory's share of foreign investment in China for joint ventures and project finance is much greater than the United States, Japan and other developed nations because Hong Kong businessmen are less risk-averse than most foreign businessmen in committing funds to concrete projects.

In view of the importance that Hong Kong has to China as a foreign exchange earner, as a source of capital infusion, and as a window on the Western world, it is unlikely that the PRC would knowingly want to disturb the existing patterns of trade. In fact, to the contrary, it would be in China's best interest to further enhance Hong Kong's trading position in the world.

Re-exports

Re-exports are a significant component of Hong Kong's trade, which comprise those products re-exported (after importation) without having undergone a manufacturing process in Hong Kong. This element of trade increased in value by 16 percent in 1986, reflecting a strong revival in the territory's entrepot trade.

Such trade, in large measure, involves either something from some part of the world which is destined for China, or goods from China which are destined for some part of the world. For instance, in 1984, either as a market or as a source of supply, China accounted for 74 percent of Hong Kong's re-export trade.

Also, and most importantly, Hong Kong is the middleman between China on the one hand and Taiwan and South Korea on the other.

There are additional cost and infrastructural related reasons why goods are shipped into Hong Kong and then on-forwarded to China. The PRC lacks the infrastructural support to handle big containerized ships at many of its ports; it also lacks the necessary equipment to off-load the goods; and the warehousing space to hold them. There is also insufficient internal transportation within China to move the goods from point A to B. Thus goods are consigned to Hong Kong where the freight forwarding agents can best determine how to dispatch them to China. The same applies for China's exports. In 1986:

* Re-exports of consumer goods accounted for 40 percent in value of the total; capital goods 13 percent; foodstuffs six percent and fuels less than one percent.
* The value, price and volume of most re-exports increased, although the value of capital goods declined, the prices of fuels, raw materials and semi-manufactures dropped and the volume of capital goods decreased.
* China accounted for 33 percent of value of re-exports; the US was second with an 18 percent share, Japan, Taiwan and South Korea each held a five percent share.

* Demand for Hong Kong's re-exports increased by 52 percent in the USA, 51 percent in South Korea, Taiwan 37 percent and Japan 22 percent, but China's decreased by 11 percent.
* Of re-exported goods, 42 percent originated in China, 15 percent in Japan, nine percent in the US, Taiwan seven percent and South Korea three percent. The value of re-exports from the US and China increased while those of Japan, Taiwan and South Korea decreased.

On balance, there are just a few questions which put the future of Hong Kong's re-exports into sharper focus:

* Will the political reasons for this trade continue to exist?
* Will the infrastructure deficiencies of other countries persist so that Hong Kong transhipment is needed in the future?
* Will global demand be sustained or increase to benefit Hong Kong's re-export trade?

The answer to these questions which do not strictly lie in the statistics on past performance is probably yes, on all counts. That is to say that the invisible trade between China, Taiwan and South Korea will probably continue to be conducted through Hong Kong.

The likelihood of China and other Asian countries having sufficient transportation facilities in the near term is minimal so, it is conceivable there will be a continual need for Hong Kong's transhipment role.

As for global demand prospects, the statistics can help with this and through them it can be observed that increases occurred almost every year for every country.

Signposts

What combination of factors will actually improve Hong Kong's trading prospects? Part of the answer may lie in factors over which Hong Kong has no direct control. For instance, if the US dollar is depreciated or appreciated it could enhance or detract from the territory's exports. The macroeconomic policies of Western nations which manipulate interest rates could also combine to have either a negative or positive impact on trade.

Similarly, externalities like oil prices and external trade policies exert significant influences on global trade within which Hong Kong trade is conducted.

As to the proactive role Hong Kong can take to enhance its future trade, the signs, in view of the increasing competition, seem to point to the need for greater diversification and upgrading of exports. Such diversification could entail establishing new industries or diversifying products within established and new industries. In order to effect this growth Hong Kong manufacturers will likely need more industrial training, technology support and adequate land.

Exactly what role the government should play to facilitate these objectives will likely be a subject of future debate, both before and after 1997.

Sharon Freeman Horton is
Joint Managing Partner of
Lark-Horton Connections Ltd.

Bibliography

1. *Hong Kong Trade Review 1985*, Hong Kong Trade Development Council
2. *Overseas Business Reports Oct 1985 Marketing in Hong Kong*, US Department of Commerce, ITA
3. *1986 U.S. Foreign Trade Highlights*, U.S. Department of Commerce, ITA
4. *Hong Kong Annual Digest of Statistics 1986 Edition*, Census & Statistics Department, Hong Kong
5. *Hong Kong Review of Overseas Trade in 1986*, Census & Statistics Department, Hong Kong
6. *Hong Kong 1984*, Editor : Melinda J. Parsons Government Information Services Census & Statistics Department
7. *Hong Kong Trade Statistics Imports, Exports, Re-exports*, Census & Statistics Department
8. *The Economy of Hong Kong Revised Edition 1985* by Cheng Tong Yong
9. *The Business Environment in Hong Kong* 2nd Edition Editor: David Lethbridge

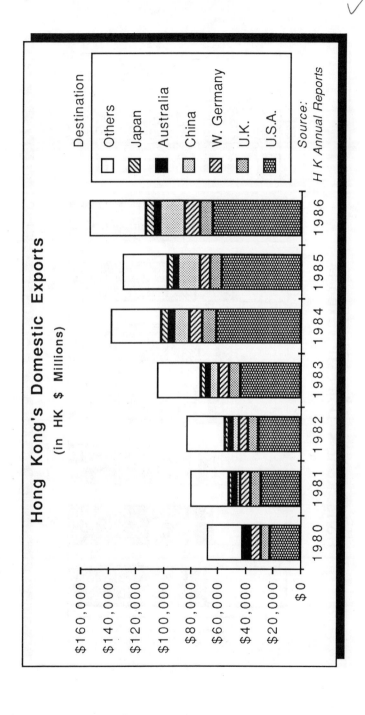

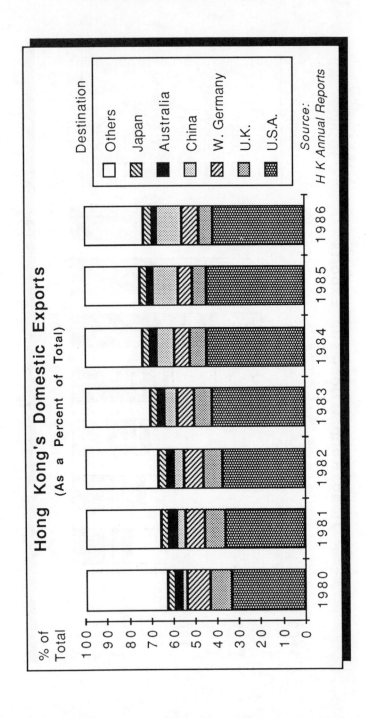

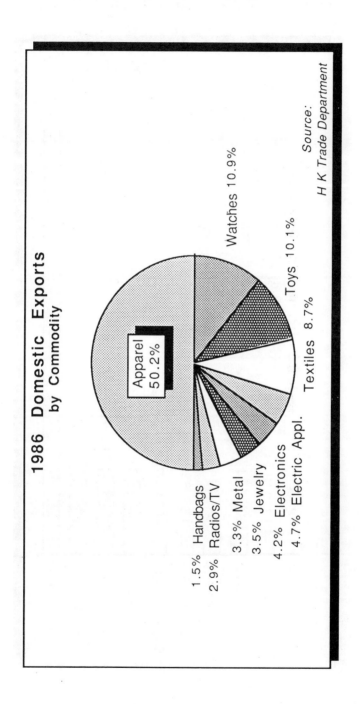

1986 **Domestic Exports**
by Commodity

Apparel 50.2%

Watches 10.9%

Toys 10.1%

Textiles 8.7%

4.7% Electric Appl.

4.2% Electronics

3.5% Jewelry

3.3% Metal

2.9% Radios/TV

1.5% Handbags

Source:

H K Trade Department

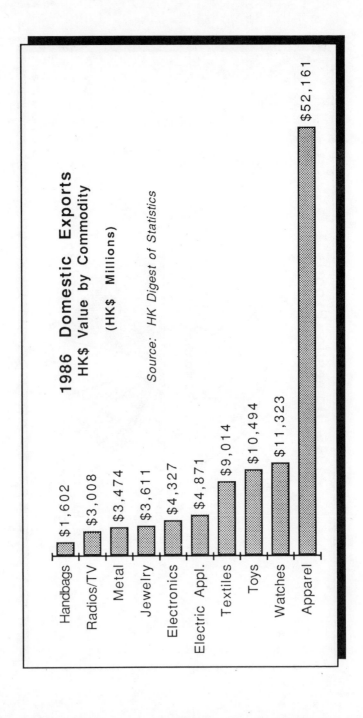

1986 Domestic Exports
HK$ Value by Commodity
(HK$ Millions)

Source: *HK Digest of Statistics*

Commodity	Value
Handbags	$1,602
Radios/TV	$3,008
Metal	$3,474
Jewelry	$3,611
Electronics	$4,327
Electric Appl.	$4,871
Textiles	$9,014
Toys	$10,494
Watches	$11,323
Apparel	$52,161

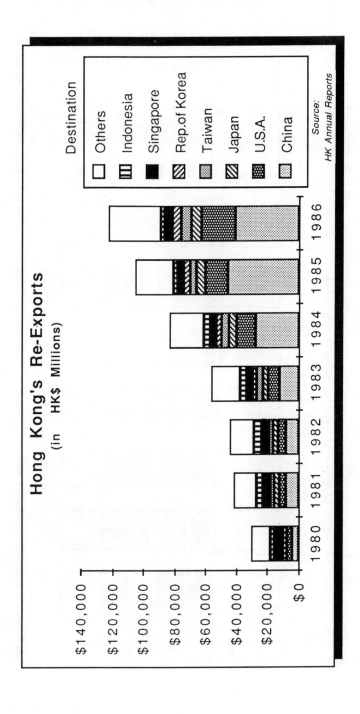

Hong Kong's Re-Exports
(in HK$ Millions)

Destination

Others
Indonesia
Singapore
Rep. of Korea
Taiwan
Japan
U.S.A.
China

Source:
HK Annual Reports

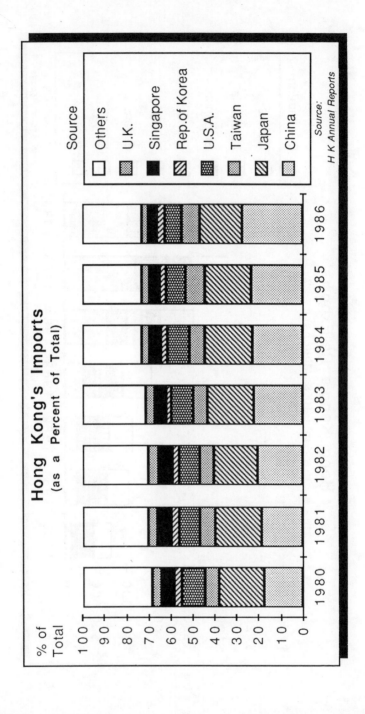

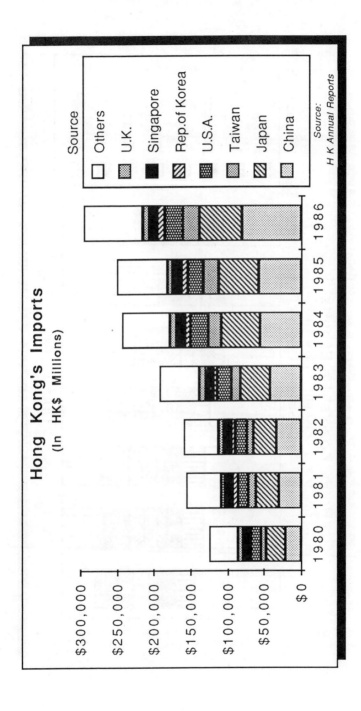

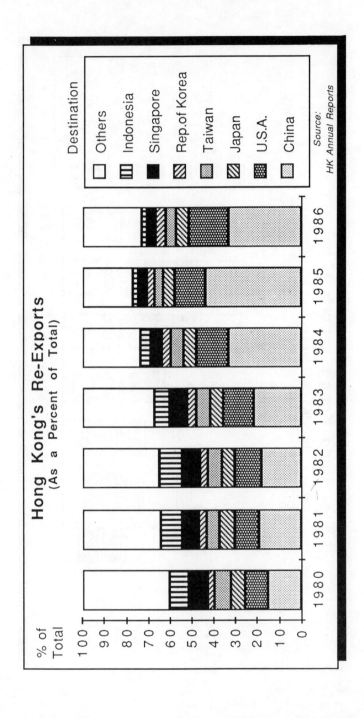

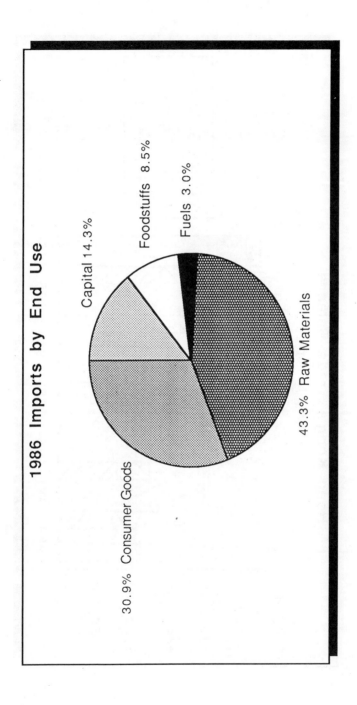

1986 Imports by End Use

Capital 14.3%

Foodstuffs 8.5%

Fuels 3.0%

43.3% Raw Materials

30.9% Consumer Goods

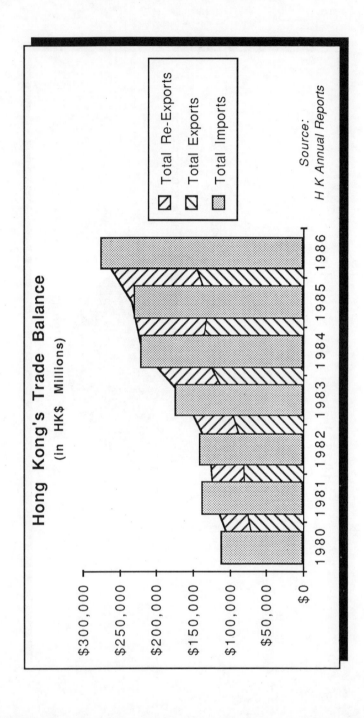

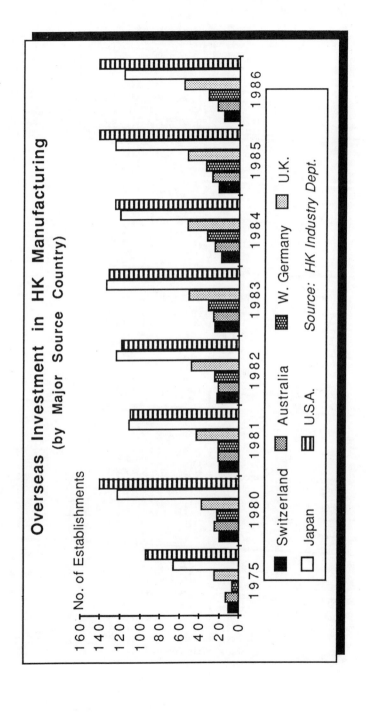

Overseas Investment in HK Manufacturing
(by Major Source Country)

No. of Establishments

Switzerland Australia W. Germany U.K.

Japan U.S.A. *Source: HK Industry Dept.*

Chapter 6

A Staging Point for China Trade

by Thomas D. Gorman

Hong Kong is frequently compared to Beijing and other Chinese cities as an operations base for the China market. For this comparison to stand, we should examine what the advantages may be, for example, for many companies, it is not an "either-or" decision. Proximity to major customers, whether in China's capital or in her other business centers, ultimately requires a full-time presence through one or more offices. Usually, however, the early stages of market development do not necessarily require an office in Beijing, Shanghai, or Guangzhou (Canton).

It is for these relatively new-to-the-market companies, or companies whose China business occupies a small share of their Asian regional business, that Hong Kong emerges as an attractive alternative. Its geographical position, free port status, and well-developed infrastructure offer enhanced access to other Asian markets besides China.

The main attractions can be grouped into two categories: Business Efficiency and Quality of Life. Business efficiency refers to factors which relate to a corporation's ability to function effectively and profitably: tax environment, infrastructure, legal and regulatory situation, availability and cost of labor and service support, etc. Quality of life includes factors related to a company's ability to recruit and maintain key executives in a lifestyle acceptable to them.

Although both categories figure in the decision-making process, factors related to business efficiency carry more weight than those related to quality of life. Business efficiency is precisely the area in which Hong Kong excels, not only in comparison to Chinese or Asian cities, but by world standards.

Hong Kong is arguably the most efficient business center in the world, with well-developed facilities geared to fast, competitively-priced service. Compared to Beijing and other Chinese cities, the territory unquestionably reigns supreme in this respect. A full range of business services is available at generally reasonable (and in some cases exceptionally low) prices, with turn-around times so short that newcomers are often surprised.

It should be noted that Hong Kong faces an extraordinary transformation in the years before and after 1997, the year when the transition to administration by the People's Republic of China will take place. This fact introduces an element of uncertainty into business planning, as the process of political change unfolds. It is clearly the stated policy of China's current leadership to maintain the attractiveness of Hong Kong to international investors. Whether this will be feasible, in light of domestic political and economic considerations, remains to be seen.

Business Efficiency

A checklist of some of the most frequently cited advantages in terms of business efficiency which Hong Kong offers in comparison to Beijing, Shanghai and other Chinese cities would include the following:

* Availability of professional, competitively-priced, customer-oriented support services including legal, tax, accounting, advertising and public relations, architecture, design, packaging, shipping and freight forwarding, executive recruitment, personnel, surveying, translation, printing, market research, software development, travel agency, specialized financial and investment services, management consulting, training, etc.
   i) basically no restrictions or unfair limitations imposed on international suppliers in competition with local suppliers;
  ii) good availability of English-speaking sales and service personnel among suppliers of business services and products;
 iii) no restrictions on payment in local versus foreign currency;
  iv) no officially endorsed or government-initiated price discrimination between local and international companies for services or products used by businesses.

* Company law is simple and straightforward; corporate profits taxation is clear and reasonable.

   i) incorporation process inexpensive and fast;
  ii) environment favorable to foreign investors;
 iii) well-developed regulatory framework; answers and clarifications on general issues available with ease;
  iv) advice and counsel on legal and tax matters available from wide variety of local and international companies;
   v) foreign investors may compete freely with local companies.

* Freely convertible currency with no restrictions on foreign currency remittances overseas.

Hong Kong dollar currently pegged to US dollar but freely convertible.

* Full range of financial institutions and services; good availability of funds for venture capital; open access to lending for commercial and individual purposes.

* Free port status; limited range of products subject to import duty.

Business equipment and office products available from worldwide suppliers at duty-free prices; most major suppliers present in market with good distribution and service support capabilities.

* Hong Kong government basically does not restrict companies from doing business with any country or region of the world.

* Good availability of office premises at prices competitive with major world business centers.

Lesses and contracts are protected by law and effectively enforced.

* World class communications facilities with few government restrictions on usage of telecommunications by business.

  i) competitive pricing; local and international companies charged at the same rate; efficient domestic service;
 ii) geographical compactness of main business districts good, inexpensive local transport.

* Good availability of trained staff for many technical and most clerical job functions.

  i) English language skills widespread;
 ii) hiring and firing not regulated by government;
iii) no restrictions on incentive-based management;
 iv) business travel by locals outside of Hong Kong generally possible with employer's support;
  v) staff hired direct rather than through government agency;
 vi) generally positive attitude by workforce towards overtime work, given extra pay incentive;
vii) unions generally cooperative with business;
viii)working for foreign enterprises on a career basis widely regarded as positive rather than negative;
 ix) employment visas generally available with a minimum of red tape and time where imported jobs are not displacing local workforce.

* Well-managed government civil service which operates efficiently and with minimal corruption.

Quality of Life

The factors most often cited by American executives as Hong

Kong's positive attitudes when compared with Chinese cities include:

* Variety, quality and cost of housing.
* Availability of a wide range of imported foods and beverages at reasonable cost.
* Widespread English capability in shops, restaurants, government offices, etc. expedites the processing of day to day personal business.
* Customer service in many retail, foodservice, and other consumer organizations is better.
* Range of clubs and recreational facilities and activities.
* For linguistic and other reasons, easier to establish contacts and to make friends with local as well as foreign nationals; participation in community and civic life not restricted by race or nationality.
* English-speaking domestic help available at very reasonable rates.
* Better range and price of products for home furnishing and daily household requirements.
* Full spectrum of religious faiths with practising congregations.
* Good schools with curricula compatible with most US and international standards for higher education.
* Domestic services including interior design, repair and maintenance widely available at reasonable cost.
* Familiar legal environment vis a vis civil conduct and personal freedoms; local media and press content mostly free from government control; limited censorship of political or moral content of films, television, etc; foreigners and locals enjoy equal status before the law.
* Unrestricted shipment of personal effects in and out with minimal Customs red tape or duty.
* Wide range of international air carriers serving worldwide destinations expedites making of personal travel arrangements; travel agencies offering personalized service available; wide access to international hotel and rental car reservation systems.
* Growing range of Asian and international cultural events and entertainment.
* Availability of high quality medical treatment from general as well as specialized practitioners in public and private facilities; English language widespread.

Hong Kong's Changing Role

The foreign trade of the People's Republic of China increased more than tenfold between the mid-1970s and mid-1980s, and Hong

Kong's role in this fast growing import-export business expanded exponentially. As China opened the door to foreign investment during this period, Hong Kong took on added importance as a 'user-friendly' environment for foreign companies. It expanded beyond being a place in which to obtain information on doing business in China, into a place to base part or all of one's China operations. China's direct investments in Hong Kong also grew explosively during this period of time, in volume of investment, sectors of business involved, and number of enterprises incorporated. From the dozen or so principal corporations in Hong Kong representing units under the Ministry of Foreign Trade during the early 1970s, many hundreds of PRC Chinese companies now represent the interests of various entities within the Ministry of Foreign Trade, Chinese provincial and municipal trade and economic departments, and Sino-foreign joint ventures. Access to these companies can facilitate the establishment of new business ventures in various parts of China.

So many 'PRC companies' are now operating in Hong Kong that it can be difficult to distinguish between the official and the unofficial, or to separate the bona fide representatives from those who exaggerate their capabilities. Privately, some executives of the older, long-established PRC companies in Hong Kong express disdain at the sometimes confusing proliferation of new-to-market 'PRC companies'. However, the influx has been a good thing for Hong Kong and for foreign business operating here. The territory's blend of Chinese and international business efficiency has clearly attracted many Chinese enterprises to set up shop, and take advantage of the expertise, economy, and access to foreign markets. Some Chinese enterprises maintain significant amounts of foreign currency in Hong Kong for purchases of products to be imported and used in China.

Hong Kong has the opportunity to be the designer, production supervisor, and marketing agent for many of China's export products. The disappointing results of offshore oil exploration in the South China Sea during the early 1980s underlined the urgency of improving the quality and range of Chinese exports, since oil cannot be expected to provide the hoped-for surge in foreign currency earnings by the late 1980s.

To the extent that increased responsiveness to overseas market trends, and new product ideas, will contribute to the growth of Chinese exports, Hong Kong has an important and growing role to play. How this role will change before and after 1997 is a subject which will continue to be debated.

Thomas D. Gorman is President of
China Consultants International (HK) Ltd.

Chapter 7

Hong Kong and China: A Trade Profile

By John T. W. Chu

China has grown enormously in significance as Hong Kong's major trading partner in the past few years. In 1978, domestic exports from the territory to China were worth HK$81 million, placing it well below the United States, Japan, the United Kingdom, West Germany and Canada. But by 1986 that figure had leapt to over HK$18,022 million, making the PRC second only to the US as an export market for Hong Kong.

Of even greater significance is re-export growth. Measured by country of destination, China has reinforced its position as by far Hong Kong's most important re-export market, with almost HK$40,894 million worth of re-exports in 1986, up from HK$214 million in 1978. Currently, sales to China account for some 12 percent of Hong Kong's domestic exports and 44 percent of its re-exports.

Imports from China to Hong Kong have also grown, though less dramatically, from HK$10,550 million in 1978 to almost HK$81,633 million in 1986. The PRC now ranks as Hong Kong's leading import source, with Japan second.

The overall story, then, is one of enormous growth in China's importance as a trading partner to Hong Kong since the country adopted its open door policy, or, to put it another way, during the period of the Sixth Five-year Plan. China's future economic performance will undoubtedly have a profound effect on Hong Kong's own growth and prosperity.

Hong Kong's Trade with and Investment in China

Two essential elements affecting China's trade with the outside world are its ability to export and the amount of foreign exchange it can manage to muster. On both counts, Hong Kong is playing, and will continue to play, a crucial role.

The key to China's ability to export is the growth of its productive capacity, leading to increased supply of exportable commodities/products. However, this has to be complemented by an expansion of its marketing network and will require the support of an efficient infrastructure, for the growth of foreign trade in China is currently constrained by the lack of efficient facilities such as transportation and telecommunications.

Hong Kong has the necessary infrastructure to support China's expansion in world trade. The territory ranks as one of the three best natural harbors of the world, and besides being very conveniently located geographically at the crossroads of international trade and cargo movements in the Far East, it is one of the best equipped and most efficient ports anywhere. Some importers and exporters involved in trade with China have requested that their cargo be handled through Hong Kong. In many instances, it is much cheaper and more punctual. Furthermore, cargo space in Chinese ocean-going vessels can be difficult to book, whereas there is often available space on the frequent routes linking Hong Kong and many overseas ports.

Besides the growth of the Chinese economy as a way to increase the amount of exportable commodities, another way China trade can be expanded is through the acquisition of more foreign exchange. In this respect Hong Kong is again of strategic value to China. The trade balance between Hong Kong and China has been to China's favor. Many have claimed that Hong Kong is the largest and most profitable market for many PRC products.

Hong Kong-China Trade, 1970–86 (HK$ million)

	1970	1978	1981	1982	1983	1984	1985	1986
HK exports to China	30	81	2924	3806	6223	11283	15189	18022
Re-exports to China	34	214	8044	7992	12183	28064	46023	40894
Total exports and re-exports to China	64	295	10968	11790	18406	39347	61212	58916
Imports from China	2830	10550	29510	32935	42821	55753	58963	81633
Trade balance	−2766	−10255	−18542	−21145	−24415	−16,406	+ 2,249	−22717

Source: Census and Statistics Department, Hong Kong

It is clear that the growth and continuation of the Hong Kong market is of significant value to China. In fact, the PRC's exports to Hong Kong (including re-exports through Hong Kong) is itself a substantial part of the total China trade as it represents roughly one-third of total China exports.

Besides its trade surplus with Hong Kong, China also earns foreign exchange from business operations in the territory. This, together with its Hong Kong trade surplus and remittances from Hong Kong and overseas Chinese through Hong Kong, contribute a substantial share of China's annual foreign exchange earnings. Through the Bank of China and its 12 sister banks in Hong

Kong (which have over 250 offices and is the second largest banking network in Hong Kong) China can avail itself of the low cost short-term deposit market of which the BOC group's share is substantial. The group has also made loans to Hong Kong business for China projects.

China's modernization program has acquired more support from Hong Kong than any other source. The PRC established four special economic zones in 1980 with an eye to attacting capital and expertise largely from overseas Chinese communities. Shenzhen, in particular, was set up with the idea that it would develop close ties to Hong Kong. Although reliable statistics are not available, it is generally accepted that Hong Kong has provided about 90 percent of Shenzhen's total investment to date and contributed about 60 percent of the total direct foreign investment in China. This figure becomes even higher if projects are taken into account in which a Hong Kong middleman played a role.

China's Economic Activities in Hong Kong

China has increased its economic activities in Hong Kong through the expansion of existing business operations and the establishment of new organizations directly involved in trade and investment. China's investments in Hong Kong are difficult to quantify, with estimates ranging from HK$25 billion to HK$40 billion. The investment comes in every conceivable form, from ownership of commercial, residential, and industrial property to interests in manufacturing, shipping, and trade.

Many Chinese firms have been set up in Hong Kong during the past few years. They range from diversified companies employing hundreds of people and representing a large province, to one-man shops. The range of services·and reliability are similarly broad.

These companies are independent of the long-term establishments, such as China Resources (Holdings) Co, the official arm of the Ministry of Foreign Economic Relations and Trade, and China Merchants and Steam Navigation, which represents the Ministry of Communications. The two most prominent among these companies are Guangdong Enterprises (Holdings) and Fujian Enterprises (Holdings) Co. Not only do these coastal provinces produce a large variety of goods and offer convenient transportation, they are at the forefront of China's economic reforms. Both also have special economic zones (Shenzhen, Zhuhai and Shantou in Guangdong, and Xiamen in Fujian).

Several of the larger firms became holding companies in 1985. Among the subsidiaries are representatives of branches of national import and export companies. For example, Guangdong Light Industrial Products Co, an agent for China National Light Industrial Products Import and Export Corp, exports a variety of products, including electrical household appliances, shoes and sporting goods. The Guangdong subsidiary can handle all negotiations for price, specifications and delivery and sign contracts so that the foreign trader need not leave Hong Kong. Fujian Enterprises is also one of those companies. It has grown from an export agent to a diversified holding company, with 18 wholly or jointly owned subsidiaries.

In addition to the long-established offices representing ministerial and provincial level enterprises, other areas have also established some presence in Hong Kong. The Dalian International Co, for example, was set up in 1985 by 18 foreign trade companies in the northeastern port city. Many of the provinces and cities have held smaller versions of the Guangzhou Trade and Commodities Fair (usually called Symposium on Technical and Economic Cooperation) to introduce lists of projects for foreign investment or products for exports. These fairs have been in Hong Kong and the respective provinces/cities.

The presence of these representatives makes Hong Kong a convenient place for foreign businessmen. Many other types of business, including trade and investment, can be coordinated by representatives of most provinces and large cities in the country. The Hong Kong Trade Development Council publishes a list of key China organizations in Hong Kong.

A Favorable Environment for Foreign Companies

For foreign companies doing or seeking to do business with China, Hong Kong offers a favorable environment in view of its unparalleled transportation and communication infrastructure, favorable government policy, established links with the rest of the world, geographic proximity, and its dynamic and educated managerial workforce. With the belief that economic and technological cooperation with China holds out considerable promise, and for the above reasons, there has been an influx of overseas businesses setting up trade offices and manufacturing facilities in Hong Kong.

Many overseas businesses, led by Americans and Japanese, have stepped up their plans for tapping the China market by using Hong

Kong as a bridgehead. Sitting on the doorstep in Hong Kong, the foreign companies are better positioned to look for investment and trade opportunities in China.

American multinational firms operating on a global strategy tend to be more willing to take risks, and appear likely to stay involved in long-term projects and in high-tech industries. The total amount of Japanese investment in Hong Kong has been on the increase, and the focus has been more on distributive trades and financial services. A tremendous amount of Southeast Asian capital has also been flowing into Hong Kong since the Sino-British agreement.

Trade organizations in Hong Kong including the American Chamber of Commerce, the Hong Kong General Chamber of Commerce, the Trade Development Council and the Hong Kong Management Association have all been actively promoting trade with China. The TDC has a representative office in Beijing with the objective of promoting Hong Kong's image in China and is very active, including the staging of a 'Made in Hong Kong' trade exhibition. All of these organizations have set up groups/committees to examine PRC trade opportunities. The China Commercial Relations Committee of AmCham has been a very active organization providing useful up-to-date information to member companies.

International banks with a strong presence in China can be particularly helpful to foreign companies doing or seeking to do business with China. These banks, with their China specialists based in Hong Kong and key cities of China, can help companies develop contacts and provide the required financial services. For example, some American bank branches in Hong Kong have established direct correspondent bank relationships with domestic branches of the Bank of China and can provide efficient bills services to their customers involved in China trade.

China's Seventh Five-year Plan (1986–1990)

Hong Kong's performance in her trade with China during the Sixth Five-year Plan (1981-1985) was remarkable. The PRC's Seventh Five-year Plan (1986-1990) was formally ratified by the National People's Congress in April 1986. What guidelines to the future does the Seventh Five-year Plan offer?

The plan is intended to restructure China into a more market-oriented economy and lay the foundation for long-term economic development plans. The aim is to quadruple the gross value of the country's industrial and agricultural output from the year 1981 to the year 2000.

According to the Seventh Five-year Plan, real GDP is targeted to grow an average 7.5 percent a year, agriculture output four percent, and industrial output eight percent. These targets are low when seen in the light of the 12 percent growth achieved in 1984-85.

The plan has three major features. First, the adoption of tighter credit controls, and the curtailing of capital spending plans. Central government control over the economy will actually be enhanced in this period, especially in areas such as international trade and banking.

The restrictive trade policies adopted in 1985 are expected to be maintained. These policies include tight controls over foreign exchange usage, import surcharges on selected items, and mandatory counter-purchase in exchange for the imports of certain products. Imports of whole plants, such as nuclear power plants, have been curbed in order to conserve foreign exchange. The central bank has continued to set binding quarterly lending quotas for all banks in order to prevent a recurrence of the rapid credit growth witnessed during fourth-quarter 1985. The second major feature of the plan is the implementation of large-scale administrative and urban economic reforms. There is to be a huge transfer of administrative power from central authorities to local government and a removal of government administration from business and industry at all levels.

The plan states that manufacturers, wholesalers and retailers must have full authority for their own management and full responsibility for their own profits and losses.

Increasingly, market forces—rather than government decree—will balance supply and demand. The number of goods under production quotas will be reduced; prices will be gradually decontrolled and subsidies will be cut. The number of consumer goods distributed by the state will be reduced and manufacturers will have to find their own markets and distribution channels for their products.

As market forces are increasingly allowed to be operative and the effectiveness of macroeconomic policy tools such as exchange rates, customs duties, taxes and export credits improves, the plan calls for local authorities and industries to make more export and import decisions.

Third, although not explicitly stated in the plan, China intends to raise large amounts of foreign capital, which it needs to achieve its goals of economic re-structuring. Direct foreign investment will be encouraged and foreign borrowings will be increased. Because of

China's lack of foreign exchange and the constant need to increase exports, overseas investment in export-oriented industries will take top priority. Technology transfer will also be emphasized to upgrade China's technological manufacturing capability.

Other key elements of the Seventh Five-year Plan include:

i) the continued emphasis on rural enterprises, which will concentrate on agriculture-related businesses (eg, food processing);

ii) increased production of consumer goods and construction of residential buildings;

iii) the implementation of key projects to reduce bottlenecks in energy, transport, telecommunications, and raw and semi-finished materials eg, iron and steel;

iv) the accelerated development of the services industry;

v) the modernization of existing factories as an alternative to building new ones.

The Implications for Hong Kong

There can be little doubt that the combined effect of restrictive economic policies, the drop in oil export revenues and the need to conserve foreign exchange reserves all spell slower import demand by China, at least for the present.

Any upturn is to a great extent dependent on the course of oil prices. Oil exports have contributed over 25 percent of China's total export revenue but with world prices down, the resultant foreign exchange constraints will cause China to curtail its imports.

Import demand will focus on raw materials, semi-finished goods, the capital goods needed to upgrade China's factories, and technology. Imports of consumer goods, especially durables, will be curtailed.

The implication for Hong Kong's exports to China is clear. Hong Kong will likely experience a decline in its domestic exports and re-exports to China. Trading companies that major in exporting to the PRC will likely see a downturn in their performance; they will probably find better business opportunities in importing goods from China and exporting them to other countries.

China's emphasis on exports will also affect Hong Kong's manufacturing sectors.

Many local manufacturers have been shifting part of their operations into China in order to take advantage of its inexpensive labor. These investments have taken the form of wholly-owned subsidiaries, joint-ventures, compensation trade, and/or co-production. Investors will likely be expected to export more.

Such exports will compete in both the local and overseas markets with products made in Hong Kong. Competition will be most severe for products belonging to the middle to low-end markets. What could possibly happen with the opening of China to foreign investment is that there will be a shift of manufacturing activities from Hong Kong to China. This will be particularly evident for the toys, machinery, and the electronics assembly industries. Garments will probably remain stable in Hong Kong because of the quotas imposed by the US and the EEC countries.

The gradual shift of manufacturing activities to China from Hong Kong will contribute to the upgrading/renovation of China's factories. The shift will also accelerate the structural change in Hong Kong's economy, which is expected to become increasingly services-oriented and less-reliant on manufacturing. For example, Hong Kong can provide services in the area of technical and production management and marketing disciplines as China establishes its own industries. With their management and technical know-how, their understanding of China's requirements, and their established links with overseas markets, Hong Kong companies can help China source the needed technology and equipment, and export its products to other countries.

Many Hong Kong companies which have a good understanding of both Chinese end-users' requirements and foreign suppliers' capability, have helped arrange numerous deals involving transfer of technology and Chinese imports of equipment. There are also technical and support services, relating to equipment and technology imports, which Hong Kong can offer. Hong Kong has the engineering manpower trained by local and overseas universities and technical colleges.

Over the longer term, assuming that the administrative and economic reforms of the Seventh Five-year Plan will be successfully implemented, foreign investors and traders will likely find it easier to do business with China. Prices will be more reflective of product quality and availability; business decisions will be more dynamic and market-oriented; and there will be less bureaucratic red tape.

The Future

Hong Kong benefitted by its location at the centre of the growth region of the world in the late 1960s and 1970s. In the 1980s, because of the dedicated modernization program of China, the favorable location of Hong Kong would seem to be further strengthened. The past five year's performance of the territory as a China trade base gives good support for such optimism.

Hong Kong's role as an entrepot for China should strengthen further. Its well developed transportation and communication infrastructure and established links with the rest of the world will be of great value to China, which will continue to expand its external trade and to modernize its economy. Hong Kong will continue to offer the attractive environment through which overseas businessmen can develop links with China.

As China gradually matures and decentralises in the coming years, Hong Kong will progress inexorably towards a service-based economy, fueled, at least in part, by China's open door policy. The next two years will not be easy for product trade with China, but even here, the move to a market-oriented economy within China will lead to market opportunities as this decade draws to a close.

This move, and the whole thrust of the Seventh Five-year Plan, also augurs well for harmonious economic cooperation between Hong Kong and China into the 1990s and beyond.

John T. W. Chu is a
Vice President of Bank of America,
N.Y.

Chapter 8

Textiles

intro
glimpses of one of HK's many successful industries.

by Thomas E. Goetz

Overview

* Hong Kong inherited the elite of China's pre-revolutionary textile and apparel industrialists.
* Hong Kong's textile industry provides spinning, weaving, dyeing and finishing operations of varying, but generally good, quality.
* High quality apparel comprises Hong Kong's most famous export commodity, owing to the high standards and extraordinary diversity of the industry.
* The United States is Hong Kong's largest buyer of apparel, though even greater market demand goes unsatisfied because of severe trade agreements and export quotas.
* Overseas buyers are advised to work through experienced Hong Kong-based agencies.
* As protectionist sentiments rise in the United States, Hong Kong may respond by seeking manufacturers overseas, taking on the role of administrative center for world-wide textile and apparel industries.

The origins of Hong Kong's major export industry are found in the exodus of Shanghai's industrial families to Hong Kong in the early 1950s.

Before the Chinese revolution of 1949, Shanghai (and to a lesser extent, Tianjin) possessed the major factories and expertise in spinning, weaving and apparel manufacture. Other regions boasted of magnificent silk weaving and hand-crafted garments, but those two major industrial cities contained the most modern and extensive facilities both for domestic and export markets.

When the Communists finally controlled these two great northern ports, the business community of Shanghai made an explicit point of demanding a guarantee of autonomy from the new government. But when the Communists quickly broke their initial promise and began to nationalize key industries, the Shanghai capitalists in turn fled south to Hong Kong, bringing their expertise and capital to the then relatively sleepy trading port.

At the same time, hundreds of thousands of other Chinese were also seeking refuge and freedom in Hong Kong. This combination of knowledge, capital and low priced labor, gathered together on the edge of one of the world's great harbors, was able to overcome many of Hong Kong's major handicaps, such as the need to import raw materials and energy to run the mills.

The year 1985 was a major turning point for Hong Kong's textile industry, as measured by the mix of exports. Hong Kong's trade with the United States, its major buyer with over 50 percent of the total exports, reached record levels, even though this trade is restrained under a bilateral agreement sanctioned under the Multi-Fiber Arrangement (MFA).

The MFA and American Protectionism

The MFA, which was renewed for the fourth time on August 1, 1986, now extends its coverage from cotton wool and man-made fiber to include all vegetable fibers and silk blends. It restrains virtually all textiles and garments under a complex system of categorization.

Categories are based upon the chief value of the fiber content of a product, combined with its usage description. For example, a chief value cotton shirt falls in one category, while a chief value synthetic shirt lands in another. The chief value of a fiber refers to the chief material from which it is composed, ie a chief value cotton shirt is made from a higher percentage of cotton than of any other material.

Items composed of (or blends comprising a chief value of) silk, ramie and linen were exempt from quota controls and restraints, and were not covered by the previous MFA, which expired on July 31, 1986. This latter fiber group alone accounted for an increase in volume in 1985 of textile and apparel products to the United States amounting to 11 percent over the 1984 total, proving that even though Hong Kong had reached the limit of its allowable restraints under the bilateral agreements over the past two years, the value and expertise of its products enjoy a market in the United States far beyond the allowable limitations.

American trade legislation, as exemplified by the ''Textile and Apparel Trade Enforcement Act of 1985'' (better known as the 'Jenkins Bill'), attempted to counter this Hong Kong 'sellers' market' with the threat of even greater restraints then currently exist. The trend in the second half of the eighties is increasingly constrictive in this area of trade.

If the American buyers' appetite and budget would prefer even more of Hong Kong's products, a well organized and financed domestic textile and apparel industry is nonetheless determined to push back Hong Kong imports.

The American domestic textile industry is already one of the most protected: according to the US Department of Commerce, the total of all textile and apparel imports represented only 21 percent and 26 percent of the US market, respectively, in 1984.

The future of textile trade with the United States appears even more restrictive under the new MFA agreement, as only garments which contain 70 percent or more by weight of silk are not subject to restraint of any sort. Furthermore, the new agreement places a ceiling on the quantity of all fiber apparel and non-apparel of cotton, wool and man-made fiber that can be exported to the US each year, and it is likely that other categories will eventually be included. How will Hong Kong react? Most likely by remaining as a corporate and administrative base for the textile and apparel trade, but with branch factories reaching around the globe, established in which ever country offers market access and low priced labor.

Textiles and Yarns

The textiles and yarns segment of the industry has had its ups and downs in the past three decades, but today appears to be enjoying a rebirth due to the strong Japanese yen, and, in the finishing and printing sectors, to ever more sophisticated greige goods available from China. Hong Kong imports all its raw materials, and although there are representations here of almost every aspect of the spinning and weaving industries, the quality of such products does not match those of Japan or even meet the standards of some of Hong Kong's top fashion garment manufacturers.

Woven Textiles

The typical Hong Kong woven fabric is an all-cotton or synthetic-cotton blend intended for usage in the medium- to low-price market. Typically, products include denims, corduroys, broadcloths, sheetings, ducks and twills.

A second major category of fabric readily available in Hong Kong comprises goods woven in China and dyed, finished or printed in Hong Kong. These include the fabrics listed in the previous paragraph in addition to linens, ramies, and an incredible range of beautiful silks and silk blends.

Not found locally are the synthetics, such as nylons, rayons and acetates, which are imported from Taiwan, Korea or Japan.

Finishing Operations

Dyeing is a fairly modern operation in Hong Kong. Continuous dye baths are available for long runs of one color, from which various components will be cut (such as jackets and skirts) when a close color match is required. The flexibility of jet dyeing is not available, however, so that smaller increments of 1,000 meters or so must still be done in Japan.

Dyestuffs come from Japan and Europe, and such processing generally costs less in Hong Kong than in Japan or the United States.

Hong Kong printing operations employ hand screens (for samples and small runs), automatic or rotary screens, and roller printing, including wide presses for the bed linen trade.
Quality is medium to low, with the better quality items imported from Japan or Europe.

Finishing operations, such as pre-shrinking, mercerization, etc, are available. Of special interest is a wide range of PV and PVC (types of plastic) coatings, for use in apparel, upholstery, handbags, and other diverse products.

Yarns

Hong Kong spins yarn for weaving, knitting and sewing thread, but the industry is a 'spotty' one.

For the circular knit and woven fabric industry, semi-combed or combed cotton and blends are spun without benefit of such enhancements as mercerization or gassing. Again, better quality yarns come from Japan, and a large amount is also purchased from Taiwan and China.

For flat-bed (sweater) knitting, a local worsted spun industry of quite good quality exists, with woolen spun yarns coming from Taiwan, South Korea and Japan (and ever growing imports from Europe as Hong Kong upgrades its sweaters).

Dyeing of yarn on banks or cones is readily available, and, as with the weaving and finishing industries in general, enjoys a brisk business.

While this busy aspect of the trade is good for the mills, it means the buyers must wait longer to get their orders filled; Hong Kong no longer offers overnight delivery. Average dyeing and finishing orders take about one month after a firm order is placed.

Apparel

Apparel is the product category that made Hong Kong famous, the finished article that has introduced consumers world-wide to this remarkable city state.

'Made in Hong Kong' (or 'Made in the British Crown Colony of Hong Kong', as some buyers still prefer) has come to mean a medium- to up-market product, usually accompanied by the brand name of a top designer label or quality retailer. In fact, the ranking of Hong Kong in the American consumer's mind is third on a rating list topped only by 'Made in Europe' (or UK) and 'Made in Japan' (albeit the Japanese quality image is more synonymous with cars, cameras and stereos). Our other Southeast Asian neighbors rank well below Hong Kong in terms of assumed integrity of product. Ironically, the catalyst behind this enhanced image was the application of the above-mentioned restraints.

Woven Garments

This category comprises a gamut of products, from men's business shirts to women's intimate apparel. Hong Kong makes it all: blouses, dresses, skirts, trousers, shorts, jackets, blousons, raincoats—in fact almost every item of apparel imaginable, except children's wear (exports are minor, as the restrictions cause 'smaller' or less profitable garments to be set aside in favor of higher priced adult clothing) and men's tailored suits and jackets (though this latter category is of great importance to the extensive custom tailoring trade within the city).

Circular Knits

Hong Kong manufactures the best knit shirts and garments in the region because it has invested in the most advanced knitting technology.

Although there are a number of very large vertical operations, encompassing knitting, dyeing, cutting and sewing, most of the industry is segmented either into knitting or garment making. It is this separation that provides the competition and flexibility which makes Hong Kong number one in this category.

From simple T-shirts to sophisticated velours, and with an unbelievable range of printing, flocking, elaborate piecing, and even beading, this flexible industry continues to outpace the designers' ingenuity. As world demand for casual and comfortable sportswear grows, the only limitations will be the protectionist restraints.

Already, Singapore, Manila, Penang, and Bangkok are cutting fabrics knit in Hong Kong.

Sweaters

A recent ruling by the United States government formally disallowed the practice of knitting sweater panels (made of cotton, wool and man-made fiber) in China, and then looping (sewing together), washing, pressing and packaging the same in Hong Kong, if the product is exported to the US with a Hong Kong export visa. Under the new regulation, adopted April 4, 1985, such sweaters would be considered as products of China, not Hong Kong, and would require a Chinese export visa to enter the United States. All other countries of the world continue to follow the previous system of establishing country of origin on the basis of assembly.

As a result of this abrupt change of the globally-accepted rules by the United States, the Hong Kong sweater factories had to quickly replace the low-cost, labor-intensive hand flat knitting machines in China with competitive knitting in Hong Kong. The result was that during the uncertain period following the announcement of Hong Kong's return to China in 1997, the sweater industry was forced to choose between investing millions of US dollars in modern computer knitting or go out of business.

The gambling spirit of the Hong Kong businessman prevailed, even among those Shanghainese who had been deceived before by the mainland government. Their courage in buying (or leasing) the hundreds of machines necessary to replace the 60,000 or so hand flat machines, upgraded Hong Kong's sweater industry to an absolute state-of-the-art standard unmatched by any other country in the world. The valuable restraint levels continued to be met and production in silk and other vegetable fibers was used to achieve higher levels of shipments in 1985 and the first half of 1986 before they came under restraint in the current 1986-1991 agreement.

This incident reflects the tenacity of the Hong Kong apparel industry to thrive and grow even in the face of adversity. The Hong Kong government also assisted by providing a completely new import regulation system to establish the validity of origin of Hong Kong's sweater panels.

In addition to the now computerized knitting industry, Hong Kong offers more traditional techniques, as well as sophisticated decoration of sweaters, such as printing, beading and embroidered applique.

Leathers and Furs

This specialized aspect of apparel has become big business for the medium-price markets of the world. Ironically, in the fur industry, the top quality garments are still painstakingly made in New York or Europe.

The leather garment industry, however, can more than match the quality of European or American garments, importing the leather skins from around the world to achieve this high standard.

Accessories and Findings

In this critical aspect, Hong Kong falters. Buyers of better-quality garments often must arrange for the importation of such trimmings from Europe or Japan.

Although a vast selection of buttons, snaps, zippers, lace, etc, is found in the specialized neighborhood of Shum Shui Po in Kowloon, the quality is often not up to world standards.

Zippers, for example, are virtually dominated by YKK of Japan, and therefore delivery of their semi-custom styles can take up to 60 days. In 1986, YKK greatly expanded its facilities in Hong Kong, and some of the pressure has been diminished.

Top quality buttons and snaps are sourced from Japan, Europe and the United States, especially for unique patterns and designs. A wide range of trim tapes, strings and cordings are available locally, however, along with embroideries. Laces and related items are imported and sold locally in specialized shops.

Fashion Design

In this most important aspect of creativity, Hong Kong is truly lacking. Although a few local designers have exported their collections and achieved some acclaim outside Hong Kong, their uniqueness stems as much from the novelty of being from Hong Kong as from the marketability of their collections. It is certain that future generations will produce more viable fashion designers, but for now, 'Made in Hong Kong' means 'Designed Outside.'

√ Trade

American Trade

As pointed out earlier in the chapter, the relationship with Hong Kong's largest buyer is at best quite complex, and at times, antagonistic. This same trade relationship, however, has been the major factor in causing Hong Kong to become the highest quality apparel source in the region. The reason for this is quite ironic.

When Hong Kong began exporting garments in the 1950s, almost the entire industry used only natural fibers—100 percent cotton and wool. As business grew, it continued to rely on such raw materials, as the Far East, outside of Japan, had not yet established any of the then relatively new polyester-producing facilities.

By the time the trading partners of Hong Kong founded the MFA and established restraint levels, the apparel trade was not only at a very sizable level, but was almost entirely in natural fibers. Only the United States, under pressure from its synthetic fiber industry, chose to categorize each product not only by usage (shirt, skirt, etc) and gender, but also by fiber (chief value cotton, etc).

This resulted in Hong Kong receiving almost all its viable quotas in natural fiber categories. With the emergence of the 1960s, Americans began to equate 'natural' with 'better,' and today's affluent yuppie is a product of such philosophy.

Consequently, the better apparel business in the United States will only accept natural fibers, and only Hong Kong has sizable quantities available. This is because the neighboring countries in the region achieved their restraint limits by producing 'threatening quantities' (as viewed by American protectionists) at a later time when synthetic and synthetic blends had become commonplace and relatively cheap.

As the value of being able to provide natural fiber products became more and more important, Hong Kong's buyers demanded better and more sophisticated garments—and so natural fiber quotas caused Hong Kong to become the favored source for designer collections and up-market retailers. This in turn caused a 'me-too' effect, whence lesser brands and stores wanted to have that very acceptable 'Made in Hong Kong' label.

And when Hong Kong could ship no more cotton and wool owing to restraints, it rediscovered that most ancient of natural fibers, ramie.

Ramie is a type of hemp known to have been used 10,000 years ago during the late Stone Age. The ancient Egyptians cultivated hemp for textiles and wrapped their mummies in it. In Asia, use of ramie was recorded as early as 600 AD in garments worn by Japanese dancers and singers performing in temples and shrines. More recently, ramie has been used for tablecloths, napkins, home furnishing, fabrics, fishing nets, etc. Luckily for Hong Kong, two of its neighbors number among the world's three greatest producers of ramie—China and the Philippines (the third is Brazil).

As Hong Kong manufacturers studied the bilateral agreements, looking for every possible means of increasing their output beyond the restraint levels, it became obvious that the US category of non-MFA fibers, labeled 'chief value vegetable fiber,' held heretofore undiscovered opportunities.

Vegetable fibers include ramie, flax/linen, hemp, jute, abaca and henequin (the latter two are types of banana plants).

Linen was always a part of the spring/summer fashion scene,

especially in up-market collections, so it seemed natural (no pun intended) that ramie, which was more abundant, and lower priced than linen, could find acceptance in the US market.

Within one year, American consumers who had never heard of ramie, learned to accept this crisp, flax-like fiber in everything from sweaters to blouses to jeans. In fact, ramie is most commonly blended with cotton to produce a product that is a rustic version of a pure cotton yarn or fabric.

Ramie sweaters especially were a great success, and since ramie was unrestricted in any shape or form, once again Hong Kong knitters could legally knit panels across the border in China and assemble the sweaters in Hong Kong.

This resulted in the United States initiating a request to modify the 1980-1987 bilateral agreement in March 1986 to include ramie and other fibers, which were then not subject to restraint. The extension of coverage to include these fibers resulted in the 1986-1991 bilateral agreement.

To list all of the categories and their current limitations would take pages, and it is recommended that those who wish to examine the details more closely contact the Hong Kong Trade Department. Complete listings are also available of all the factories that hold permanent quotas for restrained items.

European Trade

Although the MFA is a world-wide agreement, each nation negotiates directly with another as to quantities and category definitions, as we have already seen in the case of the United States.

All European Economic Community (EEC, or Common Market) countries share a common classification system much simpler than the American version. Basically, a garment is defined by usage (blouse, skirt, etc), regardless of fiber. A cotton blouse and synthetic blouse are therefore placed in the same category. Non-MFA fibers are treated the same as they are in the United States, though there remains the question of whether the Common Market will restrain ramie.

Since country of origin identifies country of assembly in the Common Market, the European customer benefits from the lower cost of knitting panels in China. This doesn't mean that these countries import Hong Kong apparel without resistance, however; obtaining all of the necessary export visas and importing country's licenses can be challenging.

Of interest from a marketing standpoint is the fact that the United States today successfully exports its design creativity to

European consumers via Hong Kong manufacturers. The resulting product with a 'Made in Hong Kong' label has all but broken European resistance to Hong Kong origins in quality apparel. Even France and Italy now accept such garments. West Germany and some of the Benelux countries do not require a 'country of origin' label, so their consumers are spared that particular emotional aspect of buying fashion.

Other Trade

The other markets of the world for Hong Kong textiles and apparel are of lesser importance, with the exception of Japan.

Japan resisted buying apparel from its neighbors long after the US and EEC had signed agreements limiting the same, but with the advent of American designers penetrating the Japanese market with Hong Kong-made apparel, it has become quite acceptable to an ever growing number of Japanese consumers. (European designers sell European-made garments in Japan; the Americans either license their designs or import Hong Kong products.)

With a strengthened yen, Japan will be an ever increasing market for Hong Kong, and as yet, one without any restraints.

Quotas

The introduction to this chapter and the section above refer to restraints upon the number of garments which Hong Kong can ship to a given country. These restraints are the quotas imposed upon Hong Kong for different categories of its manufactured textiles.

A quota should be considered as a penalty for performance above and beyond that level which another country considers threatening to its own domestic industry or to its trade balance in general.

Quotas were not 'given' to Hong Kong; rather they were *imposed* upon Hong Kong. The semantic distinction is critical, though Hong Kong has made the best of what might otherwise have been a bad situation: the Hong Kong government allows the sale of quotas, which results in profits.

But first, the history of quota allocation.

When the first bilateral agreements were negotiated, and the Hong Kong government officials returned home with a list of restraints, their first responsibility was to distribute the newly acquired 'ceilings' fairly.

As the trading partners of Hong Kong had used the previously achieved annual shipments within each category as a basis for the new restraints, it was decided to allocate these restraints to the manufacturing community on the same basis.

That is, if Hong Kong had negotiated a restraint of 100 pieces of a particular category based upon the previous year's performance, and Factory X had produced 10 pieces the previous year, then it was only fair to allocate to Factory X a restraint level equal to its actual previous performance. So Factory X received a quota of 10 pieces. This meant that Factory X would *always* be able to ship 10 pieces of that category to the country in question.

What follows is a classic example of how Hong Kong deals with adversity, or, 'the glass is still half full' as opposed to 'the glass is already half empty.'

Factory X was able to continue shipping, at least as long as the bilateral agreement which imposed such restraints would last. (Being quite pragmatic in these matters, Hong Kong calls such quota 'Permanent Quota'.)

The country imposing such quotas doesn't care which factory actually *manufactured* the item in question. The quota specifies only that a factory can *ship* such items; it doesn't necessarily have to *manufacture* them. Equally important to get the quota game going is Factory Y. Factory Y doesn't hold any permanent quota for this hypothetical category, but for some reason, has an order for such a restrained item.

Now assuming that Factory X is experiencing a normal market softening among its old customers, resulting in unsold quota items, and Factory Y wants to obtain such quota, we have a potential buyer and a seller.

The Hong Kong government attempted to support its apparel industry by allowing for as much flexibility as possible under the undesirable restraints. Therefore, it was planned for and officially endorsed that a permanent quota holder such as Factory X could lend its quota to Factory Y to minimize any disruption of the apparel manufacturing community. After all, when a factory held (or 'owned' as it is called) permanent quota that it did not need, and another factory wanted it, there was a logical reason for money to change hands. This lending is called a 'Temporary Quota Transfer.' It requires filling out official government forms, which must be signed by the Hong Kong Trade Department.

As Hong Kong's apparel business thrived and grew faster than even the automatic annual increases, which most bilateral trade agreements allow, competition for quota became a very real part of the apparel business.

Once Factory Z came into the picture to bid against Factory Y for the quota they both wanted, the value of Factory X's quota went up.

And so a new business was formed, neither illegal nor scorned, but nonetheless of a somewhat parasitical nature, thriving upon the essential need to export. It became apparent to certain permanent quota owners that they held the next best thing to land in Hong Kong, a rare commodity that others would pay for. These 'quota brokers' began to flourish.

The 'others' who pay the bill, of course, are the very consumers of the country that sought to protect itself. So protectionism and resultant restraints boomeranged while leaving behind a wealthier new class of quota holders. Once it became apparent that quotas were of real value, many factories closed their manufacturing operations and became solely 'quota factories,' living grandly off the value of their 'penalties of restraint.'

The Hong Kong government had originally built in a safety valve in an attempt to prevent this from happening, by limiting the amount of temporary quota which could be sold in any given year to 50 percent of the company's quota holdings. Various schemes and paper shuffles were created to bypass this clause, however. On January 1, 1986, when temporary quota transfers were reduced to 35 percent of one's total, the selling price of such temporary quota rose still higher. (By the end of that year, the temporary transfer rule was revised again—back to 50 percent.)

The money involved in quota broking is tremendous, and by virtue of mark-ups being done on a percentage basis in this industry, the cost to the consumer is outrageous.

In a study prepared in 1984 by the US Federal Trade Commissioner, entitled: 'Import Quotas on Textiles: The Welfare Effects of United States Restrictions On Hong Kong,' one conclusion was that in 1980, '...the annual social cost on the US economy (was) $308 million.'

At the same time, the study examined the potential effect upon the US apparel industry of removing such quotas. It reported, 'we estimate that additional imports would reduce domestic employment in these industries by 8,900 workers and involve a cost of unemployment of $17 million.' However, 'if the quotas were eliminated, the benefits would continue year after year, indefinitely, while most of the unemployment costs would occur over a short period, less than a year, and would end once the workers displaced by the additional imports found new jobs.'

It can be concluded that US quotas created the up-market fashion apparel dominance of Hong Kong, and enriched many local businessmen, all at the expense of the American consumer.

For the potential investor who wishes to obtain a quota, either temporary or permanent (which may also be bought and sold), the Hong Kong Exporters Association offers an excellent service at nominal cost, and available to non-members, by listing quotas that subscribers are looking to buy or sell. Offers are listed by country. The listings are updated weekly and distributed by facsimile directly to the subscribers. The service encompasses both US and EEC quotas.

Industry Profile

Buying Offices

Off-shore buyers of textiles and apparel are advised to work with an established agency in Hong Kong. Such offices provide communications, merchandising (finding the best manufacturers and following up on orders) and monitoring of quality control.

Most of these service organizations are located in the Tsim Sha Tsui area, although many have recently started to set up business in industrial neighborhoods.

Buying offices range in size from one-man operations to huge multinational companies with offices throughout the region. Many large buyers prefer to establish their own corporate buying office, and even structure such businesses as profit centers.

The drawback to having one's own office is that the expense should not exceed four to five percent of the dollar volume (FOB value) of the shipments involved, as it would then be more economical to engage the services of an outside company. Also, independent agents of any size are often more attuned to market conditions (especially as regards quotas), and offer multinational sourcing.

Below are a few questions to keep in mind when evaluating a buying agency:
 i) are the offices clean and well organized? Poor housekeeping and a 'cheap' mentality will be reflected in their evaluation of *your* product;
 ii) do they have a definitive system of policies and procedures? An agency that can't discipline itself will hardly be able to organize the buyer's details and communications professionally;
 iii) how do they monitor quality control and production? Do they use comprehensive inspection forms that will remind the inspector to check *all* the subtle details?
 iv) are their communications up to date? Hong Kong offers state-of-the-art communications, and an offshore buyer will require telex, facsimile and an adequate number of telephone lines;
 v) is the agency using computers to track production, size scales,

etc? Many agencies use computers to cross reference the many details involved in garment production and thus provide a more exact control for the buyer;

vi) does the agency's management have working experience with the buyer's market? Not only should they understand the specific needs of that market, but they should also be knowledgeable of Hong Kong trade agreements and exporting regulations that apply to the country in question;

vii) does the company have an adequate history of experience in Hong Kong, with solid relationships with factories and suppliers? Approximately five years' experience would be the minimum "history";

viii) does the company have integrity? A professional agent will respect styles, colors, and concepts as being the sole property of the buyer and will not show or share them in any way with other buyers. A brief letter of agreement outlining such conditions and responsibilities is highly recommended to prevent later misunderstandings;

ix) is the agency active in the professional community? Active membership in one or more of the various trade or commerce organizations will result in a better informed agent, and will therefore benefit the buyer;

x) how is the agency viewed by its present clients? Most agencies should be willing to offer such potential references to bolster their reputation;

xi) is the agency 'comfortable'? This last point is difficult to define, but nonetheless critical. After all, the agent will be your off-shore management and must therefore be selected carefully. How do you *feel* about the agency? Do they understand your product, your image and your needs? Do they presently handle buyers that are of the same standard as your company? Does the agency management represent your ideal of a business partner? It is impossible to list all of the existing agents or even to attempt to narrow the field, so it is advisable to contact the offices of the Hong Kong Trade Development Council (HKTDC), an excellent source of information for any aspect of Hong Kong overseas trade. It is a quasi-government statutory body with offices around the world. Its trade enquiry section is computerized and includes over 22,000 local manufacturers, exporters and importers.

The US Foreign Commercial Service of the American Consulate General in Hong Kong is likewise very professional and helpful in these matters, and another highly informative source is the Hong Kong Exporters Association.

It should be mentioned that the American Chamber of Commerce in Hong Kong, through its Business Briefing Committee, can arrange a breakfast briefing with various representatives of the apparel and textile community, and possibly a representative from the Hong Kong Trade Department, to elaborate further on the industry.

Garment and Textile Factories

There are thousands of garment factories in Hong Kong. The best guide to them is a good agent, though you can also contact the offices mentioned above (especially the HKTDC) for advice.

Perhaps the best source of advice about garment factories is the Federation of Hong Kong Industries. This most professional association is the only organization authorized by a Hong Kong government statute to issue an official seal of quality for products manufactured in Hong Kong, the Hong Kong Quality Mark (HKQ-Mark).

Federation membership is open to all manufacturers, and list of all members are provided upon request.

There are a number of particular questions which can be asked of each factory in order to assess its viability.

The Trade Development Council and the Federation of Hong Kong Industries are equally suitable as a means of sourcing weavers and spinners. In addition, the Association of Textile Bleachers, Dyers, Printers and Finishers Ltd; the Federation of HK Cotton Weavers; and the Hongkong Cotton Spinners Association can also be of assistance.

Publications

An interesting periodical available to the textile and apparel industry in the Hong Kong region is *Textile Asia*. This monthly publication is indispensable for professionals in both apparel and textile related industries. The articles, editorials and features run the gamut from machinery and manufacturing techniques, to trade issues and fashion notes.

In addition, there are regional updates, exhibition reviews, and a host of technical equipment articles.

Subscriptions are also available in countries outside Hong Kong, China and Macau for under US$50 per year (surface mail); write to Textile Asia Business Press Ltd, GPO Box 185, Hong Kong.

The Future

Protectionism and restraints head the list of issues having influenced the development of Hong Kong's textile and apparel industry and most affecting its future. As stated in the introduction, Hong Kong faces a shrinking world market because of US and ECC protectionism. Although Japan offers some hope for expanded exports, that market will be further limited as other countries in the region compete with lower prices.

On a more positive note is the emergence of Hong Kong as a regional center for the expansion and improvement of the industry, as local corporations invest in other countries in order to maintain growth. This "headquarters" concept not only has positive bearing on the future of Hong Kong as a banking center (in addition to providing comfort to the local hotel and airline industries), but bodes well for Hong Kong's continued growth in importance as a regional (and possibly world-wide) booking center for the off-shore (outside Hong Kong) manufacture of textiles and apparel.

Certainly China is the best venue for such lower labor cost sourcing, provided that the PRC government is successful in fighting back protective trade ceilings and eventually gains full member status in GATT, which would require China to change many of its foreign trade rules and procedures. The Sino-British agreement may yet prove to be a factor in the further conversion of China to an open market mentality.

For More Information

A now-famous anecdote among Hong Kong's apparel industry tells of an Italian who sought to replace a favorite shirt, which had been burned by a cigarette. When he brought it to a Hong Kong factory and was assured that 12 identical copies would be ready by the following week, he departed with praise for the skill and efficiency of Hong Kong's apparel industry. Upon returning to collect his order, he was even more impressed. The shirt had been reproduced 12 times exactly like the original, right down to the cigarette hole.

The moral of the story is that, despite Hong Kong's Western veneer, a wall of misunderstanding still divides cultures. Factory mentality can be very literal. Never assume anything. Manufacturers are not in focus on the end use of the product, but on the profit.

Another misunderstanding that often crops up is the problem of face: factories don't like to admit that they can't complete an order on time. Many manufacturers will accept an order, assuring a buyer that all commitments can be met, when in fact they know for certain that it won't.   One solution for foreign buyers is to work with an experienced agent familiar with the ways of Hong Kong.

Where to subscribe to the report on quotas:

The Hong Kong Exporter's Association, 825 Star House, Tsim Sha Tsui, Hong Kong Tel. 3-699851 Tx. 57905 EXASO HX.

The Federation of Hong Kong Industries, 407 Hankow Centre 5 Hankow Road Tsim Sha Tsui, Hong Kong. Tel: 3-7230818; telex: 84652 HKIND HX; fax: 3-7213494.

The Association of Textile Bleachers, Dyers, Printers and Finishers Ltd, CMA Building, 4/F, 64 Connaught Road Central, Hong Kong. Tel: 5-456166; cable address: 'MAFTS'; telex: 63526 MAFTS HX.

The Federation of HK Cotton Weavers, Astoria Building, 14/F, Block B 24 Ashley Road, Kowloon, Hong Kong. Tel: 3-672383.

Hongkong Cotton Spinners Association, 1041 Swire House, Hong Kong. Tel: 5-235634, 5-237203; cable address: 'SPINNERS'.

Thomas E. Goetz is Director of
Intertex Goetz International Ltd.

Chapter 9

Electronics

By James T.Y. Fok

In 1986, Hong Kong exported some US$4 billion of electronics goods. Compared with the 1977 figure of around US$800 million, the 1986 figure represents a five-fold increase over a nine-year period, or a nominal annual growth rate of 20 percent before adjusting for inflation.

Hong Kong's electronics industry came into existence almost accidentally. Until the late fifties, when the first radio factories were established by Japanese companies, there was practically no manufacturing of electronics products in Hong Kong. The main reason these transistor radio factories were set up in Hong Kong was the availability of low-cost labor and low-cost electronic components at that time. Being a free port, Hong Kong served as the Far East center of the spot market for the excess stock of electronic parts and components.

The success of the Japanese ventures demonstrated the viability of using Hong Kong as a base to assemble electronics products. This development caught the eye of some American electronics companies which were dissatisfied with the relatively low productivity of their manufacturing subsidiaries in Central and South America. Consequently, some of these American companies set up assembly plants in Hong Kong, making consumer products and semi-conductor components to benefit from the low-cost but hard-working labor force. In the mid-sixties, nearly every major American consumer electronics company and semi-conductor house had their products assembled in the territory.

Although nearly all companies were initially attracted by the low-cost labor, some of them recognised the high quality and skills of the local engineering and professional staff, and have diversified their activities away from pure assembly work. As Hong Kong is no longer a low labor cost region, those companies that are solely interested in assembly work have by now moved their operations elsewhere.

The diffusion of management and production technology brought in by the American companies enabled the establishment of many indigenous companies to cash in on the successive boom of consumer electronics products starting in the mid-seventies. The surge in demand for these products, such as LED digital watches, LED calculators, LCD watches, LCD calculators, hand-held video games, tv-based video games, pulse-dialling telephones and personal computers overlapped with each other and ended in 1985 with the slump of the world electronics market.

The opening up of the PRC has enabled local electronics companies to take advantage of the low-cost labor across the border and meet the upsurge in demand.

Structure of the Electronics Industry

The major characteristics of the Hong Kong electronics industry are fragmented in that it is populated by many small companies.

Number of establishments and persons engaged in electronics industry by employment size

Employment size	No. of establishments				
	1982	1983	1984	1985	1986
1-4	262	259	284	250	201
5-9	222	192	202	144	155
10-19	205	225	262	218	220
20-49	264	292	306	247	224
50-99	156	161	153	121	122
100-199	95	87	110	97	76
200-499	71	75	79	75	66
500-999	28	32	29	23	20
1000-1999	6	10	14	6	5
2000-4999	—	1	—	—	1
Total	1305	1335	1441	1181	1090

Employment size	No. of persons engaged				
	1982	1983	1984	1985	1986
1-4	685	600	667	582	451
5-9	1550	1285	1365	966	1067
10-19	2838	3113	3667	3006	3057
20-49	8060	9074	9716	7774	7070
50-99	10683	11211	10715	8153	8366
100-199	14054	12527	15820	13204	10647
200-499	21744	21700	24809	23213	20584
500-999	18837	21012	20259	16740	15000
1000-1999	7495	12689	19395	7590	6779
2000-4999	—	2116	—	—	2152
Total	85946	95327	106413	81228	75718

Taking the figures for 1986, the average number of employees in each firm is 74, with 73 percent of the establishments being small-scale factories employing less than 50 persons in each factory. Foreign investment still plays a major role in shaping the local electronics industry.

Overseas investment in electronics industry

Year	No. of establishments	No. of employees
1981	57	27676
1982	64	29114
1983	78	29630
1984	80	34869
1985	99	33731
1986	115	32254

There are about 115 foreign-owned electronics companies in Hong Kong employing about 32,000 persons, nearly half of the total workforce in the electronics industry. The average investment of these foreign-owned companies was US$5.5 million in 1986. America is the major source of foreign investment in the electronics industry in Hong Kong.

Overseas investment in electronics industry by country source (excluding toys, and watches and clocks)

Country source	No. of establishments	Investment at original cost before depreciation (HK$m)
USA	58	3099
Japan	14	593
Netherlands	7	459
China	9	410
UK	8	137
Canada	4	116
Singapore	5	29
Germany FR	3	18
Philippines	4	1
Others	11	159
Total	115	5021

The Products

As the industry is dominated by many small-size factories, most of these companies do not have the capability to market the products which they manufacture. Therefore most of the firms are OEMers (Original Equipment Manufacturers), that is to say, they build products which are sold under other people's (usually the OEM buyer's) brand name. Several of the larger local companies have begun to experiment with selling products under their own brand name, spending large sums of money in advertisements in the overseas (such as US) markets. Although it is true that the size of the firms precludes the undertaking of basic R&D work, it is not true that the industry only assembles components for the OEM-buyers. Many firms have capabilities to develop electronic products according to descriptions provided to them by the buyers, rather than relying on the buyers to provide them with all the necessary technical information. Again it is not uncommon for foreign buyers and Hong Kong OEMers to join forces to develop new products. Sometimes the Hong Kong company would develop a product entirely on its own, using its own in-house engineering talents. After the development work has been completed, the product would be exhibited in overseas trade shows where OEM contracts with major household-name buyers are usually secured.

The products manufactured by foreign-owned companies obviously are sold under the mother companies' brandnames. For the more established subsidiaries, however, they usually have a fair degree of autonomy in their own operations. Hence they are more like OEMers for their mother companies. If the mother companies have more than one manufacturing location in this region, these Hong Kong subsidiaries would have to compete for business with their counterparts in the Asia Pacific region, if not on a worldwide scale.

Domestic export of electronics goods (HK$ m)

Exports	1982	1983	1984	1985	1986
Watches and clocks	4556	5759	6157	6236	7780
Components	1911	2443	4471	4719	5098
Radios	3493	3550	4750	3324	3864
Computer parts	1694	3833	6147	4427	4327
Telephones	321	2011	1611	1448	1673
Parts for radios	556	692	1457	1437	1612
Video tapes	110	219	278	556	1361
Computer peripherals	112	618	1459	826	1279
TV	152	345	355	544	1048
Misc consumer goods	3081	4378	3848	3445	5323
Total	15986	23848	30533	26962	33366

The range of electronics products includes radios, cassette recorders, hi-fi equipment, television sets, electronic watches and clocks, tv and handheld games, calculators, photocopying equipment, personal computers, printers, wired and cordless telephone handsets, modems, switching mode power supplies, read-write magnetic heads, facsimile machines, CD players, CAD equipment and measuring and testing equipment.

Characteristics and Trends

Flexibility

The small and medium-sized factories of the industry determine its major characteristics, that of flexibility and fast turnaround. Even for the larger firms that are listed on the Hong Kong Stock Exchange, the founder-owners are still in charge and view every order as if their livelihood depended on it. The willingness to accommodate the buyers' requirements is always evident.

Cost Engineering

Although the electronics industry in Hong Kong no longer competes on low cost labor, the cost-consciousness ingrained over the years still remains with the industry. The industrialists are more keen to seek out low-cost compatible components, to modify the products so as to lower the production costs, and to impose tight control over the production schedule. That the industry is still able to compete in the very mature products such as radio/cassette recorders and digital watches bears witness to the aggressiveness of the Hong Kong manufacturers in the control of costs.

Followers

It is understandable that with the limited resources at their disposal, Hong Kong manufacturers play the role of follower instead of leader, both in terms of product and manufacturing processes. Acting in such a manner, they benefit from the 'late-comer effect' in avoiding major mistakes. The late entry in the market or manufacturing techniques is further compensated by the speed of adoption of such products or processes.

Strategic Alliances with OEM Buyers

As the Hong Kong manufacturers possess certain capabilities in the production and product technologies but without the corresponding marketing capabilities, it is logical that these firms would form strategical alliances, sometimes formal but mostly informal, with some of their OEM buyers. Needless to say, the OEMers and the buyers concerned have already achieved good working relationships over the years.

Technology Sourcing

The range of products manufactured in Hong Kong has been diversifying, but product technology (ie the ability to design products using existing technology) has been a limiting factor in the speed of product diversification. There has been a trend to engage overseas (US and Japan) consultants in the design of part or whole of a product, and to acquire, wholly or partially, technologically advanced small firms (those in the Bay area in California are the most popular) as a means of acquiring advanced product technology and hence achieving product diversification.

The China Factor

The recent modernisation program of the People's Republic of China means that foreign investment and foreign ownership are welcome inside China. Recognizing the potential of the PRC as a vast source of low-cost labor, many of the local electronics manufacturers have been experimenting with the use of Chinese workers in the assembly of electronics products inside the PRC for the past 10 years. In the beginning, the quality of work was poor, and the discipline and motivation of the workforce a continuous cause of concern. In the past three years or so, after making many presentations to the various Chinese authorities and after a number of experimentations with various management and incentive schemes, workable solutions have been found. The amount of assembly work shifted into China increased tremendously. It is now estimated that 90 percent of Hong Kong manufacturers either have their own plants, or have subcontractors working for them inside the PRC.

Private Sector Support

The manufacture of electronics products requires many 'non-electronics' parts such as plastic casing, metal parts, printed circuit boards, tools and fixtures and many other similar items.

Most of these parts and components can be sourced locally in Hong Kong. The industry supplying these parts and components, sometimes referred to as the 'linkage' industry (as it links the raw materials with the end products), is again dominated by many small firms, employing on average about 10 persons each.

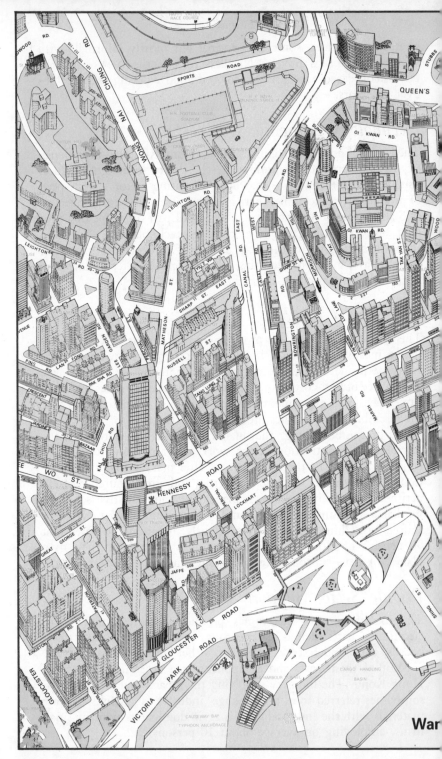

Nevertheless, the larger firms have recently invested heavily in CNC equipment. Thus the whole linkage industry provides a low-cost, high-quality and fast turnaround service to many end-users, including the local electronics industry.

The services provided can be grouped under three major headings: Mould Making, Metal Plating and Metal Working. A brief description is given below, but the more serious user sourcing for suitable vendors may contact one of the several trade organizations, the Trade Development Council, or the Hong Kong Productivity Council. HKPC has been conducting a detailed survey of the linkage industry, determining both the capability and the equipment in use in each firm. The survey results are contained in the publication Hong Kong Linkage Industry, which can be purchased from HKPC.

Mould Making

There are about 1500 mould making jobshops, employing about 10,000 workers. Roughly half of these jobshops are tool and die makers, and the other half, plastic mould makers. The types of dies and moulds available from these jobshops include: plastic injection moulds for calculator casings, cassette and video tape casings etc; diecasting moulds for computer housings, metal parts etc; stamping dies for electronic components; encapsulation moulds for plastic DIP IC's and discrete semi-conductor components.

Metal Plating

There are about 800 metal plating jobshops, employing about 15,000 workers. Most of these jobshops are in the ornamental plating field, with about 300 of them engaged in plating for the various electronic parts and components. There are about 100 PCB plating shops, doing both double-sided and multi-layer boards. A few jobshops also do plating for IC leadframes, and facilities are also available to do plating for glass to metal seal header, the only facilities available in Asia outside Japan.

Metal Working

There are about 300 diecasting jobshops employing about 5000 workers. These shops can provide diecast casings and mechanical parts for computers and other electronics products. Many jobshops can provide machining for metal casings and parts, and metal parts such as springs, washers and screws are also available locally.

Testing Laboratories

A number of testing laboratories provide services in product testing, chemical analysis, environmental testing, production and pre-shipment inspection and technical consultancy. Some of these laboratories are related to industrial organisations, such as the Hong Kong Standard and Testing Centre, which was originally set up by the Federation of Hong Kong Industries, and the CMA Testing and Certification Laboratory, which is part of the Chinese Manufacturers Association of Hong Kong, while others are commercial laboratories. Information concerning these can be obtained from the Association of Testing Laboratories.

Public Sector and the Electronics Industry

Unlike the other three 'tigers' where the respective governments adopt a very aggressive industrial policy, with special emphasis placed on the electronics industry, the Hong Kong government is said to adopt a laissez faire or positive non-intervention policy towards the manufacturing industries. Whereas what is meant by non-intervention has not been explicitly defined, the general concensus is that the Hong Kong government has limited itself to the provision of industrial support facilities in areas of common concern to all manufacturing industries. These areas include the basic resources such as manpower training and the provision of industrial land, and technical support such as standards and calibration and the use of CAD/CAM. Recently the government is seen to be more concerned with the industrial support of specific industries, of which electronics is one.

Examples of recent government actions in the field of electronics are the establishment of an ASIC engineer training scheme which promotes the overseas training of ASIC designers and the proposed establishment of a surface mounting technology laboratory and a radio-frequency/digital-communication laboratory at the Hong Kong Productivity Council.

Educational Institutes

The educational system in Hong Kong basically follows the British system, with six years of primary schooling, five years of high school, and for those wishing to attend universities which run three-year Bachelor Degree courses, two more years in high schools before sitting for the university entrance examinations. (The Chinese University of Hong Kong runs four-year Bachelor Degree courses and potential applicants may take its entrance examination after one extra year at high school rather than two years.)

There are two universities in Hong Kong which provide undergraduate and post-graduate education in electronics and in related disciplines such as physics and chemistry. One of the two universities, the University of Hong Kong, also has departments in mechanical engineering and in industrial engineering. A third university, devoted to producing graduates in science, engineering and management disciplines only, is under planning and is expected to take its first students in 1991.

Besides the two universities, there are also two polytechnics (the Hong Kong Polytechnic and the City Polytechnic of Hong Kong) which produce graduates and postgraduates in electronics, mechanical engineering and production and industrial engineering, as well as technician engineers in the above disciplines. Craftsmen and technician training are also provided by the technical institutes operated and maintained by the Vocational Training Council.

Vocational Training Council

A statutory organization, the Vocational Training Council operates and maintains seven technical institutes and two industrial training center complexes. The technical institutes provide courses at craft and technician level for many engineering disciplines including electronics, technical engineering and chemistry. These courses can be taken full time, or through block-release, part-time day release and part-time evening attendance in the two training center complexes. Basic off-the-job vocational training in electronics, machine shop and metal working, plastics and precision tooling are available for a wide spectrum of technical personnel, from operative to technologist level. One of the recent additions of interest to the electronics industry is the training of CAD/CAM personnel. The council has also set up a training scheme to enable practicing graduate electronics engineers to receive overseas training in the design of ASIC circuits.

The VTC has 19 training boards, each covering a sector of industry. Two major duties of these boards are the assessment of the manpower requirement of the respective industry, and the design of the appropriate training programs for use in the training centers. In the areas of electronics, the VTC has an Electronics Training Board which is composed of representatives from the electronics industry and other related organizations.

142

Enquiries and suggestions concerning the training of electronics personnel at all levels can be made to the secretary of the Electronics Training Board at the VTC.

Trade Development Council

The Trade Development Council (TDC) is a statutory body responsible for promoting and developing Hong Kong's overseas trade. The council consists of representatives of major trade associations, leading industrialists and businessmen, and two senior government officials. It is financed principally by the net proceeds of an ad valorem levy on all exports and on imports other than foodstuffs.

TDC has a wide spectrum of activities covering the organisation of local trade shows, participation in overseas trade fairs, market research and publications. Of particular interest to the electronics industry is its computerised trade inquiry service which assists in the location of local manufacturers of equipment, parts and components. TDC also publishes a monthly Hong Kong Enterprise which although is not dedicated to the electronics industry, is a wealth of information on the range of electronics products manufactured locally.

Hong Kong Productivity Council

The Hong Kong Productivity Council (HKPC) is a statutory body responsible for the promotion of increased industrial productivity in Hong Kong. The council consists of members representing management, labor, academic and professional interests as well as government departments closely associated with productivity. HKPC is financed partly by an annual government subvention and partly by fees earned from its services. HKPC is a multi-disciplinary consulting and training organisation. It conducts a wide range of short training courses and seminars in industrial technology, management techniques and computer related topics. It also organises industrial exhibitions and overseas study missions on the most recent and advanced industrial and managerial technologies. Tailor-made in-factory training on specific topics is also undertaken on assignment basis.

HKPC provides consultancy services to assist foreign and local investors to locate suitable industrial premises, recruit key personnel, plan plant layout, control potential sources of pollution, and reduce energy consumption. On-line information retrieval services are available to do patent and technical literature search on a worldwide basis. A monthly publication, the Electronics Bulletin, provides information on recent developments in electronics, both locally and world-wide. A new publication and an associated computerised enquiry service will be available soon to help manufacturers to locate mould and die plating and metal working jobshops. Detailed information on the types of equipment and expertise available in each jobshop will be provided. HKPC also has laboratories in electroplating and metal-finishing, heat treatment of tools, and diecasting. These laboratories provide bureau service and consultancies to all interested parties. An integrated CAD/CAM center with CAD workstations and multi-station CNC work centers has the capability to design and make high precision moulds and tools using only computer-based equipment.

In the area of electronics, HKPC has a microprocessor applications laboratory which provides training and consultancy in the use of microprocessors, particularly in the design of customised automatic production and testing equipment. In 1988, a surface mounting technology laboratory and a radio-frequency/digital communications laboratory will be established to provide technical assistance in the use of SMT and the design and production of communication equipment respectively.

Industry Department

In addition to the roles of policy formulation and adminstration typical of any government department, the industry department also runs a standards and calibration laboratory which maintains reference standards tracable to international standard institutions and provides calibration services for electrical and electronic measuring equipment. The department is wholly responsible for promoting industrial investment in Hong Kong with a view of introducing into Hong Kong manufacturing operations which help to upgrade the local capabilities in manufacturing processes and management.

Towards this end, the department maintains a 'One Stop Unit' which assists prospective investors in matters relating to the establishment of manufacturing facilities in Hong Kong, such as the search for suitable labor and industrial accommodation.

James T.Y. Fok is Divisional
Manager, Hong Kong
Productivity Council

Chapter 10

Land and Premises

by Peter Churchouse

Overview

* Only about 15 percent of Hong Kong's 420 square-mile land area is readily developable.
* All land in Hong Kong is owned by the government, which sells or grants leasehold interests.
* The Sino-British agreement guarantees extension of land leases beyond 1997 up to the year 2047.
* The property market has proved particularly volatile in recent years.
* A good range of sophisticated buildings is available.
* Hong Kong has three main office locations: Central District, Wan Chai/Causeway Bay and Tsim Sha Tsui.
* Central District is the traditional office center, and has highest rents and prices.
* Office rentals are generally lower in Hong Kong than in the other main financial centers of New York, London and Tokyo.
* Manufacturing is largely located in high-rise, compartmentalized factory buildings, but there is a trend towards developing more specialized buildings.
* Housing is geared very much towards apartment living.
* Hong Kong Island is the most popular residential location for foreigners.
* Residential prices on Hong Kong Island are highest, with Kowloon prices normally about 75 percent of these levels.

Known as the Manhattan of Asia and the Pearl of the Orient, Hong Kong never fails to impress the first-time visitor with its stunning topography and intensity of life. This exciting physical environment is the visitor's first taste of a community in which almost anything goes and where almost everything seems possible.

The lofty, tree-clad heights of Victoria Peak on Hong Kong Island provide a dramatic backdrop to the densely packed high-rise city strung out for miles along the waterfront. Buildings of every hue, from somber browns to glistening gold, dominate the urban landscape, as high-tech structures like the Hongkong Bank headquarters and Hong Kong Land Property Company's Exchange Square stand out as monuments to modern architecture. The Kowloon Peninsula, although as densely developed as the Hong Kong shore, presents a more monotonous skyline, with buildings limited in height by the nearby airport's approach routes.

With a total land area of only about 420 square miles, of which less than 15 percent is considered readily developable, land is indeed a scarce commodity in Hong Kong. The city has responded to this lack of good building sites with extensive land reclamation schemes, a process that has already created most of the high-rent commercial and industrial real estate in Hong Kong and Kowloon, including most of Central District and East Tsim Sha Tsui.

Property plays a more important role in Hong Kong's economy than it does in the economies of most other countries. This stems partly from the shortage of easily developable land and partly from a highly entrepreneurial business environment that encourages investors at all levels of society to exploit the financial opportunities of property development. Hong Kong's stock market is dominated by property companies, and even firms whose primary operations are in other spheres often have substantial property interests.

The volatility of Hong Kong's property sector is well known. This has been dramatically illustrated within the last five years, when property value increases of over 150 percent a year were sometimes followed almost immediately by equally rapid declines. As a vitally important part of Hong Kong's economy, property is subject to the forces of supply and demand, and is particularly sensitive to the political uncertainties facing the Territory in the lead-up to 1997.

Leasehold Laws

All land in Hong Kong is owned by the British government, referred to as the Crown. The Crown never actually sells the land, but only sells or grants leasehold interests for certain periods of time. In the past, such Crown leases extended for periods of 75, 99 or 999 years. This was later standardized in Hong Kong and Kowloon to terms of 75 years, usually renewable for a further 75 years, with other rules holding sway in the New Territories. Despite the ephemeral nature of such arrangements, property is still said to be bought and sold when it changes hands under long-term leasehold.

The Sino-British agreement has altered the terms of leasehold agreement, to the advantage of the long-term leaseholder. Signed in October 1984, the agreement assures a measure of stability in land and property dealings, enabling business operations to continue up to and after 1997 with a greater degree of certainty regarding land and property rights.

Under the Agreement, all new long-term leases are granted for 50 years beyond 1997, up to the year 2047. All current leases extending beyond the year 1997 will be honored. All existing long-term leases that do not extend beyond the year 1997 will be extended to 2047 without additional premium payments, though annual rent increases equivalent to three percent of the rateable value of property will be charged. (For more information, see Annex III of the White Paper agreement of 26 September 1984.)

General Principles of Acquiring Property

Foreign businesses, whether coming to Hong Kong for the first time or already here, are normally concerned with office, residential or industrial property. In all three sectors, the potential occupant is likely to have a wide range of choices as to location, quality and price.

There are a number of issues that occupiers should bear in mind, some of which will be peculiar to the Hong Kong context. Likewise, each property sector has its characteristic problems, though many considerations of property leasing or purchase are common to all three. Before examining the peculiarities of each, it is worthwhile examining some of these general issues.

Definition of floor area and basis of quotation: Probably in common with other areas, many property owners are prone to exaggeration when quoting details of the size of property being let or sold. Various practices are employed in Hong Kong, with the quotation of price and rents often done on the basis of a confusing range of definitions—*net, gross, lettable, usable*, etc. Irrespective of definition used, the prospective buyer or tenant should be very clear about what space he is entitled to, what is being paid for and how much of it is actually usable for the activity concerned.

Measurements: Although Hong Kong has officially gone metric, the property business has been slow to adapt. Areas are typically quoted in square feet by most operators in the business.

Lease: The length of lease periods varies by contract, but most kinds of property are leased on a two- or three-year basis. Longer leases with right-of-renewal clauses are becoming increasingly common.

Fixtures, fittings, management and air-conditioning: Landlords' provisions for fittings and decorations vary widely in quality and number, and can significantly affect total occupation costs. In virtually every case, management and air-conditioning costs are charged separately to the occupier. Quality and cost of building management may vary considerably between specific buildings.

Government taxes: A number of taxes are levied against both tenants and purchasers, including property tax, rates and stamp duties. Property tax is usually paid by the property owner, but may be passed on to the occupier. Rates are typically paid by the occupier. Both rates and property taxes are regular payments.

Stamp duties: Stamp duties are paid on execution of lease, whether for office, industrial or *registered* residential properties, amounting to 0.5 percent of the annual rental, exclusive of management and utilities charges. A lawyer may advise on various ways to reduce stamp duty.

Agent and legal fees: Agents' fees are normally, but not always, paid by the landlord or owner. Both parties are usually expected to bear their own legal fees arising from the property transaction, but in some instances the tenant will be expected to pay the landlord's legal fees or a proportion of them.

Deposits: In most tenancy situations the occupier is required to lodge a deposit with the landlord, usually equivalent to two months' rent. This is held by the landlord until expiry of the lease and normally does not bear interest.

Rent-free periods: For office and industrial properties, landlords normally offer a rent-free period to allow tenants to undertake the fitting out of their premises. The length of the rent-free period typically varies according to prevailing market conditions; when supply is tight, rent-free periods are reduced, and vice versa. Generally, however, these are shorter than the norm in the United States and Europe.

By now, it is probably fairly clear that general leasing and purchasing conditions in Hong Kong tend to be heavily weighted in the landlord's favor. In the true spirit of Hong Kong business, however, many aspects are often negotiable, making it important that purchasers and tenants seek good professional advice both to smooth the way and to ensure that the best possible deal is struck for the prevailing market context.

Office Market

Location

Over the last five to seven years, Hong Kong has developed a relatively sophisticated office market with a wide range of good quality premises. The new generation of office developments in Hong Kong now offers facilities on a par with the best available in the world's other major financial centers—though the actual amount of space per worker is probably tighter. Potential tenants will have to sort through a number of factors in choosing an office, foremost of which are size, prestige, cost and location.

Total Hong Kong office space amounts to around 48 million square feet. Grade 'A' office space—which is loosely defined as well designed, constructed and managed buildings with central air-conditioning systems and in good locations—comprises about 50 percent of total office stock. Most Grade A office floors are in the range of 10 thousand to 15 thousand square feet.

The three main office locations are Hong Kong Island's Central and Wan Chai/Causeway Bay districts, and Tsim Sha Tsui on the southern tip of the Kowloon Peninsula. Although good quality buildings are available in all three locations, prices vary significantly. Central has traditionally been the focus of office-based commercial activities and is very much the heart of Hong Kong's financial, banking and stockbroking businesses. Although Central's share of office stock has declined from over 44 percent in 1976 to around 26 percent in 1985, it remains the prime office location.

Wan Chai and Causeway Bay support a broader mixture of land uses. Causeway Bay is noted as a shopping, dining and hotel district. Wan Chai, immortalized in *The World of Suzie Wong*, still hosts the late-night exploits of sailors and others of nocturnal persuasion, but its heyday during the Vietnam War has long passed. As high-rent pressure on Central increases, a considerable number of good quality office buildings have been developed in Wan Chai and Causeway Bay, attracting a particularly large number of service-oriented consulting agencies, eg, advertisers, traders and building contractors. Major office development in Tsim Sha Tsui, the center of the tourist and hotel industry, is also a relatively recent phenomenon.

This area appeals to manufacturing company offices locating within striking distance of their factories or suppliers in Kowloon and the New Territories. Tsim Sha Tsui is popular with many China traders and import-export firms, as well as companies that need to be near the airport or train depot.

Method of Floor Area Quotation

Floor areas in office buildings are quoted in square feet and may be measured by four different methods: i) gross area; ii) lettable area; iii) net area; and iv) net usable area.

Landlords have different interpretations of these methods, and potential tenants or purchasers should be aware that, depending on the method quoted and the measurement method used, they may be expected to pay for such areas as lobbies, stairs, toilets, kitchens, lift shafts, corridors and columns.

The *gross area* is usually taken as the area within the perimeter of the outside walls, and includes wall thicknesses, elevator lobbies, stairwells, freight elevators, interior and external walls, kitchens and bathrooms. The amount of usable space normally represents between 75 and 85 percent of the gross area quoted.

At the other end of the scale, the *net usable area* can be defined as the main office area, typically excluding columns and partitions, bathrooms, walls, elevator lobbies and the like. This method of measurement implies that you are able to use 100 percent of what you are paying rent on. Not many offices in Hong Kong are rented on this basis. The *net area* can be defined as the net usable area plus all of the internal columns and the floor space up to the face of all external windows.

The definition of *lettable floor space* generally includes the net usable area as well as the lift lobby areas. Under this definition, the usable space will usually amount to between 90 and 95 percent of what you are paying rent on.

Air-conditioning and Management Charges

Air-conditioning and management charges are normally quoted on a per-square-foot basis. In some instances, the area on which rental is quoted may not be the same as the area on which management is quoted. Typically, management and air-conditioning charges include the costs of providing cool air to the premises, building security, window cleaning, building management and, in some instances, cleaning of the office premises. In most instances, the landlord charges a fixed amount, usually around HK$2.50 per square foot per month, and may adjust this on an annual basis. In some instances, a fully cost-accounted approach is adopted, where a set amount is charged per month and adjustments may be made at the end of the year when the management accounts have been settled.

In considering the management of the building, tenants should consider the following questions:

i) What is building security like, particularly after normal business hours? ii) Is air-conditioning provided outside of normal business hours? If so, is there an additional charge made? iii) What hours are elevators in operation? (In many buildings, they may be shut off at 6:30 pm.) iv) What hours can tenants gain access to the building? v) How often are windows cleaned? vi) What is maintenance like for common areas and toilets? Consideration should also be given to the ownership structure of the building itself, ie whether the building is owned by a major institutional or individual landlord. The larger institutional landlord may offer a tenant certain advantages with regard to flexibility for expansion. For example, if the tenant finds that he needs to expand his premises after one year of his lease period, the larger institutional landlord may allow the tenant to break the original lease if he is moving into another office within that landlord's portfolio.

Buildings that are owned by more than one owner may suffer certain management problems and also often have a lower net to gross floor-space ratio.

Lease Terms

Three-year leases on office premises have long been standard in Hong Kong, though more tenants are now taking either a three-year lease with an option for a three-year renewal, or a straight six-year lease. Such longer leases may contain provisions for modifying the rent after the third year—usually stipulating only a rent increase.

Expansion and Sub-letting

Many companies commonly lease slightly more space than they need to allow for expansion at a later date, and then sub-let the space over a short term. Tenants should determine before signing a lease whether the landlord will permit this type of arrangement. Generally speaking, landlords will make any covenant that is applicable to the tenant also applicable to any sub-tenant.

Rent-free Period

Rent-free periods offered by landlords vary according to the market situation at the time of the lease negotiation. Rent-free periods have been traditionally viewed by tenants and landlords as a simple discount on the rental value. Until recently, the standard rent-free period has been three months, but two months is now typical, and many rent-free periods are even shorter. Many landlords now talk of a 'fitting-out period' rather than a 'rent-free period,' allowing tenants perhaps as little as one month to fit out their office and start paying rent.

Landlord Provisions

The extent of facilities provided by landlords varies widely. At one extreme, the landlord might provide simply a bare concrete shell, leaving all modifications to the occupier. At the other extreme, in buildings like Exchange Square, the landlord's provisions might include all air-conditioning ducts, diffusers, sprinkler systems, high quality ceilings, under-floor trunking, and allowances for carpets, electrical sockets and telephone plugs.

Obviously, the extent of provision by the landlord affects the costs of remodeling and decorating the office. Where virtually nothing is provided by the landlord, for instance, fit-out costs can run in the order of HK$200 per square foot, compared with HK$120-130 per square foot at the other extreme.

It should be noted that most buildings in Hong Kong do not have under-floor trunking, or channels for conduit and wiring. Floors are normally bare concrete slabs across which renovators are required to chase cable runs for electrical sockets and communication lines—typically by chipping a channel with a hammer and chisel. Unlike the United States and Europe, there are no developments available in Hong Kong providing raised floors.

There is a trend for some companies in Hong Kong to include decorating and fitting-out costs in their rent. Landlords are not keen to do this because it has an effect on property taxes, but there are leasing companies and banks that will consider this approach.

Reinstatement

Generally speaking, the tenant is expected to reinstate the office premises on departure to exactly the same condition as when handed over at the beginning of the tenancy period. A landlord will rarely permit the out-going tenant to leave all interior fittings and decorations in place. Ripping out the fittings can result in additional cost to the tenant of around HK$10 per square foot. If a carpet was originally provided by the landlord, the tenant may be required to replace the carpet on departure from the premises with a carpet of the same standard and value as the original. If carpet allowance was given by the landlord, this would not be necessary.

Inter-tenancy Walls

Walls between tenants on any one floor are usually provided by the landlord and are often very simple structures. These usually reach only from the floor to the ceiling and do not extend above the ceiling to the roof. Most international companies do not find this arrangement satisfactory for sound-proofing, privacy and security.

Water Supply and Washrooms

Hong Kong office buildings generally do not provide executive washrooms and showers. An important consideration may be whether additional toilets can be provided within the building and whether water can be provided to a kitchen area.

Legal Considerations

Tenants and landlords normally pay their own legal costs for the drawing up of tenancy agreements. Sometimes, however, the landlord may ask a tenant to pay half of his legal costs.

The procedure for taking a lease typically entails an oral agreement between landlord and tenant, followed up by an offer letter setting down the general terms agreed. This is normally valid for one or two weeks and is returned to the landlord, signed and marked 'Subject to contract', usually with two months' deposit for rental, air-conditioning and management charges. (This two months' rental deposit is held by the landlord until the end of the tenancy, when it is returned to the tenant without interest.) If the landlord has not sent a tenancy agreement with the offer letter, he or she usually does so now. Once the tenancy agreement has been signed by the tenant and landlord, the tenancy must be registered and stamp duty paid. This may be split equally between landlord and tenant. On the signing of the tenancy agreement, one month's rent is usually payable in advance. All charges and rents are paid monthly. There may be variations in this procedure, and the tenant is advised to seek professional advice from the agent throughout. Agent fees are normally paid in Hong Kong by the landlord.

Utilities and Government Rates

Water rates are normally charged to the landlord's account and then passed on to the tenant. Electricity and telephone are metered and charged direct to the tenant by the respective utility company.

Government rates are typically paid by the landlord and charged back to the tenant. These are set by government as a percentage of the assessed rental value. In 1986, for instance, government rates were set at six percent of the assessed rental in 1983.

Other Issues

There are many other issues which may concern international companies in considering any prospective building.

Is the ceiling height sufficient to enable the construction of raised floors for offices or computer rooms? Are the windows double-glazed and thus likely to provide good sound insulation and to conserve energy? Can additional air-conditioning be installed for specialized areas, such as computer rooms? Does the building offer central telex, telephone or computer systems, conference facilities, or secretarial and business services? Are the toilets adequate for the numbers of staff?

Does the landlord provide cleaning services? If so, at what time of the day do the cleaners come? Does the building module design allow for the form of interior renovation that the company prefers in terms of ceiling grids, windows, column spacing, air-conditioning ducts, etc.? Does the building have provisions for parking? Most Hong Kong buildings do not, and those that do generally have only a modest number. In Central District, there four public parking lot buildings, which now charge about HK$1,400 to HK$1,500 per parking space per month. These spaces are not allocated, so parking is on a first-come-first-served basis. Generally, buildings that do provide parking spaces within the office building allocate specific spaces for tenants.

Rents and Office Prices

Rental and price movements in recent years are illustrated in Figures 2 and 3. Rental movements have generally lagged behind price movements, while fluctuating less. On average, rents in Tsim Sha Tsui, Wan Chai and Causeway Bay have consistently remained at about 65 to 75 percent of those prevailing in Central.

It should be noted that Figures 3 and 4 represent average values and that rents for prime buildings can be expected to reach much higher levels. Top rents in Central currently run about HK$29 per square foot net per month, though HK$25 to HK$27 is typical for prime buildings in prime locations. In Tsim Sha Tsui, an increasingly popular office location, Grade A rentals run in the range of HK$19 to HK$24 per square foot net per month, while in Wan Chai and Causeway Bay, rents are in the HK$15 to HK$18 range.

Selling prices of office property also show a marked variation even between buildings within the same areas. For buildings in Central District, prices for good quality premises typically range between HK$2,400 and HK$2,800 per square foot, gross, though premises in slightly less prestigious buildings in fringe locations can be obtained for HK$1,500 to HK$1,800 per square foot. Prices in Wan Chai and Causeway Bay are typically lower, running between HK$1,000 and HK$1,400 for better quality premises.

Prospects

New, good quality office space that came onto the market in 1986 amounted to only about one quarter of the same in each of the previous five years, on average. The result is a generally tight office market, with year-end vacancies at around 2.7 percent, the lowest rate for many years. Despite approximately 2.6 million square feet becoming available in 1987, it is likely that the year-end vacancy rate will be a modest 5–6 percent, well below vacancy rates for the 1981-1985 period. 1988 should see some 3.2 million square feet of Grade A space come available, with almost half of that in Central.

Significant amounts of space will become available in Central then, when the Bank of China's new headquarters building, located on the eastern fringe of Central, is completed. This new supply should help to moderate prices and rents. During this same period, the Tsim Sha Tsui market is likely to remain tight, with very little new supply, though some 1.26 million square feet of new space in 1988 should ease pressure on that market.

At present, only relatively modest levels of new supply seem likely to come onto the market in 1989 and 1990—1.65 million and 1.8 million square feet, respectively—significantly lower than the average of 2.6 million square feet per year during the 1981-1985 period.

Thus, it should be expected that a generally tight office market will persist until the end of the 1980s, with perhaps some softening in 1988. If Hong Kong's economy continues to grow at present rates, a healthy level of demand for office space will also continue; with relatively modest levels of new supply, the market should witness continued upward pressure on rentals and prices, though it's unlikely that the spectacular rates of increase achieved in the 1978-1981 period will be repeated.

Industrial Premises

American Industrial Investment

Despite the growing importance of financial and business services, the manufacturing sector remains the economic mainstay of Hong Kong, contributing approximately one quarter of the total Gross Domestic Product and employing some 42 percent of the work force. The manufacturing base has traditionally been rooted in light industries, particularly textiles and electronics. The textiles sector, including clothing manufacturers, employs approximately 44 percent of the territory's manufacturing work force.

The role of American trade and the impact of the American economy on Hong Kong has increased significantly over the past

10 years, giving greater support to the old adage that when America sneezes, Hong Kong catches pneumonia. Swings in the American economy's performance are reflected almost immediately in the order books of Hong Kong's manufacturers. The United States now takes some 45 percent of Hong Kong's domestic exports, up from 32 percent in 1975. It is therefore not without good reason that Hong Kong's manufacturers keep close watch on developments in the American economy and political sentiments. American involvement in manufacturing has increased by over 600 percent since 1980. The US has recently overtaken Japan as the leading source of foreign involvement in manufacturing with an investment of more than HK$6 billion, 50 percent of which is focused on the electronics industry.

Industrial Locations

Most Hong Kong manufacturers are located in high-rise flatted factory buildings. (The term 'flatted' means that the building is divided into separate apartments, which can be sold or leased to different occupants.) Most of these buildings have been neither designed nor built to particularly high standards, and cannot compare favorably with purpose-built developments in the US and Europe. Most of these industrial buildings were developed for speculation and leased to end-users, or sold, floor by floor, unit by unit.

Fortunately, the number of customized industrial buildings of exacting specifications is increasing in Hong Kong. Industrialists, particularly, are developing their own buildings, both to ensure a higher quality industrial environment and to retain better control of their buildings. Many are increasingly prepared to move from traditional industrial locations in the urban areas to more open, better quality environments, such as the new towns in the New Territories. Sha Tin has proved particularly popular among industrialists. Two low-rise industrial estates in Tai Po and Yuen Long are currently being developed by the Industrial Estates Corporation to provide industrial space for industries that cannot be readily accommodated in traditional flatted factories, or for special industries that the government wishes to encourage. The bulk of industrial space is concentrated in the Kowloon area, between Tsuen Wan in the west and Kwun Tong in the east.

These areas generally have good access to labor and major transport links, including the Mass Transit Railway. The Kwai Chung area is popular with companies desiring proximity to the major container terminal, while To Kwa Wan and San Po Kong to the east are popular with companies preferring ready access to the airport.

Generally speaking, industrial areas closest to the urban areas fetch the highest prices and rents, while those further out in the New Territories—such as Tuen Mun, Sha Tin, Yuen Long and Tai Po—are significantly cheaper.

At the end of 1985, Hong Kong had a total of 141.25 million square feet of flatted factory space, this having increased 134 percent since 1976.

Newcomer's Options

In establishing an industrial operation in Hong Kong, the prospective operator is faced with four main options.

#*Option One*: Lease or buy standard space in an existing high rise factory building or in a brand new building. These may have been developed by speculative developers for rent or sale, or may have been developed by other end-users, who then lease or sell surplus space. This option is the most popular among new businesses in Hong Kong.

#*Option Two*: Buy a plot of land, either from a private sector seller or at government auction, and develop your own industrial building to specific requirements. Companies pursuing this option are strongly advised to appoint a professional project manager to oversee the development of the building.

#*Option Three*: Find a developer to build the industrial building to specifications and requirements set down by the end-user, who is committed in advance to buy or lease it, usually in its entirety. Again, it is important to ensure that strong project management is maintained from beginning to end.

#*Option Four*: Purchase land or standard factory space in one of the two estates in Tai Po or Yuen Long currently developed by the Industrial Estates Corporation.

Availability of Labor

Availability of labor within easy commuting range of the factory will be an important consideration for industrialists. Labor in Hong Kong tends to be quite mobile, with often fairly high labor turnover. Availability of efficient, cheap public transport, cafeterias, restaurants and other personal services, such as banks, within the industrial area is an important incentive to attract labor, and can also result in lower labor costs. With the growth of the new towns, areas like Sha Tin, Tai Po and Tuen Mun now have established sizable local labor pools that help to make their areas more attractive to industrialists.

Floor Area Quotation and Other Costs

Industrial rents and prices are normally quoted on the gross floor areas. This typically includes walls, columns and common areas, like elevators and stairwells. The usable space usually amounts to approximately 80 percent of the gross floor space, though some older, smaller buildings can be as low as 60 percent, and some of the more modern warehouse buildings can be as high as 90 percent.

Rents are normally quoted as Hong Kong dollars per square foot per month on the gross area, exclusive of government rates and management charges. Management charges are normally about HK$.30 to HK$.35 per square foot per month on the gross area. Rates are six percent of the 1983 assessed rental value and are paid quarterly by the occupier whether the occupier is a tenant or an owner. All utilities, such as water, electricity and gas, are added to the tenant's account. Parking spaces and exclusive unloading space are paid as a separate charge. In early 1987, parking spaces for cars typically cost around HK$800 per month each, while spaces for trucks cost around HK$1,000 per month and spaces for shipping containers around HK$1,500.

Ceiling and Floor Considerations

An important point to bear in mind when examining industrial buildings is ceiling height. This is normally quoted as the height from the floor to the ceiling slab above, but this can be misleading, as the height from the floor to the under-beam ceiling is the more important measure. Typically, this height is around nine feet in most industrial buildings and up to 11 feet in some of the better buildings. Many warehouses have a floor to under-beam height of around 16 feet.

Another important consideration is the floor loading characteristics of the building. Most floors can withstand floor loading pressures of around 150 pounds per square foot, though some specialized buildings can have floor loadings of up to 350 pounds per square foot.

Ground floor space in industrial buildings typically has greater ceiling heights and floor loadings, as well as better access, than upper floors. Rents and prices are likewise higher for ground level space, usually double the rents and prices of the upper floors.

Leasing Industrial Space

Leases are typically of three years' duration, and sometimes five years with a review after three years. There are various options on conditions of the review, which can be based on open market values or subject to a minimum of the initial rent paid in the first period of the tenancy. Sometimes a fixed increase or a fixed minimum and maximum can be set. It is possible to negotiate longer term leases at the outset, though this is rare. Options to renew are often difficult to negotiate with some landlords.

Tenants are normally expected to pay two to three months' rent as a deposit and also two to three months' management fee. Stamp duties are paid by both the tenant and landlord. Agency fees are normally paid by the landlord. Rent-free periods for industrial buildings in Hong Kong are usually one month, even for large buildings. General tenancy conditions in industrial buildings are heavily weighted in favor of the landlord and many of the larger industrial property owners will not entertain any modification of the tenancy conditions set down by them.

Prospective occupiers should find out if the building under consideration is wholly owned by one party or if it has been subdivided among many owners under strata title. In the latter case, particularly, the quality and reliability of the building management is important to determine before signing papers.

Purchasing Industrial Space

When buying space in an industrial building, the buyer is purchasing undivided shares in the building and the land up to 1997, plus 50 years beyond. Similar conditions apply in the purchase of industrial land. The price of land is based on the amount of developable floor space that can be built on the land, dictated by a designated plot ratio. Purchase prices of industrial buildings are usually quoted as Hong Kong dollars per square foot, gross. After negotiating the general terms of a sale, a 10 percent deposit is paid on signing the sale and purchase agreement. The balance is paid within 30 days of completing the documentation. Each party bears its own legal costs, and stamp duty is paid by the buyer. Agency fees are normally paid by the seller. All occupation costs, such as rates, utilities and parking spaces, are to purchaser's account. If a building is bought while under construction, the buyer may pay by installment throughout the construction period.

If a user is considering purchasing space within a building under a strata title, careful attention needs to be given the Deed of Mutual Covenant (DMC). This document sets out the conditions, controls and management procedures for the operation of the building. A purchaser normally will acquire voting rights for building operation under the terms of the DMC. The DMC may also make provisions for noise, vibrations, odors, offensive trades and other conditions within the building. This may have implications for insurance on the building as a whole and also for insurance of the purchaser's own space.

Industrial Estates Corporation

The Industrial Estates Corporation, established by the government in 1977 as an autonomous, government-funded, non-profit organization, is responsible for providing industrial land for uses and processes that cannot conveniently be accommodated within standard high rise factory buildings.

The corporation gives priority to certain types of industries: i) industries using levels of technology higher than normal in Hong Kong, and providing employment in high skill areas; ii) industries making products new to Hong Kong, or exporting a significant proportion of their production; and iii) industries producing goods or components of high domestic value.

Two estates have been developed, one in Tai Po in the northeastern New Territories and the other in Yuen Long in the northwestern New Territories.

These did not prove particularly popular in the early days, when they were considered rather remote from the urban areas and labor supply. They were also covered by relatively strict controls on industrial processes and uses. Since the opening of the electrified rail line, however, the estate at Tai Po has proven more popular and is now 80 to 85 percent occupied.

Within these industrial estates, tenants may be allowed to postpone paying full property costs until the factory has gone into production.

Industrialists wishing to take up space in either of these two estates should proceed by one of two options. Firstly, one can purchase a 15-year lease and construct the desired factory space to a maximum designated plot ratio of 2.5:1 (2.5 square feet of floor area for every one square foot of ground area).

Secondly, one can take standard factory space, built typically to standards commonly found in the United States. These factories are typically single story buildings with walls about 23 feet high and ceilings 32 feet high at the building's centre. These are available for purchase or rent.

Rents and Prices

Industrial rents and prices vary widely throughout Hong Kong, reflecting location, quality of building, access and environment.

Prices tend to be higher in Hong Kong and Kowloon, and lower further out in the New Territories. Within individual buildings, ground floors with greater floor loadings, higher ceilings and better access fetch higher rents and prices than upper floors.

Trends

With increasing sophistication of Hong Kong's industrial base and manufacturing investment from the United States, Japan and other countries, a number of trends are being observed in the industrial property market:

—Demand is increasing for high quality space with greater ceiling heights and floor loadings.

—Demand is also increasing for low-rise buildings that can accommodate a single company in its own medium-sized building (100,000 to 150,000 square feet).

—Large space users are increasingly requiring around 50,000 square feet on a single floor and exclusive use of elevators and loading bays.

—Many companies are prepared to move to less traditional locations to secure the above requirements, along with a better working environment.

—There is a trend towards larger companies developing their own purpose-built factories, particularly in Kowloon Bay and more distant locations, such as Sha Tin and Yuen Long.

—There is increasing divergence between the type of accommodation which dominates existing supply and that required by many new industrial processes.

Residential Property

Finding a home anywhere can be a lengthy and frustrating experience, and in Hong Kong the house-hunter is faced with certain unique problems. Some adjustment to the territory's dense population, cosmopolitan atmosphere and bustling economy is usually necessary for the newcomer.

Residential accommodation is geared almost exclusively to apartment living, a lifestyle quite alien to many people from less densely populated parts of the world. And while low-rise developments are available, the residential environment is dominated by high-rise blocks, necessitating a vital adjustment to one's housing expectations. Still, a fulfilling and comfortable style of living is attainable to those who are prepared to look for it with some perseverance and an open mind. Selecting the most appropriate accommodation, particularly for a family, is inevitably somewhat of an emotional decision, but can result in one of the most rewarding compensations for the transfer away from 'home'.

The expatriate coming to Hong Kong is usually looking for a much larger flat than average on a housing market that is dominated by small flats. Less than three percent of Hong Kong's private housing stock comprise units of over 1,700 square feet. In fact, approximately 85 percent of private housing is in units of less than 750 square feet, gross, an indication of the very crowded living conditions in Hong Kong.

The larger flat market is dominated by the corporate sector, where housing is provided for senior staff by employers. This sector of the market is very much a rented market rather than an owner-occupier market and is affected very much by the general health of the economy, and particularly foreign business involvement in Hong Kong. In consequence, this market is more volatile than other residential sectors.

Choosing a Neighborhood

When looking for housing in Hong Kong, the prospective tenant or purchaser must decide where he or she wants to live. The first problem is to choose between Hong Kong Island and Kowloon or the New Territories. Though Kowloon and the New Territories have become more popular in recent years, Hong Kong Island is still the most popular choice for new arrivals.

Within Hong Kong Island there are broadly two choices: the south of the island or the north side.

The south side includes locations like Repulse Bay, Shouson Hill, Stanley and Chung Hom Kok, and is characterized by a far higher proportion of low-rise apartment blocks than elsewhere on the island. Though further from the Central business district, these areas have a quieter living environment and ready access to beaches and country parks.

Victoria Peak, the traditional housing area for Hong Kong's taipans, also has a predominance of low-rise residential development, often with spectacular views (when not enshrouded in mist or clouds) of Hong Kong's harbor or the islands to the south. The Mid-Levels area stretches along the north side of the island, midway (as the name suggests) between the shoreline and the Peak. Mid-Levels has good access to Central and Wan Chai, and is characterized by high-rise apartment blocks, often with good harbor views. This area is often chosen by people who may trade off the environmental benefits of the south side of the island for convenience.

In Kowloon and the New Territories, the most popular areas for expatriates are Clearwater Bay and Sai Kung to the east of the territory, and Kowloon Tong. Clearwater Bay and Sai Kung, which contain mainly low-rise developments and many detached houses, are each about 45 minutes' drive from Central if traffic is not too heavy. Kowloon Tong, which also has many low-rise developments, is convenient for Tsim Sha Tsui, but is located under the flight path to the airport and is consequently not the quietest of environments.

In Tsim Sha Tsui proper, two individual developments are worth noting—Harbour City on Canton Road and New World Apartments in New World Centre. Both provide good quality premises in the heart of the busy tourist district.

Methods of Quotation

Rents are normally quoted on a monthly basis exclusive of all management charges, utilities and government rates. While landlords typically quote the gross area of the apartment, rents are almost always quoted as a lump sum for the flat, not on a per-square-foot basis as in other property sectors. The gross area, if quoted, normally includes elevator lobbies, elevators and stairwells apportioned to the flat.

Most larger units include one or two parking spaces within the rental figure.

For sales, likewise, prices are normally quoted as a total price rather than on a per-square-foot basis.

Management Fee

The amount of the management fee depends on the age of the building and the services and amenities provided in the development. The fee is normally paid directly by the occupier.

The charge typically contributes towards security guards, caretakers, gardens, communal facilities, cleaning and some general maintenance of the building and public areas. As a general guide, this charge can vary from HK$200 to HK$300 per month in some older blocks to as much as HK$2,000 per month for some newer, smaller developments with such facilities as a swimming pool.

Agent's Fees

When leasing, the agent's fee normally equals one month's rent, and is split between landlord and tenant. When the flat is sold, the fee is sometimes paid by the seller, but purchasers may be required to pay it in certain situations.

Legal Costs

The costs of drawing up the tenancy agreement are usually borne both by the landlord and tenant. If the tenant engages the services of another solicitor to act on his behalf, this cost goes to the tenant's account.

Property sellers and buyers normally pay their own legal costs, which are set on a sliding scale according to the value of the property. If the buyer is taking a mortgage from a bank, the bank's legal fees are usually paid by the purchaser.

Government Rates, Stamp Duty and Utilities

Government taxes are paid quarterly and amount to a percentage of the 1983 rental value assessed by government. In early 1987, this amounted to six percent of the 1983 assessed rental value, but it is periodically changed by the government. An apartment currently renting at around HK$35,000 per month, for example, might expect to have rates payable of about HK$1,800 per month (HK$5,400 per quarter).

Stamp duty is mandatory only for registered residential leases. This amounts to one half of one percent of the annual rent on the premises. It is paid on the stamping of the lease agreement, and is normally apportioned equally between the landlord and tenant. For residential sales, stamp duty is paid by the buyer, and is calculated as 2.75 percent of sales value on prices over HK$500,000.

All utilities, such as electricity, gas and water charges, are borne by the occupier.

Tenure

Leases normally last for a two-year period. A break option after one year may sometimes be granted. An option to extend a lease for a third year is also often built in. Rights of tenure exist after the two-year lease period provided the tenant pays a market rent, which will be assessed by the Lands Tribunal when the parties are unable to agree a value.

In purchasing property, it is important to bear in mind that what is being purchased is a leasehold interest, not a freehold interest. All new long-term leases can be granted for 50 years beyond 1997, up to the year 2047.

Standards of Finish, Fixtures, and Fittings

Standards of finish, design and facilities in many residential blocks containing larger units have improved significantly in recent years. Better quality developments now typically have such facilities as a swimming pool, tennis court, squash court, sauna, gym and resident's club. Within flats themselves, standards of kitchens have also improved to meet Western demands; in the past, kitchens have been very basic affairs with a minimum of facilities.

Most flats in the expatriate market typically have three or four bedrooms with two bathrooms, one *en suite*, and possibly a guest toilet. Servants' quarters with separate shower and toilet are normally located adjacent to the kitchen. Some larger flats may have a utilities room.

Floors throughout are often wood parquet, finished in polyurethane varnish or polished. Walls are plastered and normally painted white. Bathrooms are tiled. Electrical facilities and water heaters may not be provided, but there are recent trends in some developments to provide such items as an oven, refrigerator and washing machine.

Where central air-conditioning is provided, operating costs are borne by the occupier.

Many newer developments have entry phone and closed circuit security systems.

Buying Property

Conditions for property purchase have been made easier recently by a relaxation in lending policies of the major financial institutions. Banks have increased the amounts they are prepared to lend for house purchase to 80 or 90 percent of the property's value, and mortgage periods have been extended to 20 years and longer. With interest rates lower than in the early 1980s, monthly repayments have been significantly reduced. Since 1984, a larger number of financial institutions have entered the home mortgage market, opening up new avenues to financing and creating a greater degree of competition among banks, all to the benefit of the home buyer.

Prices and Rents

Of the three main locations, Hong Kong Island, Kowloon and the New Territories, prices for residential property on the island are highest, with the New Territories lowest. Generally, unit prices in Kowloon are around 75 percent of those on Hong Kong Island, while prices in the New Territories are 55 to 60 percent.

Within Hong Kong Island, properties on the Peak and on the south side are most expensive. Mid-levels property prices tend to be around 75 to 85 percent of those. The market for larger residential units, however, is the most volatile sector of the residential market, being very much dependent on general economic performance and business confidence.

Typically the tenant would expect to pay a rent of HK$30,000 to HK$40,000 per month for a large apartment of, say, 2,700 to 3,300 square feet, gross, in a good location. Smaller units in the 2,000 to 2,500 square-foot range typically command rents of HK$20,000 to HK$25,000 per month.

Purchase prices have also recovered since 1984 to the extent that good quality larger units typically sell for HK$1,200 to HK$1,500 per square foot, gross. It is noteworthy that in the Hong Kong market prices tend to be more volatile than rentals, reflecting the greater risks involved in owning rather than renting property. Historically, also, there has been a distinct trend for movements in rentals to lag behind movements in prices.

General Trends and Prospects

It is probably clear that the Hong Kong property market is indeed a volatile one, and that this volatility cuts across all sectors and types of property. This was dramatically illustrated from 1978 to 1985, when property values in some sectors showed annual rates of increase of over 150 percent per annum. A downturn in this spiral was inevitable. Although popular belief and the media have often ascribed the price slump to the political factors surrounding Hong Kong's uncertain future and the Sino-British negotiations, closer analysis of the facts suggests that underlying causes are clearly economic in nature.

Notwithstanding political factors, the dramatic fall in prices can be attributed largely to the considerable over-supply in most sectors of the market. Levels of real demand could not be expected to keep pace with the high levels of new supply which were spurred on by earlier rapid price increases and speculative activity.

By the end of 1984, following the signing of the Sino-British agreement, an equilibrium in supply and demand seemed to have been reached in most sectors of the market; the political agreement is generally cited as the catalyst of this calming effect. Due to the generally long lead times involved in high-rise property development, and the consequent delay of reaction to perceived shortfalls and surpluses, supply of new stock often fluctuates widely from year to year. Demand for floor-space, on the other hand, tends to be more stable than supply. The combination of these factors can have a significant impact on prices and rents, with upward or downward pressures being felt quickly in the market.

Assuming that the economy performs reasonably well in the period up to the end of the 1980s, and there are no major political bombshells, it is possible to make some general observations on the likely characteristics of the market over this period.

The generally tight supply in the office market is likely to persist until 1988. Because new supply is unevenly distributed between Hong Kong, Tsim Sha Tsui and the Wan Chai/Causeway Bay area, market pressures will be different for each area. Tsim Sha Tsui will have the widest fluctuation, though in the short term, values are likely to continue to increase at a greater rate than other areas, approaching Central District rents. Significant amounts of space will become available in Central from late 1987 through 1988, including the Bank of China's new headquarters building. Located on the eastern fringe of Central, this new stock should help to moderate prices and rentals over this time. In the residential market, significant increases in the supply of large, good quality flats in 1987 and 1988 should provide plenty of choice for accommodation, effectively stabilizing prices and rentals. Much of the new supply of larger flats will be on the south side of Hong Kong Island.

An interesting trend emerged in 1986 in most sectors of the property market: owners were earning increasing yields on property investment brought about by rents rising faster than sales prices. Perhaps this reflects the greater risks and lower flexibility involved in owning property compared to renting. To a certain extent it may be postulated that the uncertainty surrounding the future after 1997 acts to fuel this phenomenon. If in fact correct, we may reasonably expect rents to continue to rise faster than prices, with even higher property yields, as 1997 draws closer. This, however, lies as much in the area of political speculation as it docs in the area of economic and property market forecasting.

For More Information Property Listings appear daily in the *South China Morning Post* and *Hong Kong Standard*.

JLW Property Index, Jones Lang Wootton. A quarterly publication charting movements and trends in the Hong Kong property market. By subscription.

Your Rates in 1984–1985, Rating and Valuation Department, Hong Kong Government.

Hong Kong 1987, Hong Kong Government Bookshop. An annual publication by Hong Kong government.

Asian Property Review, Jones Lang Wootton. Published at the beginning of each year.
Hong Kong Industrial Property Review, 1987, Jones Lang Wootton. Published annually.
Property Review 1987, Rating and Valuation Department, Hong Kong government. Published annually.
Tenants Guide, Jones Lang Wootton.

Next Steps

The first step in locating property in Hong Kong is to approach one of the firms of chartered surveyors. Such firms have fully qualified staff trained in all aspects of property and whose members belong to the professional bodies of the Royal Institution of Chartered Surveyors and the Hong Kong Institute of Surveyors. Membership of these institutions, which govern professional standards and codes of professional conduct, ensures clients of high standards of service.

There are many firms who act only as brokers or agents and are affiliated to either of these professional bodies.

Apart from helping you locate appropriate property, such firms can advise on procedures in leasing and buying, other costs and taxes, and potential problems or pitfalls.

Final Word

The newspaper article below is from the front page of Hong Kong's leading English language newspaper, reporting on a land auction; it serves to indicate the sort of excitement and importance of property in the daily life of Hong Kong. In very few parts of the world would a similar event receive such media or public attention or be surrounded by such an air of theatre.

The City Hall Theatre was packed to the rafters yesterday as hundreds of curious stockbrokers, bankers, property consultants and reporters gathered to witness another of Hong Kong's great commercial dramas being played out.

Only a sprinkling of the territory's biggest financiers and conglomerates were able to afford the anticipated $1 billion for the site, ... and it was to see the tycoons in action that the crowds had gathered.

They were not disappointed.

CHINA

Deep Bay

LAU FAU SHAN

YUEN LONG

SAN TIN

SHEK KONG

LO W

TUEN MUN

TAI LAM CHUNG

SHAM TSENG

TSUEN WAN

MA WAN

TSING YI

LA

THE
BROTHERS

CHEK LAP KOK
ISLAND

TUNG
CHUNG

PENG
CHAU

MUI WO

TAI O

CHI MA WAN
PENINSULA

CHEUNG
CHAU

West Lamma Channel

Lantau Channel

SOKO ISLANDS

IS

scale
1:200 000

km 0   2   4   6   8   10   12   14 km

Series   AR/I/LU
Edition 2 1982   (Reprinted 1986)

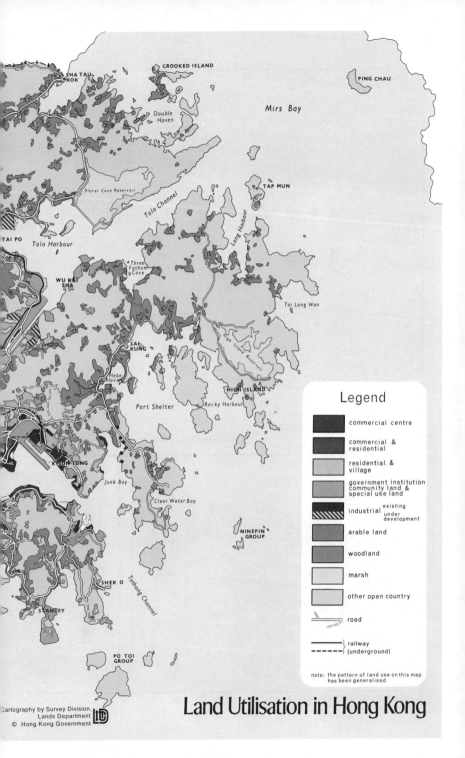

Land Utilisation in Hong Kong

Legend

- commercial centre
- commercial & residential
- residential & village
- government institution community land & special use land
- industrial — existing / under development
- arable land
- woodland
- marsh
- other open country
- road
- railway
- (underground)

note: the pattern of land use on this map has been generalised.

Cartography by Survey Division, Lands Department
© Hong Kong Government

Map labels: CROOKED ISLAND, PING CHAU, SHA TAU KOK, Double Haven, Mirs Bay, Plover Cove Reservoir, Tolo Channel, TAP MUN, TAI PO, Tolo Harbour, Long Harbour, WU KAI SHA, Three Fathom Cove, Tai Long Wan, High Island Reservoir, SAI KUNG, Hebe Haven, HIGH ISLAND, Port Shelter, Rocky Harbour, KWUN TONG, Junk Bay, Clear Water Bay, NINEPIN GROUP, SHEK O, Tathong Channel, STANLEY, PO TOI GROUP

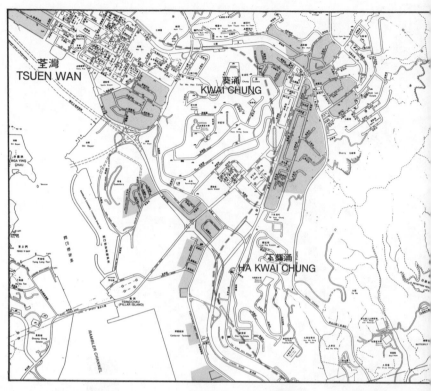

荃灣
TSUEN WAN

葵涌
KWAI CHUNG

下葵涌
HA KWAI CHUNG

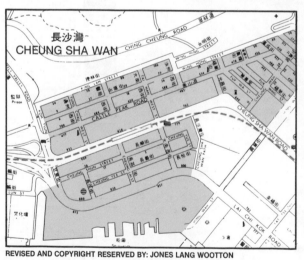

長沙灣
CHEUNG SHA WAN

CHING CHEUNG ROAD

CASTLE PEAK ROAD

CHEUNG SHA WAN ROAD

LAI CHI KOK ROAD

屯門
TUEN MUN NEW TO

HO TIN ST

KIN WING STREET

KIN KWAN ST

PUI TO RO

REVISED AND COPYRIGHT RESERVED BY: JONES LANG WOOTTON

172

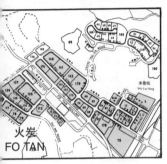

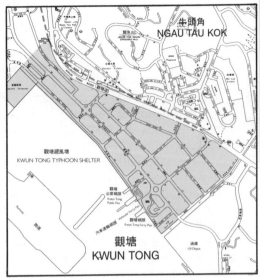

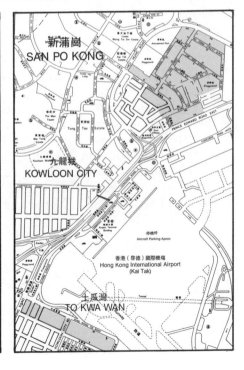

Five minutes after the scheduled time for the opening of bidding the territory's most powerful property mogul, Mr Li Ka-shing, entered the room, to be met with gasps of recognition from the crowd.

With an impeccable sense of theatrical timing, and to the accompaniment of television arc lights and camera flashes, Mr Li took his seat.

The game was on!

... the auctioneer immediately launched the formal proceedings, asking for bids at $850 million, to a chorus of '*Wah!*' from onlookers.

... the $850 million opening gambit signalled to the gathering that auctioneer Jim Hughes was in a no-nonsense frame of mind.

Predictably, a hand shot up from the Cheung Kong/Hutchison encampment, and it belonged to no less than Mr Li Ka-shing himself.

The sighs of wonderment began afresh, as bidding moved briskly to $950 million in only four minutes... Mr Li's mobile telephone rang, causing him to leave ahead of the final bid, as the price had clearly moved beyond the level he regarded as reasonable.

At $925 million Swire, in the form of David Mahoney, entered the bidding for the first time, eliciting a buzz of excitement as Mr Chen stood up and moved several rows to the rear to sit beside Mr Kwok Tak-seng, Kwok family patriarch and chairman of Sun Hung Kai Properties.

High drama again as another member of the Kwok family approached Mr Mahoney, clearly offering some form of joint action, but the response was a firm 'No deal'.

Sun Hung Kai then offered the magical 'one billion dollars'.

But this was undoubtedly as far as the Kwok interests were prepared to go, and Swire's $1.005 billion won the day... '1997 seems a long way off,' quipped one analyst. (*South China Morning Post*, 28th May 1986.)

Peter Churchouse is the
Director, Research Department of
Jones Lang Wootton.

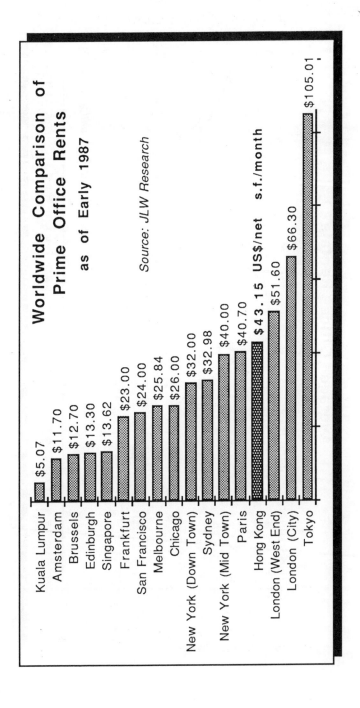

Worldwide Comparison of Prime Office Rents

as of Early 1987

Source: JLW Research

$43.15 US$/net s.f./month

Kuala Lumpur	$5.07
Amsterdam	$11.70
Brussels	$12.70
Edinburgh	$13.30
Singapore	$13.62
Frankfurt	$23.00
San Francisco	$24.00
Melbourne	$25.84
Chicago	$26.00
New York (Down Town)	$32.00
Sydney	$32.98
New York (Mid Town)	$40.00
Paris	$40.70
Hong Kong	$43.15
London (West End)	$51.60
London (City)	$66.30
Tokyo	$105.01

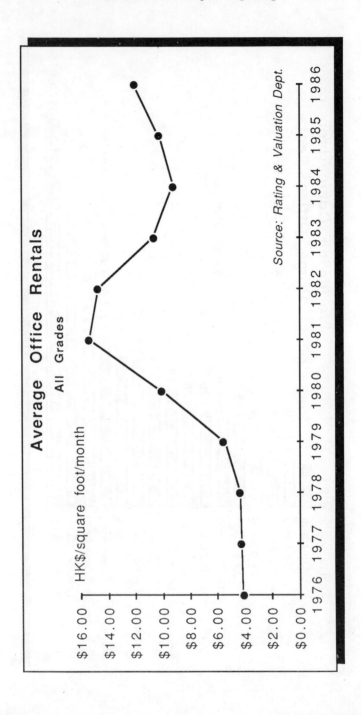

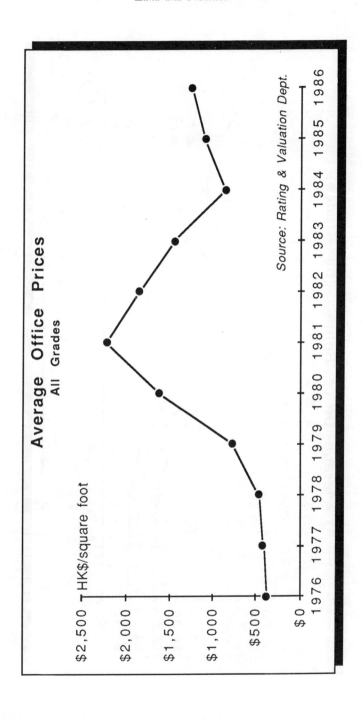

Average Office Prices
All Grades

HK$/square foot

Source: Rating & Valuation Dept.

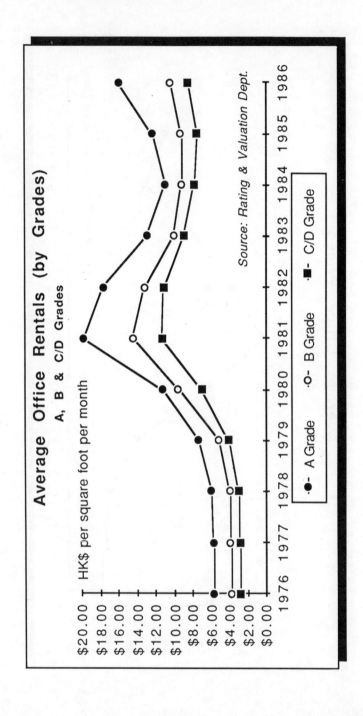

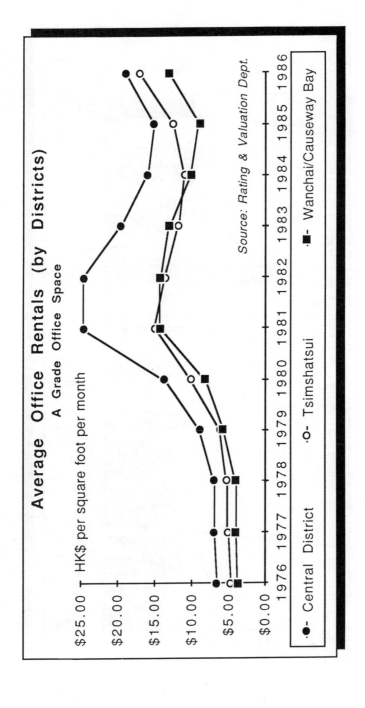

Average Office Rentals (by Districts)

A Grade Office Space

HK$ per square foot per month

Source: Rating & Valuation Dept.

●- Central District   ·○- Tsimshatsui   ■- Wanchai/Causeway Bay

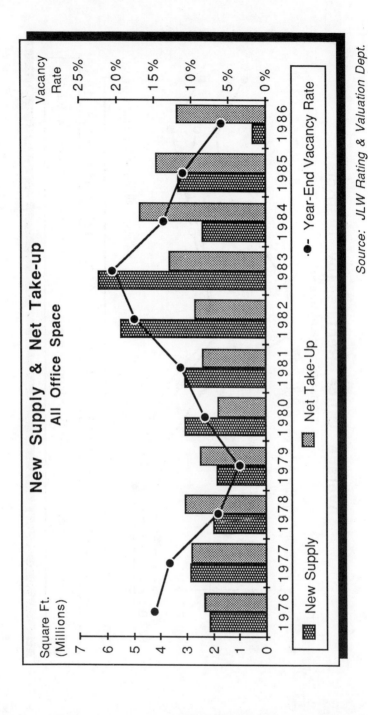

New Supply & Net Take-up
All Office Space

Source: JLW Rating & Valuation Dept.

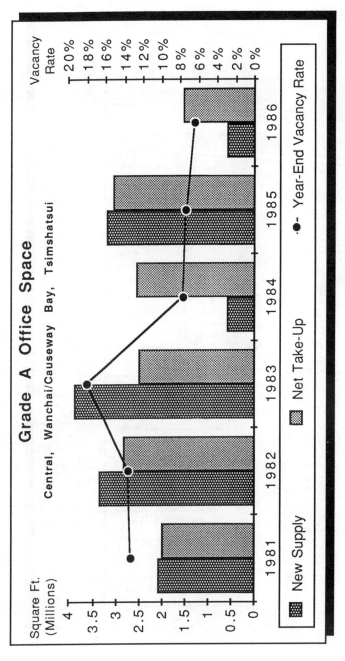

Grade A Office Space
Central, Wanchai/Causeway Bay, Tsimshatsui

Square Ft.
(Millions)

Vacancy
Rate

■ New Supply   ▨ Net Take-Up   ●- Year-End Vacancy Rate

Source: JLW Research, Rating & Valuation Dept.

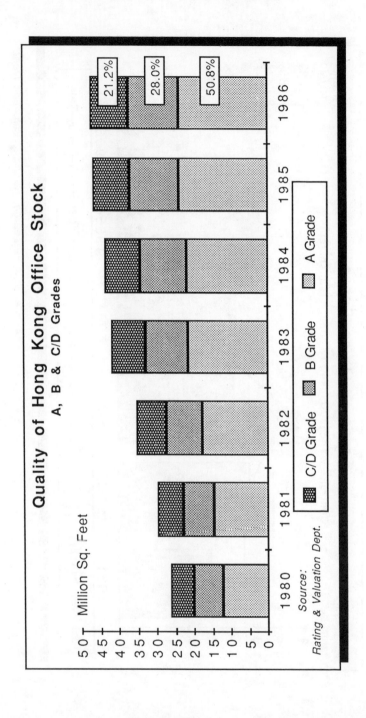

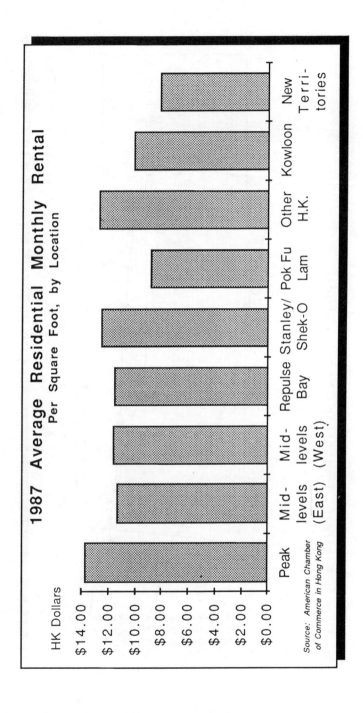

1987 Average Residential Monthly Rental
Per Square Foot, by Location

HK Dollars

Peak | Mid-levels (East) | Mid-levels (West) | Repulse Bay | Stanley/ Shek-O | Pok Fu Lam | Other H.K. | Kowloon | New Terri-tories

$14.00 $12.00 $10.00 $8.00 $6.00 $4.00 $2.00 $0.00

Source: American Chamber of Commerce in Hong Kong

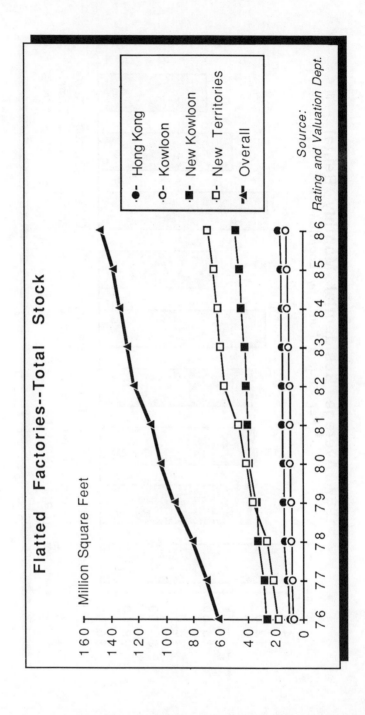

Flatted Factories--Total Stock

Million Square Feet

Legend:
- Hong Kong
- Kowloon
- New Kowloon
- New Territories
- Overall

Source: *Rating and Valuation Dept.*

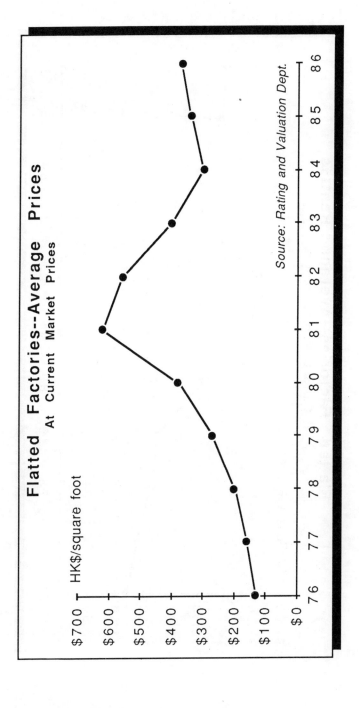

Flatted Factories--Average Prices
At Current Market Prices

HK$/square foot

Source: Rating and Valuation Dept.

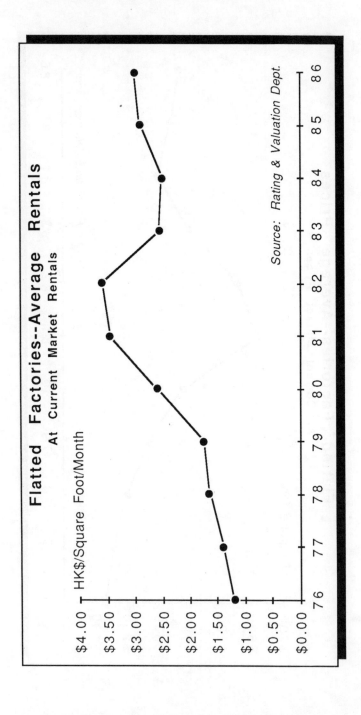

Flatted Factories--Average Rentals

At Current Market Rentals

HK$/Square Foot/Month

Source: Rating & Valuation Dept.

Chapter 11

Employment

by Kenneth Barrett

Hong Kong's resourceful and energetic workforce is one of the mainsprings of the territory's success on the world's markets. Hardworking, and increasingly well-educated, it is Hong Kong's single greatest asset. There is a pool of some 2.64 million workers available, and owing to the buoyant local economy there is very little unemployment: at the end of 1986, only 2.2 percent of those considered to be economically active were unemployed. In fact, in certain sectors such as construction, and in many of the manufacturing sectors, there is a shortage of skilled labor. Shortages of suitable people also occur in some of the non-manufacturing sectors, notably hotels, banks and real estate companies.

Long gone are the days of the sweat-shop image, and much has been done in recent years to secure a steady improvement in working conditions and terms of employment, through an extensive program of labor legislation.

As a dependent territory of the United Kingdom, Hong Kong is not a member of the International Labor Organization (ILO) and is therefore not called upon to ratify any international conventions which set labor standards. However, the UK government can make declarations on behalf of Hong Kong with regard to the application of conventions it ratifies. This is done after full consultation with the Hong Kong government.

At the end of 1986, Hong Kong had applied 48 conventions, which exceeded the number ratified by most member nations in the region.

Working Conditions

The Employment Ordinance provides the framework for a comprehensive code of employment. It governs the payment of wages, the termination of employment contracts and the operation of employment agencies.

The law provides, among other benefits, statutory holidays with pay, sick leave, sickness allowance, paid maternity leave, rest days, and seven days' annual leave with pay for most employees. All employees have statutory protection against anti-union discrimination. There is provision for severance payment to workers made redundant, and workers with long service who are dismissed otherwise than for reasons of redundancy or on disciplinary grounds, and who are entitled to long service payment. An employee whose employer becomes insolvent and who is owed wages may also apply for ex-gratia payment from the Protection of Wages on Insolvency Fund, which is financed by an annual levy of $100 on all business registration certificates.

The Employment of Children Regulations prohibit the employment of children under 15 in all economic sectors. However, children of 13 and over and who are attending school may take part-time employment in the non-industrial sector, subject to certain restrictions aimed at protecting their health and morals.

The Women and Young Persons (Industry) Regulations limit the standard working hours of women and young persons aged 15 to 17 to eight hours a day and 48 hours a week. The maximum annual overtime which may be worked by women is 200 hours. Overtime by young persons is prohibited. Female workers are also given maternity protection.

There is no statutory restriction on the hours of work for male workers aged 18 and over. An eight-hour day is normally observed in larger industrial establishments. Many cotton-spinning mills and large weaving factories operate on three eight-hour shifts, whereas garment, plastics and metalware factories generally work only a single shift.

Rest Days and Holidays

All manual workers and other employees earning not more than $10,500 a month are entitled to one rest day in seven days. Most factories stop work completely one day a week, usually on Sundays. Some factories have a five-day or five-and-a-half day week.

There are 11 statutory holidays a year, and if the employee has worked continuously for his employer for three months preceding the holiday, he is entitled to pay for that day.

All employees covered by the ordinance are entitled to seven days annual leave with pay after serving a period of 12 months under a continuous contract with the same employer. Many employers in the manufacturing sector grant their employees paid annual leave at the same period as the three statutory holidays during the Lunar New Year.

Sickness and Maternity Leave

Sickness allowance is calculated at two-thirds of an employee's pay, and he may accumulate his entitlement at the rate of two paid sickness days for every completed month of service in the first 12 months of employment, and subsequently, four paid sickness days per month of service, up to a maximum of 120 days.

Female employees who have served the same employer continuously for 26 weeks are entitled to 10 weeks' maternity leave. Those with 40 weeks' service and up to two children are entitled to pay during maternity leave at the rate of two-thirds of normal wages.

Trade Unions and Industrial Disputes

Trade union activity in Hong Kong tends to be peacable. All unions have to be registered under the Trade Unions Ordinance, which is administered by the Registrar of Trade Unions. Once registered, they are corporate bodies and enjoy immunity from certain civil suits. At the end of 1986 there were 448 registered trade unions, consisting of 403 employees' unions, 30 employers' associations and 15 mixed organizations of employers and employees. The total declared membership was around 392,500.

The majority of the blue collar employees' unions are affiliated to one of the two bodies registered under the Societies Ordinance: the Hong Kong Federation of Trade Unions (FTU); and the Hong Kong and Kowloon Trades Union Council (TUC). The FTU has 71 affiliated unions, mostly in the shipyards, textile mills, public transport, public utilities and the printing and carpentry trades. The TUC has 68 affiliated unions, mainly in the catering and building trades. The remaining 264 employees unions are mostly drawn from the civil service and the teaching profession. Most government departments and many large establishments have set up formal joint consultative committees. Over 90 percent of Hong Kong's manufacturing establishments are small in size, employing not more than 50 workers each. In these, informal consultation usually takes place as and when the need arises.

Hong Kong has an outstandingly good record of industrial peace. In 1986, it lost 2.10 working days per 1,000 workers. There were just nine work stoppages, with the number of actual working days lost totalling 4,907. This was in fact an increase over the all-time low of the previous year, when only 0.52 working days per 1,000 employees were lost. The 1986 increase was attributable to two cases involving a comparatively large number of workers, which led to a loss of 4,470 working days.

Labor Tribunal

The Labor Tribunal provides a quick, inexpensive and informal method of settling certain types of dispute between employees and employers arising from breaches of contract or the provisions of the Employment Ordinance. The tribunal is part of the judiciary and complements the conciliation services.

During 1986, the Labor Department dealt with 19,416 labor problems, most of which involved individuals in claims of wages in arrears, wages in lieu of notice, holiday pay, etc.

Industrial Safety and Health

Regulations have been made to cover the most hazardous industrial activities. These include construction work; the use of lifting appliances and gear; the use of electricity; cargo handling at wharves, quays and godowns; work in confined spaces and in compressed air; the use of abrasive wheels and cartridge-operated fixing tools; goods lifts; the spraying of flammable liquids; the guarding and operation of machinery, the use of asbestos, and electrolytic chromium processing. The protection of eyes and hearing is also mandatory for the relevant hazardous industrial operations.

Employees' Compensation

Closely allied to the field of industrial safety is the service of assisting employees or their dependents to obtain compensation which an employer is liable to pay in the event of injury or the accidental death of an employee. All employers are compulsorily required to take out insurance policies to cover their full liabilities under the ordinance and under common law.

The Employees' Compensation Ordinance handled 221 fatal accident cases and 86,800 non-fatal accident cases in 1986.

Safety in the Workplace

Anyone having the management and control of a workplace has to notify the Commissioner for Labor before the workplace commences operation. The Factory Inspectorate undertakes the inspection of industrial undertakings for the enforcement of safety, health and related provisions.

The Industrial Safety Training Center offers safety training courses, and also talks on safety which are held in a diverse number of organizations, including institutes of higher education, vocational training schools and associations of employees and employers.

Finding Employment

The Local Employment Service of the Labor Department provides a free placement service helping employers to recruit suitable staff, and job-seekers to secure employment. It operates from 15 offices linked by a facsimile system for fast distribution of vacancy information.

The Central Recruitment Unit, an extension of the Local Employment Service, acts as the central agency for all government departments in the recruitment of all Model Scale I staff such as artisans and drivers. It also coordinates employment services provided to large employers in the private sector with territory-wide recruitment needs.

The Labor Department has also established a Higher Education Employment Service to give free employment assistance to graduates of local and overseas universities, and job-seekers possessing post-secondary or professional qualifications.

Employment Assistance to the Disabled

The Selective Placement Service provides free specialized employment assistance to disabled persons seeking jobs. The service caters for the blind, the deaf, and those with disabilities of orthopaedic or medical origins. It also covers the mentally retarded and former mental patients.

Overseas Employment

The Contracts for Employment Outside Hong Kong Ordinance controls employment contracts entered into in Hong Kong between employers and manual workers who are required to work outside the territory. The number of manual workers taking up employment outside Hong Kong has recently declined somewhat, mainly due to a drop in the number of workers going to Singapore. West Germany and Canada are the largest employers of Hong Kong workers.

Employment Agencies

The licensing and operating of employment agencies are controlled by the Employment Ordinance and the Employment Agency Regulations, which are enforced by the Overseas Employment Service.

Foreign Domestic Helpers

The Labor Department provides attestation of standard contracts for foreign domestic workers in Hong Kong. These contracts must be attested before they are presented to the Director of Immigration in support of the domestic helpers' applications for entry visas. The majority of domestic helpers come from the Philippines.

Structure of Labor Market

In the fourth quarter of 1986, a government survey showed that 2,723,500 people were economically active, and that 2,664,600 were employed. Distribution of workers among the different sectors is as follows:

Sector	No. Persons	% Total economically active population
Agriculture, forestry, hunting and fishing	42,000	1.5
Mining and quarrying	800*	
Manufacturing	918,000	33.7
Electricity, gas and water	18,700	0.7
Construction	208,100	7.6
Wholesale and retail trade, restaurants and hotels	619,100	22.7
Transport, storage and communication	223,300	8.2
Financing, insurance, real estate and business services	170,000	6.3
Services	464,600	17.1
Total working population	2,664,600	97.8
Unemployed (incl job-seekers)	59,000	2.2
Total economically active population	2,723,500	100.0

Note: Figures may not add up to total due to rounding. * Less than 0.5%

The manufacturing sector is by far the largest in terms of employment of Hong Kong workers. Of these, the top five employers are: wearing apparel manufacturers (excepting footwear), with some 40 percent of the total manufacturing workers; textiles, with around 18 percent; electrical machinery and apparatus, almost 18 percent; plastic products, 14 percent; and fabricated metal products (except for machinery and equipment), almost 10 percent.

Wage Structure

There is no legal minimum wage in Hong Kong, and the wage level prevailing is essentially the result of an interplay of the economic forces of supply and demand. They are customarily fixed by individual agreement between employers and employees.

Wages are usually calculated on hourly, daily, monthly, or piece rates. Monthly-rated industrial workers are generally employed in supervisory capacities. Men and women receive the same rate for piece work, but women generally are paid less when working on a time basis.

Uniform wage structures exist in only a small number of trades and industries, usually where labor is organized, or where old customs of craft persist; here, general wage agreements would be in force and a form of collective bargaining practised.

Many workers receive additional benefits such as free medical treatment, subsidized meals, a good attendance bonus, paid rest-days, and subsidized transport to and from work. In most companies, a Lunar New Year bonus is customary. This is usually equivalent to about one month's extra pay; in some cases it may be considerably more.

Wage and Salary Movements

The Census and Statistics Department compiles wage indexes to measure changes in wage rates of both manual and non-manual workers in a selection of economic sectors, based on a quarterly survey of wages, salaries and employee benefits. The survey covers about 2,000 establishments in five sectors: manufacturing, wholesale/retail and import/export trades, restaurants and hotels; transport services; business services; and personal services.

Severance Payment

An employee with 24 or more months of continuous service who is dismissed by reason of redundancy is entitled to a severance payment calculated at the rate of 18 days' wages or two-thirds of a month's pay for every year of service up to a maximum of 12 months' wages.

Kenneth Barrett is a Hong Kong-based business journalist and regular contributor to Amcham magazine. He is the co-editor of 'Doing Business in Today's Hong Kong'.

Chapter 12

Expatriate Life

by Alan Moores

Overview

* Despite overcrowding, language barriers and a hot and humid climate, expatriate life in Hong Kong can be uniquely rewarding.
* Apartment living is a feature of Hong Kong life common to almost all residents.
* Shopping and dining constitute two of Hong Kong's most celebrated pastimes.
* A great variety of sporting and recreational opportunities, both indoor and outdoor, are available.
* The American Chamber of Commerce publishes a comprehensive and useful guide for the newly arrived expatriate family, *Living in Hong Kong*.

For the newly arrived resident or tourist, Hong Kong can be an overwhelming experience. No matter how much you might have prepared, the city—with its jam-packed streets, its splashy colors, its subtropical climate, its exotic aromas, its breathtaking skylines, its noise and its manic pace—will hit you with a bang.

The first thing to understand is that there are numerous organizations and resources in Hong Kong that exist solely to help newcomers in adjusting to life here. Perhaps the best way to start is by obtaining a copy of the American Chamber of Commerce in Hong Kong's guide, *Living in Hong Kong*.

The island of Hong Kong (from the Cantonese *heung gong*, meaning 'fragrant harbor') comprises 29 square miles, Kowloon covers a little more than three square miles, and the New Territories, which includes all land up to the Chinese border as well as some 235 islands, covers a total land area of 365 square miles. The territory has been a colony of the British government since 1841, but is to be handed over to the People's Republic of China on 1 July 1997. As part of a joint declaration signed by Great Britain and China in December 1984, Hong Kong will be a special administrative region under the jurisdiction of the Chinese communist government, but for 50 years (Deng Xiaoping has stated that this will be 100 years) after 1997 will be allowed to retain its current political, social, commercial, and legal systems, including the capitalist economy and trade that have made the territory an international center of finance, industry and commerce.

Hong Kong's population is approximately 5.4 million persons, 98 percent of whom are Chinese. The other two percent comprise Filipinos, Indians, Americans, British, Thais, Malaysians and numerous other national groups. Hong Kong has two official languages, English and Cantonese, though English is the language of the law and the courts. Cantonese is a dialect spoken by most southern Chinese from Canton (Guangzhou) and some of the surrounding Guangdong province. The vast majority of Hong Kong's residents originally came from Guangdong province—hence, the use of Cantonese here.

With its nine or more tones, Cantonese seems an extremely forbidding language for the non-Chinese person to learn—but most who attempt it soon agree that it's not so difficult as its reputation belies. If nothing else, it is rewarding to learn even just a few Cantonese expressions; there are many excellent schools and private tutors available to teach you. For information, just consult the 'Tuition' section of the classified advertising pages of the *Hong Kong Standard* or the *South China Morning Post*, or the 'Language Schools' section of the local Yellow Pages.

Despite the fact that Hong Kong is an extraordinarily overcrowded city, living conditions in general are actually quite favorable to the newly arrived expatriate. Health standards are very high, the crime rate is relatively low, the cost of living (apart from housing) is also low, services are among the best in Asia, the variety and cost of food is excellent and schooling (if one can afford it) is also quite good.

Vital Information

Health

The general health standards of Hong Kong are fairly high compared with other Asian cities. Infectious diseases are on the decrease. There are isolated cases of cholera, hepatitis, tuberculosis, and malaria, but if you take the most basic precautions you will be at absolutely no risk of contracting anything more serious than a common cold or a bout of the flu.

Drinking water is safe almost anywhere in Hong Kong, but some residents prefer to boil their water first, or purchase bottled water. Food is considered to be fairly hygienic, but cases of food poisoning—particularly contracted from cooked food stalls (*dai pai dongs*)—are not uncommon. Food served in almost any restaurant —especially one that carries the approval of the Hong Kong Tourist Association—should be safe.

There are many excellent hospitals in Hong Kong, including the Baptist Hospital, Hong Kong Adventist Hospital, Mathilda Hospital, and Canossa Hospital—all private centers. They maintain high standards for their general and specialized facilities, including convalescence, maternity care, pediatrics and orthopedics. There are also a number of good government hospitals. Hong Kong has many highly trained doctors practising Western medicine. A list of all registered medical practitioners is published twice each year in the *Government Gazette*.

Recommendations for a family doctor, dentist or specialist can best be obtained from friends, from your national consulate, or from your employer.

Along with fine medical care, Hong Kong offers numerous counseling services for English-speaking and Chinese families and individuals. These services handle such problems as alcoholism and hard-drug abuse, over-eating, family problems, stress and virtually any other psychological problem.

Housing

Perhaps the most acute and visible problem in Hong Kong is housing. With some of the most densely populated neighborhoods in the world, the territory has chronically suffered from a shortage of good, reasonably priced accommodation. If you have been brought here by your company, chances are that you receive a housing allowance of some kind, which makes good accommodation much easier to find.

Your first housing experience here will most likely be in a hotel. The Hong Kong Tourist Association issues a free leaflet, *Hotels in Hong Kong*, which lists hotels, guest houses, and hostels in Hong Kong and Macau. You can also find an extensive list of hotels in *Living in Hong Kong* and in Appendix XIII of this book. Some important points to keep in mind: You might have trouble getting reservations if you plan to arrive during the peak tourist and conference months of April-May and October-November. On the other hand, you might be able to obtain corporate or long-term discounts. If your family will be staying with you in the hotel, you will want one that has good family accommodation. Consider also the distance from the hotel to your office, your children's school, stores and recreational facilities.

You might also wish to consider renting a leave flat, which is a fully furnished apartment that is sub-let for a short period by the tenant while he or she is away on home leave. Negotiating a lease can be a relatively simple matter, and the price compares favorably with that of a hotel room. A leave flat can also provide you with many amenities—cooking facilities, washer, dryer, perhaps a residential neighborhood, or an amah (a maid)—which might not be available in a hotel. You will, however, be locked into a lease, even if a short-term one, and you might feel a bit awkward trying to make yourself comfortable in someone else's home. Leave flats, more readily available during the summer months, can be found through the classified ads of the *South China Morning Post* and the *Hongkong Standard*.

When you do finally decide to settle into more permanent housing, there are several questions to ask yourself: How much can I afford to pay? Do I want to live in the more rural New Territories, or near the action of Hong Kong Island and Kowloon? How long will it take to travel to the office? What about schools in the area?

Without some financial assistance from their employers, most expatriates will find the cost of Hong Kong housing prohibitive. For those without such assistance, there are older buildings with flats that are rather small, perhaps offering less-than-spectacular views, and set in a higher-density neighborhood. Despite the obvious drawbacks, there might be strong advantages, such as easier access to markets and transport as well as the sense that you indeed live in Asia and not a home-country suburb. For those with more money to spend, the sky (almost literally) is the limit. You can find palatial apartments with outstanding harbor views plus such recreational facilities as tennis courts and a swimming pool.

Most expatriate families live on Hong Kong Island. Rents, however, are much cheaper beyond Kowloon Tong into the New Territories, and commuting on the Kowloon Canton Railway (KCR) and the Mass Transit Railway (MTR) subway is fast, convenient, relatively comfortable and very safe.

The New Territories life-style is most readily adopted by people who prefer suburban life to that of the city, or who are willing to sacrifice easier commuting for more spacious living facilities.

The south side of Hong Kong Island, Mid-Levels and the Peak are the most popular places for foreigners to live. (They are discussed at length in the chapter, 'Land and Premises.') Pok Fu Lam, on the western side of the island, has become a very popular residential area in recent years, offering excellent views of the harbor as well as a number of low-rise apartments with garden areas.

Happy Valley, Causeway Bay and Wan Chai contain some high-rise blocks of flats that appeal to expatriates. Generally, the flats are smaller there, but one can find some good harbor views, plus excellent shopping and transport facilities.

Among the Kowloon locations where many expatriates choose to live are Waterloo Hill and Homantin Hill, areas of high-rise buildings with excellent access to public transport and supermarkets. Here and there, they offer terraces and good views. Beware of airport noise, however.

Kowloon Tong and Yau Yat Chuen are more suburban in feel. One- and two-story buildings, surrounded by gardens and set on quiet streets, are available in completely residential settings. Again, beware of airport noise.

Mei Foo Sun Chuen is a self-contained high-rise community in Lai Chi Kok. Flats for bachelors, couples and families are small but allow for people of all ages, family composition and income. While it can be noisy and crowded, it does offer great harbor views, good shopping facilities, restaurants, parks and play areas.

The New Territories have seen many new magnificent town-house-type developments in recent years, particularly around Sai Kung and Clearwater Bay. Previously overlooked by expatriates who were put off by the long commute and isolation, the New Territories have recently become much more accessible and attractive. Rents are still reasonable, and the region is a pleasant change from the bustle of Hong Kong Island and Kowloon.

Discovery Bay on Lantau Island is a new development comprising townhouses and some high-rise apartments. It is becoming a victim of its own success, however: with its low rents, greenery, quiet and fairly easy access to Hong Kong Island, Discovery Bay is attracting ever more people.

Schools

Where you ultimately decide to live could largely be determined by the schools you would like your children to attend. For students whose first language is other than Chinese, there are a number of excellent schools available. *Living in Hong Kong* details nearly all of them, including age group, address, composition and number of students, subjects taught and tuition fees.

Non-Chinese schools fall into three general categories: private schools (which receive no financial assistance), grant-aided schools (which do receive some funds) and British army schools. The private schools provide education for children of many nationalities. The grant-aided schools are managed by the English Schools Foundation (ESF) and are attended by the majority of English-speaking children. The British army schools are almost always filled to capacity and are therefore rarely able to accommodate children other than entitled military dependents. ESF schools generally have a high standard of education, and children who attend them have no difficulty in adapting to schools in their home country when they return. For information on the ESF, contact: The Secretary, English Schools Foundation, 43B Stubbs Road, Hong Kong, or telephone 5-742351.

There are nine private schools that cater to a number of different nationalities. These schools are the Chinese International School in Causeway Bay, the German Swiss International School on the Peak, Hong Kong Japanese School in Happy Valley, Hong Lok Yuen School in the New Territories, Kellett School in Pok Fu Lam, L'Ecole Francaise Internationale in Jardine's Lookout, Royden House School in the Mid-Levels, the Sears Rogers International School in Kowloon, and the Hong Kong International School in Repulse Bay. The latter is one of the most popular among American students.

It can be difficult for parents to enroll their children into these schools, given the demand for quality education in Hong Kong. One possibility, however, is the purchase of a debenture from a particular school, which gives that school much-needed working capital. Children of debenture holders have first priority in enrolling. The sum is returned when the student leaves the school.

There is also a good variety of pre-school facilities in Hong Kong, consisting of kindergartens, child care centers and Western-style play groups. Kindergartens emphasize formal learning in a classroom environment; child-care centers, for babies and toddlers under the age of four, are informal, with much free time and open interaction among the children; and Western-style play groups cater mainly to children aged three to five whose first language is English. For further information, contact the Child Care Centres Advisory Inspectorate (telephone 5-754321, extension 44).

Finally, there are some post-secondary opportunities in Hong Kong for expatriates. For those already attending a university and interested in Asian and Chinese studies, it is possible to enroll as an external student at the University of Hong Kong or the Chinese University. It is usually not possible to gain admission as a regular student due to the competitive examination procedure. However, a few mature students may be accepted for full-time degree study.

Extramural courses are available at both the Chinese University and the University of Hong Kong.

The Hong Kong Baptist College in Kowloon Tong may accept full-time foreign students, who later can transfer credits earned there to American universities without much difficulty.

The University of East Asia, in Macau, also offers many degree courses to part-time and full-time students.

Communications

Almost every imaginable kind of telephone can be bought in Hong Kong. One can find a simple black dialing telephone as well as high-speed data links. All telephone lines are owned and controlled by the Hong Kong Telephone Company Ltd (Telco), your first place to visit to obtain telephone service. Aside from a monthly flat rate for service, calls anywhere within the territory are free. International calls are very easy to make, either through the International Service Operàtor or via IDD (International Direct Dialing). You can also make international calls by going to one of the Cable and Wireless offices.

Incidentally, merchants allow the public to make local calls free from their shop phones. Public pay phones have been relegated to MTR stations, hotels and other public places.

Postal services are good in Hong Kong, both within the territory and overseas. A leaflet, *Postage Rates and Services*, free at post offices, gives mailing times for every day of the week and rates for each country, as well as supplementary services available.

√ *Media*

For a city whose native English-speaking population comprises only about 50,000 persons, Hong Kong has relatively good English-language news media. There are three English-language daily newspapers: the *South China Morning Post*, the *Hongkong Standard* and the *Asian Wall Street Journal*. The *International Herald Tribune* and *USA Today* are also printed locally. The *Post* and the *Standard* have local and international coverage. While the *Asian Wall Street Journal* is regional in scope and the *International Herald Tribune* global in outlook, both have achieved a strong readership here.
In addition to these papers, there are many other overseas papers available in Hong Kong.

Among the more widely read magazines in Hong Kong are the *Far Eastern Economic Review*, *Asian Business* and *Asiaweek*. There are many American, British, Australian and European magazines at newsstands, bookstores and kiosks throughout the city.

Hong Kong has 10 radio channels. Five are operated by Radio Television Hong Kong (RTHK), three by the Hong Kong Commercial Broadcasting Company (Commercial Radio), and two by the British Forces Broadcasting Service (BFBS). Among them, you will find local and international news, discussion programs, overseas features, weather, classical music, jazz and pop music.

There are two Chinese and two English-language TV stations in Hong Kong, and some 94 percent of all the households here have at least one set. ATV and Pearl, the English-language channels, broadcast a variety of movies, news reports, local programming, and shows from Great Britain, the United States and Australia.

One of the most disappointing aspects of Hong Kong is the overall poor quality of its libraries, particularly where English-language material is concerned. The Urban Council, however, operates a public library system in some 23 locations throughout Hong Kong. The range of material includes books, newspapers, magazines, records, audio cassettes, video cassettes, slides and microfilm. The Government Information Services Library is a reference collection concerning a variety of subjects, including the laws of Hong Kong, departmental reports and official documents.

The American Library, a clean, well-lighted oasis in the United Centre, is basically focused on subjects pertaining to the US. Although it is small, it is relatively comprehensive.

There are other, smaller collections available, including those at the British Council Library, the Alliance Francaise and the Goethe Institute.

Transport

It would be very hard to find a transport system anywhere in the world that is the equal of Hong Kong's. That is not to say that the city does not experience heavy traffic, but for its compact size, Hong Kong offers an astonishing range of transport: trams, buses, minibuses, ferries, hovercraft, a commuter railway, a subway system, taxis, limousines and private cars. And the range of prices is equally surprising. For example, you can cross the harbor on the Star Ferry for just HK$.50, or travel the length of the island by tram for just HK$.60. Even taxis are favorably priced compared to those of other cities.

Shopping

If there's one thing for which Hong Kong is famous it is the outstanding shopping to be found. There are upmarket department stores like Lane Crawford and Sogo, Chinese-product department stores (including a wide range of excellent Chinese arts and crafts), good middle-of-the-scale department stores like Wing On and Sincere, high-tech shopping centers, small shops, tiny alleys devoted to one item (such as fabrics), and marvelous street markets everywhere.

While Hong Kong is not quite the bargain that it might have been 10 years ago, it nevertheless offers possibly the best selection of goods in the world. It is, however, very difficult to offer any sort of guide to shopping here because so much changes with such dazzling speed.

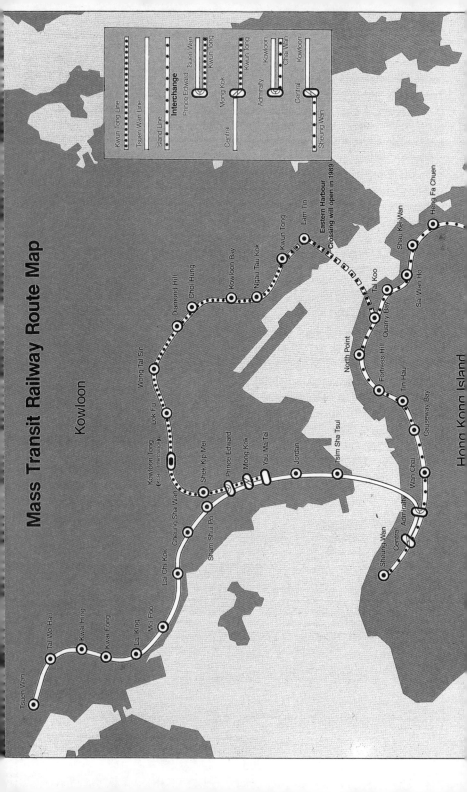

Mass Transit Railway Route Map

Kowloon

Hong Kong Island

Eastern Harbour
Crossing will open in 1989

Legend:
- Kwun Tong Line
- Tsuen Wan Line
- Island Line
- Interchange

Tsuen Wan, Tai Wo Hau, Kwai Hing, Kwai Fong, Lai King, Mei Foo, Lai Chi Kok, Cheung Sha Wan, Sham Shui Po, Shek Kip Mei, Prince Edward, Mong Kok, Yau Ma Tei, Jordan, Tsim Sha Tsui

Kowloon Tong (KCR Interchange), Lok Fu, Wong Tai Sin, Diamond Hill, Choi Hung, Kowloon Bay, Ngau Tau Kok, Kwun Tong, Lam Tin

Prince Edward, Tsuen Wan, Kwun Tong, Mong Kok, Kwun Tong, Admiralty, Kowloon, Central, Chai Wan, Kowloon, Central, Sheung Wan

Sheung Wan, Central, Admiralty, Wan Chai, Causeway Bay, Tin Hau, Fortress Hill, North Point, Quarry Bay, Tai Koo, Sai Wan Ho, Shau Kei Wan, Heng Fa Chuen

There are a few good shopping guidebooks available. Dana Goetz's *Complete Guide to Hong Kong Factory Bargains*, continually updated, is indispensable to locating the city's great outlets. There is also the Hong Kong Tourist Association's *Official Guidebook*, a monthly compendium that offers, among other information, a good shopping section. *Living in Hong Kong* also has a detailed chapter on Hong Kong shopping.

It is important to point out that since so many tourists come to Hong Kong for great buys in camera and electronic equipment, there are many stores equally willing to exploit them.

Thus, it is not uncommon for someone to pay hard-earned money for what he or she thought was a complete camera, for example, only to find that the price included only the body and not the lens.

And sometimes a 'new' camera is actually secondhand. If you are victimized, you can take your complaint to the Small Claims Tribunal, the Consumer Council or the Hong Kong Tourist Association. The best advice might be to know exactly what it is you want, examine the merchandise you would like to buy, and insist on a detailed deposit slip or receipt. And if you are cheated? Raise hell!

Leisure and Recreation

Leisure

If you are interested in learning about all the leisure activities to be found in Hong Kong, again, *Living in Hong Kong* is an excellent source. You'll find extensive listings of adult education centers, amusement parks, arts venues, boating and sports facilities, clubs, movie theaters and film societies, museums, women's organizations and activities for children. Since 'phone numbers, addresses, and times are always changing, we suggest you confirm these in the Yellow Pages, *TV & Entertainment Times*, *Dollarsaver*, the local daily papers or the Community Advice Bureau.

Many expatriate residents of Hong Kong partake of the rather British tradition of joining a club. Clubs offer their own recreational facilities in an already crowded city, as well as relaxation, leisure and dining facilities. Among the more established social and business clubs are the American Club, the Hongkong Club, the Foreign Correspondents Club, the Royal Hong Kong Yacht Club and the Pacific Club. Hong Kong also has a seemingly endless number of specialized clubs for hobbyists and sportsmen. *Living in*

Hong Kong lists many of them. They include the Hong Kong Backgammon Club, the Hong Kong Bird Watching Society, the Hong Kong Flower Club, the South China Athletic Association and many others.

Despite extreme crowding and hectic conditions, Hong Kong's parks and countryside are among the most accessible of any city's. Sprawling country parks cover much of the New Territories and the south side of Hong Kong Island, and frequent ferry services provide ready access to the rural outer islands, ideal destinations for hikers. Given Hong Kong's good climate year-round, a great variety of óutdoor activities can be enjoyed, including team sports, hiking, camping, boating, diving, fishing, swimming, windsurfing, horseback riding and many others.

And if you should fancy some leisure activities away from Hong Kong, you'll quickly discover just how accessible foreign destinations can be. Japan, Korea, the Philippines, Taiwan, Malaysia, Indonesia, Thailand and, of course, China can all be reached at a reasonable cost. There are more than 800 travel agents listed in the Yellow Pages, along with many excellent travel books, so you'll find it hard to go wrong. In addition, it's *always* easy to find someone who has vacationed at your anticipated destination who may give you some appropriate advice.

Nightlife

While Hong Kong might not have as lively (or as notorious) a night scene as its Asian neighbors, Bangkok, Manila and Tokyo, residents and visitors can find more than enough to occupy their evenings.

People with refined tastes can enjoy the ongoing performances of the Hong Kong Philharmonic Orchestra, other recitals of both Chinese and Western music, and dance performances—all at various venues throughout the city, including the Hong Kong Arts Centre. Hong Kong also hosts the annual Asian Arts Festival in the autumn and the more famous Hong Kong Arts Festival every winter, both of which bring in renowned artists from around the world.

Hong Kong is not especially noted for its movie scene, but filmgoers will find selected English-language and Cantonese (subtitled) films available throughout the city. Studio One, located at the French International School, features excellent American and European films. *TV & Entertainment Times* is a very good source for all kinds of activities taking place in Hong Kong, including theater, dance, concerts, movies, lectures and courses.

Among the more famous aspects of Hong Kong's nightlife are

its nightclubs and bars, particularly in Wan Chai and Tsim Sha Tsui. Immortalized in Richard Mason's novel of a Wan Chai hostess club, *The World of Suzie Wong*, the Wan Chai district today has been extensively gentrified, although a few scattered bars and clubs still exist. Nowadays, most of the liveliest nightlife is concentrated in Tsim Sha Tsui. Needless to say, some clubs are less scrupulous than others, and one would be well advised to know in advance which are which.

One could hardly write about leisure activities in Hong Kong without at least mentioning the outstanding restaurants. Chinese food, and particularly Cantonese, is arguably the finest in the world, and Hong Kong is certainly a world capital of dining. Besides regional Chinese, virtually every ethnic cuisine is represented: Japanese, Korea, Malaysian, Thai, Vietnamese, Indonesian, Mexican, Jewish, Australian, Italian, Swiss, French, Austrian and everything else in between. There are many good food guides available. One of the best is *Fodor's Hong Kong*, which divides restaurants into national categories. The Hong Kong Tourist Association can also guide you.

Cantonese Culture

While Hong Kong is certainly one of the most cosmopolitan cities of the world, one of the most rewarding aspects of your stay here will certainly come in learning about the Chinese culture.

The best place to start might be signing up for a Cantonese language course, which makes one's understanding of Hong Kong and its people that much more rewarding. There are many other avenues to learning about the city, however. The Government Publications Center has scores of books about Hong Kong, from its history to its plant life. You'll find that many of the clubs and organizations in Hong Kong are composed primarily of Chinese persons. Thus, you can have the opportunity of getting to know the local people while sharing common interests. The Community Advice Bureau can also direct you to organizations. *TV and Entertainment Times* is another very good source; for example, a recent issue listed classes on Chinese cooking, painting, *fung shui* and *tai chi*, as well as information on Chinese medicine, an exhibition of tea ware, a recital of Chinese music and performances of Cantonese drama.

For More Information

Hotels, Social resources, Local publications, Clubs. See Appendices.

Community Advice Bureau, St John's Cathedral, Garden Road. Tel: 5-245444. An excellent, "user-friendly" service that's especially helpful to new arrivals. It offers an orientation course.

American Women's Association, C7 Monticello, 48 Kennedy Road. Tel: 5-272961/2. This association puts its 1,500 members in touch with other women in Hong Kong, offering monthly neighborhood coffees, classes, lectures, and an extensive range of volunteer and fund-raising activities to aid local charities.

Hong Kong Council of Women, GPO Box 819. This association, established for the personal growth of women in the community, has subcommittees on Childbirth, Postnatal Support, Mastectomy, and Refuge for Battered Wives.

Alcoholics Anonymous, East Wing, 2/F, 10 Borrett Road. Tel: 5-8127244. This internationally known organization offers three basic programs: Alcoholics Anonymous, for problem drinkers; Al-Anon, for the families of problem drinkers; and Al-Ateen, for the children of problem drinkers.

Hong Kong Samaritans, Sailors and Soldiers Home, 22 Hennessy Road. With emphasis on suicide prevention, this organization has trained volunteers who provide a sympathetic ear to callers with problems associated with loneliness, drinking, work pressure, gambling, drugs, and other areas.

There are many other excellent service organizations in Hong Kong that can be found through the Community Advice Bureau. Tel: 5-245444.

Alan Moores was the editor of
'Living in Hong Kong', sixth edition
1986, a publication of The American
Chamber of Commerce in Hong Kong.

Appendix I

Support Services

The US government's support to the American business community in Hong Kong is the primary responsibility of the US and Foreign Commercial Service (US&FCS). Support for American agriculture interests is coordinated by the Foreign Agriculture Service (FAS). The US&FCS and FAS maintain offices on the 17th and 18th floors of the St John's Building, 33 Garden Road, directly opposite the main consulate building at 26 Garden Road.

Through a network of domestic and overseas offices, the US&FCS carries out the mandates of the US Department of Commerce's International Trade Administration. The US&FCS performs numerous activities to promote two-way trade and investment. In addition to counseling businessmen on local market trends and host government policies, the US&FCS also implements a number of commercially oriented programs, maintains a business information center, and is positioned to receive and respond to a variety of commercial inquiries.

Foreign Commercial Service officers assigned to US&FCS Hong Kong have business experience and Chinese language skills. Having excellent working relationships with the business community and with the Hong Kong government, US&FCS officers are ideally positioned to provide a broad perspective on issues which affect American business interests. Officers can also confirm and/or clarify host country business practices and governmental regulations. When requests fall outside an officer's area of expertise, appropriate contacts are introduced to meet the information needs.

Commercial officers also supervise a number of activities which provide specific services for local and overseas businessmen. The US&FCS offers background checks on local companies, agency/distributor searches, product sourcing, trade administration and export licensing information, support for US trade exhibitions, and also assistance in handling commercial complaint cases. US&FCS personnel are also available to assist visitors by providing US company addresses, product identification, overseas appointment requests, and research assistance.

The commercial and agriculture services also maintain comprehensive libraries in the St John's Building, which are open to the public from 9:30 am to 12:30 pm and 1:30 pm to 4:00 pm, Monday through Friday. The US&FCS business information center maintains up-to-date directories on US manufactured and agricultural products, industry sector reports on Hong Kong and China, information on local standards and practices, guides to local sales representation, company law, and investment; contact addresses for industry associations, local government contacts, directories of local US businesses, market research studies, procedural information for US export license applications, trade directories, trade statistics, background reports on the PRC, and also unclassified government reports on specific issues of commercial interest.

Other sections of the US Consulate General offer additional services. The Foreign Agriculture Service, for example, is an important contact for all businessmen who seek market information on US agricultural products. Through specific programs such as the Agricultural Information and Marketing Service (AIMS), FAS provides agricultural data, trade leads, pertinent trade information, and marketing services. FAS also maintains a library with up-to-date reports on market segments, distribution practices, labelling regulations, government contact lists, sanitary requirements etc. FAS officers maintain close liaison with Hong Kong's major food and commodity importers. In addition, FAS is supported by close relationships with five Hong Kong based US commodity cooperators: the United States Wheat Associates (USW), the US Feed Grains Council (USFGC), the Cotton Council International (CCI), the USA Poultry and Egg Export Council (PEEC), and the National Renderers Association (NRA).

The US Customs Service, located on the 11th floor of the St John's Building, is a useful contact for information on import quotas, foreign trade zones, duty refunds, facts about federal wildlife laws, ata carnet, marking country of origin on US imports, trademark information, GSP and other topics affecting exports to the United States.

The Economic Section of the US State Department is the principle local liaison for certain bilateral and multilateral treaties and obligations, such as the GSP and the GATT, which affect relations between the US and Hong Kong. The Economic Section continuously monitors economic trends in Hong Kong and some of their reports are available to the public from the US&FCS library and the US Information Service.

Notarials and affidavits are issued by the American Citizen Services (ACS) section at the main consulate building on 26 Garden Road. ACS also issues new US passports and keeps a supply of US tax forms for distribution. For local businessmen whose passports expire with a valid US visa contained within, the consulate also offers a 'drop box' service whereby an applicant can attach the old passport and the new passport to an application form with a photograph, and drop it in a box for processing without having to apply for the visa in person.

The United States Trade and Development Program (TDP) has offices on the 11th floor of the St John's Building. TDP promotes economic development in Third World countries, particularly the middle income developing countries, by financing planning services for development projects leading to the export of US goods and services. In order to be funded, projects must be high on the list of development priorities by the host country's government; they must demonstrate significant procurement potential for US goods and services; the host government must submit evidence that funding for the project implementation is available; and the planning services must facilitate and lead to project implementation.

US Consulate General

US & Foreign
Commercial Service
17th Floor,
St John's Building
33 Garden Road
Tel: 5-211467, 5-227013

US Foreign
Agriculture Service
18th Floor,
St John's Building
33 Garden Road
Hong Kong
Tel: 5-8412350

US Customs Service
11th Floor,
St John's Building
33 Garden Road
Hong Kong
Tel: 5-8412244

US Trade
Development Program
11th Floor,
St John's Building
33 Garden Road
Hong Kong
Tel: 5-8412239

Economic Section,
US Department of State
26 Garden Road
Hong Kong
Tel: 5-239011 ext 305

US Information Service
26 Garden Road
Hong Kong
Tel: 5-239011 ext 255

American Citizen Services
26 Garden Road
Hong Kong
Tel: 5-239011 ext 211

Appendix II

Foreign Consulates and Official Trade Commissions

Australia
Consulate
Harbour Centre,
23-24 floor,
25 Harbour Road
5-731881

Austria
Consulate
Room 2201
Wang Kee Building,
34-37 Connaught Road
Central
5-228086

Belgium
Consulate
9 floor, St. John's Building,
33 Garden Road 5-243111

Belize
Honorary Consulate
Room 103
Hang Chong Building,
5 Queen's Road Central
5-225587

Brazil
Consulate
1107 Shell House,
28 Queen's Road Central
5-257002

Britain
Commission
Bank of America Tower,
9 floor,
12 Harcourt Road
5-230176

Burma
Consulate
Room 2424, 24 floor,
Sun Hung Kai Centre,
30 Harbour Road
5-8913329

Canada
Commission
11-14 floor, Tower 1,
Exchange Square,
Connaught Place
5-8104321

Chile
Honorary Consulate
11 floor, Hua Hsia Building,
64 Gloucester Road
5-732139

Colombia
Consulate
Unit A, 6 floor,
CMA Building
64-66 Connaught Road
Central
5-458547

Costa Rica
Consulate
Flat C-10 Hung On Building
3 Tin Hau Temple Road
5-665181

Cuba
Consulate
10 floor, Rose Court,
115 Wong Nai Chung Road
5-760226

Cyprus
Honorary Consulate
19 floor,
United Centre,
95 Queensway
5-292161

Denmark
Consulate
Suite 2101-2102,
Great Eagle Centre,
23 Harbour Road
5-8936265

Dominican Republic
Consulate
Flat C, 4 floor, Hilton Tower
96 Granville Road,
Tsim Sha Tsui
3-7231836

Ecuador
Consulate
Flat C4, 11 floor,
Hankow Centre,
1-C Middle Road
3-692235

Egypt
Consulate
9 floor, Woodland Garden,
10 Macdonnell Road
5-244174

El Salvador
Honorary Consulate
1517 Central Building,
3 Pedder Street
5-228995

Finland
Honorary Consulate
1818 Hutchison House,
10 Harcourt Road
5-255385

France
Consulate
Admiralty Centre,
Tower 11, 26 floor,
18 Harcourt Road
5-294351

Gabon
Honorary Consulate
PO Box 54599,
North Point Post Office
5-724062

Germany
Consulate
21 floor,
United Centre,
95 Queensway
5-298855

Greece
Honorary Consulate
Rooms 1305-6,
Kam Chung Building,
54 Jaffe Road
5-200860

Guatemala
Honorary Consulate
2205 Yardley
Commercial Bldg.,
Connaught Road West
5-411300

Honduras
Honorary Consulate
24 floor,
HK Diamond Exchange Bldg.,
8-10 Duddell Street
5-226593

Iceland
Honorary Consulate
48 floor,
Hopewell Centre,
183 Queen's Road East
5-283911

India
Commissioner
Unit D,
16 floor,
United Centre,
95 Queensway
5-284029

Indonesia
Consulate
6-8 Keswick Street
5-7904421

Iran
Consulate
Rooms 1901-2,
Alliance Building,
130/136 Connaught Rd
Central
5-414745

Irish Republic
Honorary Consulate
Room 801
Prince's Building,
Hong Kong
5-226022

Israel
Consulate
Room 1122
Prince's Building
5-220177

Italy
Consulate
Room 801 Hutchison House,
10 Harcourt Road
5-220033

Jamaica
Honorary Consulate
c/o 23 floor,
Wah Kwong Bldg.,
48-62 Hennessy Road
5-8238238

Japan
Consulate
Bank of America Tower,
25 floor,
12 Harcourt Road
5-221184

Jordan
Honorary Consulate
Suite 911
World Shipping Centre,
Harbour City
3-696399

Korea
Consulate
3 floor Korea Centre Building,
119-121 Connaught Road
Central
5-430224

Liberia
Honorary Consulate
703 Admiralty Centre,
Tower 1,
18 Harcourt Road
5-201978

Luxembourg
Honorary Consulate
c/o Hilton Hotel,
2 Queen's Road Central
(GPO Box 42)
5-233111

Malaysia
Commission
24 floor,
Malaysia Building,
47-50 Gloucester Road
5-270921

Mauritius
Honorary Consulate
1 Lockhart Road,
7 floor
5-281546

Mexico
Consulate
Room 2103A
World-Wide House,
19 Des Voeux Road
Central
5-214365

Monaco
Honorary Consulate
33 floor,
Harbour Centre,
25 Harbour Road
5-8930669

Nauru
Honorary Consulate
1 floor,
Pacific Star Bldg.,
2 Canton Road
3-7233525

Netherlands
Consulate
3 floor,
China Building,
29 Queen's Road Central
5-227710

New Zealand
Commission
3414 Connaught Centre,
Connaught Road
5-255044

Nicaragua
Honorary Consulate
1202 Kincheng Bank Bldg.,
51 Des Voeux Road
5-246819

Nigeria
Commission
25 floor,
Tung Wai Commercial Bldg.,
109-111 Gloucester Road
5-8939444

Norway
Consulate
1401 AIA Building,
1 Stubbs Road
5-749253

Oman
Honorary Consulate
2210 Alexandra House,
1 Hennessy Road
5-265664

Pakistan
Consulate
Room 307-308
Asian House,
1 Hennessy Road
5-274623

Panama
Consulate
Room 1212
Wing On Centre,
111 Connaught Road
Central
5-452166

Paraguay
Consulate
Room 509
Bank Of America Tower,
12 Harcourt Road
5-231141

Peru
Honorary Consulate
Golden Plaza,
10 floor, 'F'
745-747 Nathan Road
3-803698

Philippines
Consulate
Hang Lung Bank Building,
8 floor,
8 Hysan Avenue
5-7908823

Portugal
Consulate
Room 1001-1002
Two Exchange Square,
8 Connaught Place
5-225789

St Lucia
Honorary Consulate
8 floor,
Loke Yew Building,
50-52 Queen's Road Central
5-238810

Senegal
Honorary Consulate
c/o Dragages et
Travaux Publics,
9-10 floors,
102-112 Gloucester Rd.,
5-744261

Seychelles
Honorary Consulate
12A Menon Mansion,
18-20 Homantin Street

Singapore
Commission
Unit B, 17 floor,
United Centre,
95 Queensway
5-272212

South Africa
Consulate
27 floor,
Sunning Plaza,
10 Hysan Avenue
5-773279

Spain
Consulate
1401-1403
Melbourne Plaza Bldg.,
33 Queen's Road Central
5-253041

Sweden
Consulate
8 floor,
The Hong Kong Club Bldg.,
3A Chater Road
5-211212

Switzerland
Consulate
3703 Gloucester Tower,
The Landmark,
11 Pedder Street
5-227147

Thailand
Consulate
Hyde Centre,
2 floor,
221-226 Gloucester Road
5-742201

Tonga
Honorary Consulate
Room 84,
8 floor,
New Henry House,
10 Ice House Street
5-221321

Tuvalu
Honorary Consulate
Room 402
Yuen Yick Building,
27-29 Wellington Street
5-225997

United States of America
Consulate
26 Garden Road
5-239011

Uruguay
Consulate
Flat 103 Viewpoint,
7 Bowen Road
5-248792

Venezuela
Consulate
Room 805
Star House,
Kowloon
3-678099

Other Officially Recognised Representatives

Chinese Visa Office
5 floor, Lower Block,
26 Harbour Road
5-744083

Nepal
Royal Nepalese Liaison Office
c/o HQ Brigade of Gurkhas, HMS Tamar,
BFPO 1
5-28933255

United Nations High Commissioner for Refugees
9 floor, Yau Ma Tei Carpark Building,
250 Shanghai Street
Kowloon
3-309271

Appendix III

Hong Kong Government Departments

Agriculture
and Fisheries Department,
Canton Road
Government Offices,
393 Canton Road,
Kowloon. Tel: 3-688111

Banking Commission,
Hang Chong Building,
5 Queen's Road,
Central,
Hong Kong.
Tel.: 5-242141

Births and Deaths Registry,
Li Po Chun Chambers,
185-195 Des Voeux Road,
Central,
Hong Kong.
Tel.: 5-430970

Building Authority,
c/o Public Works Department,
Murray Building,
22 Cotton Tree Drive,
Hong Kong.
Tel.: 5-251111

Census
and Statistics Department,
Kai Tak Commercial Building,
317 Des Voeux Road,
Central,
Hong Kong. Tel.: 5-455678

Colonial Secretariat,
Central Government Offices,
Main and East Wings,
Lower Albert Road,
Hong Kong.
Tel.: 5-95718

Commerce
and Industry Department,
46 Connaught Road,
Central,
Hong Kong.
Tel.: 5-447944
Kowloon branch offices:
Tung Ying Building,
5th Floor,
100 Nathan Road, and
Room 610, 664 Nathan Road,
Kowloon.
Tel.: 3-960432

Dutiable
Commodities Office,
Rumsey Street
Car Park Building,
Hong Kong.
Tel.: 5-456182

Education Department,
33-37 Hysan Avenue,
Causeway Bay,
Hong Kong.
Tel.: 5-778311

Government
Publications Centre,
Star Ferry Concourse,
Hong Kong.
Tel.: 5-234224

Immigration Department,
International Building,
141 Des Voeux Road,
Central,
Hong Kong.
Tel.: 5-456065

Industrial Estates Corporation,
c/o The Economic
Services Branch,
The Colonial Secretariat,
Lower Albert Road,
Hong Kong.
Tel.: 5-95718

Independent Commission
Against Corruption,
Operations:
Hutchison House,
6th Floor,
Harcourt Road,
Hong Kong.
Tel.: 5-282523
Administration:
New Rodney Block,
99 Queensway,
Hong Kong.
Tel.: 5-266211

Inland Revenue Department,
Central Government Offices,
West Wing, 10th Floor,
Hong Kong.
Tel.: 5-222151

Lands and Survey Office,
c/o Public Works Department,
Murray Building,
22 Cotton Tree Drive,
Hong Kong.
Tel.: 5-251111

Labour Department,
Lee Gardens,
33-37 Hysan Avenue.
Causeway Bay,
Hong Kong.
Tel.: 5-778271
Regional Offices:
New Rodney Block,
99 Queensway,
Hong Kong.
Tel.: 282523 and

Canton Road
Government Offices,
393 Canton Road,
Kowloon.
Tel.: 3-6881111

Labour Tribunal,
Huts 28, 43 and 44,
Ex-Whitfield Barracks,
Nathan Road,
Kowloon.
Tel.: 3-691367

Marine Department,
102 Connaught Road,
Central,
Hong Kong.
Tel.: 5-450181

Marriage Registry,
City Hall High Block,
City Hall,
Hong Kong.
Tel.: 5-230725

New Territories
Administration,
North Kowloon
Magistracy Building,
4th Floor, Tai Po Road,
Kowloon.
Tel.: 3-866810

Patents Registry,
The Registrar
General's Department,
16th Floor,
Melbourne Plaza,
33 Queen's Road,
Central,
Hong Kong.
Tel.: 5-229563

Post Office,
Connaught Place,
Hong Kong.
Tel.: 5-267111

Printing Department,
81-115 Java Road,
North Point,
Hong Kong.
Tel.: 5-633616

Public Works Department,
Murray Building,
22 Cotton Tree Drive,
Hong Kong.
Tel.: 5-251111

Rating and
Valuation Department,
1 Garden Road,
Hong Kong.
Tel.: 5-249021

Registrar of Companies,
The Registrar
General's Department,
Kayamally Building,
22 Queen's Road, Central,
Hong Kong.
Tel.: 5-229270

Registration of
Persons Department,
Causeway Bay
Magistracy Building,
Hong Kong.
Tel.: 5-704417
Kowloon Branch Offices:
Canton Road
Government Offices,
393 Canton Road,
Kowloon.
Tel.: 3-697354

Registry of Trade Unions,
International Building,
141 Des Voeux Road,
Central,
Hong Kong.
Tel.: 5-454159

Securities Commission,
2404 Connaught Centre,
Connaught Road, Central,
Hong Kong.
Tel.: 5-235457

Trade Marks Registry
The Registrar
General's Department,
16th Floor, Melbourne Plaza,
33 Queen's Road, Central,
Hong Kong.
Tel.: 5-229563

Transport Department,
2 Murray Road, 9th Floor,
Hong Kong.
Tel.: 5-260121

Urban Services Dept
Central Government Offices,
West Wing, 12th Floor,
Queen's Road, Central,
Hong Kong.
Tel.: 5-95555

Waterworks Office,
Murray Building,
22 Cotton Tree Drive,
Hong Kong.
Tel.: 5-225011

* Branch offices are also located throughout Hong Kong Island, Kowloon and the New Territories.

Consumer Council
3/F Asian House
1 Hennessy Road, Wanchai
Hong Kong
Tel: 5-277662

Universal Consumers
Association Ltd
c/o Mr Edmund Chow
201 Tak Wo House
17-19 D'Aguilar Street
Hong Kong
Tel: 5-214488

Emergency Telephone Numbers

To report any accidents, fires, crimes, emergencies, or to summon
an ambulance: 999

China Light & Power Co — Kowloon & N.T.
3-7288333

Hong Kong Electric Co — Hong Kong
5-230111

Hong Kong & China Gas Co — Kowloon
3-640311

5-612111 — Hong Kong
5-223171

Police Enquiries
5-284284 ext.236

Weather Information
5-456381

St John's Ambulance Brigade — Hong Kong
5-761111

3-035555 — Kowloon

0-764227 — N.T.

Appendix IV

Trade Organizations

American Chamber
of Commerce in Hong Kong
Room 1030 Swire House,
Central
5-260165

Chinese General Chamber
of Commerce
24 Connaught Road,
Central
5-256389

The Chinese Manufacturers'
Association of Hong Kong
4th Floor, CMA Building,
64-66 Connaught Road,
Central
5-456166

The Federation
of Hong Kong Industries
Hankow Centre,
5-15 Hankow Road,
Tsimshatsui
3-7230818

The Hong Kong
Exporters' Association
825 Star House,
3 Salisbury Road,
Kowloon
3-699851

The Hong Kong
General Chamber of Commerce
22/F, United Centre,
95 Queensway,
Hong Kong
5-299229

The Hong Kong
Management Association
14/F Fairmont House,
8 Cotton Tree Drive,
Central
5-266516

The Hong Kong
Productivity Council
and Productivity Centre
12th Floor
World Commerce Centre,
Harbour City,
11 Canton Road,
Tsimshatsui
3-7235656

Hong Kong
Tourist Association
Connaught Centre, 35 floor,
Connaught Road Central,
Hong Kong
5-244191

Hong Kong
Trade Development Council
31/F, Great Eagle Centre,
23 Harbour Road,
Hong Kong
5-8334333

The Indian Chamber
of Commerce Hong Kong
2/F, Hoseinee House,
69 Wyndham Street,
Hong Kong
5-233877

Hong Kong Government

Trade Department,
14th Floor
Ocean Centre
Industry Department,
15th Floor
Ocean Centre,
Canton Road,
Tsimshatsui
3-7222434

Customs and
Excise Department
7/F Harbour Building,
38 Pier Road,
Central
5-8523324

Appendix V

Financial Institutions

American Banks Licensed in Hong Kong

American Express
International Banking Corp
28/F Connaught Centre
1 Connaught Place, Central
5-243151

Bank of America,
NT & SA
Bank of America Tower
12 Harcourt Rd Central
5-2676111

Bank of Canton
(Affilate of Security
Pacific National Bank)
6 Des Voeux Road Central
5-8411811

Bankers Trust Co
Admiralty Centre,
Tower 1, 30/F
18 Harcourt Road Central
5-281211

Chase Manhattan Bank, NA
Alexandra House
7 Des Voeux Road Central
5-8414321

Chemical Bank
42/F Gloucester Tower
11 Pedder St Central
5-2673333

Citibank, NA
Citicorp Centre
18 Whitefield Rd
Causeway Bay
5-8308211

Continental Illinois Bank Ltd
32/F Edinburgh Tower
15 Queen's Rd Central
5-255345

Crocker National Bank
Midland Bank Group
24/F Prince's Bldg
10 Chater Rd Central
5-265678

First Interstate Bank
of California
3101 Connaught Centre
1 Connaught Place, Central
5-239110

First National Bank of Boston
810-819 Connaught Centre
1 Connaught Place, Central
5-264361

First National Bank
of Chicago
13/F Connaught Centre
1 Connaught Place, Central
5-8449222

Manufacturers
Hanover Trust Co
43/F Edinburgh Tower
15 Queen's Rd Central
5-8416888

Morgan Guaranty Trust Co
of New York
23/F Edinburgh Tower
15 Queen's Rd Central
5-8411311

National Bank
of North Carolina
35/F New World Tower
16-18 Queen's Rd Central
5-220192

Northern Trust Company
17/F Edinburgh Tower
15 Queen's Rd Central
5-241057

Rainier International Bank
32/F United Centre
95 Queensway, Central
5-294461

Republic National Bank
of New York
606 Connaught Centre
1 Connaught Place, Central
5-266941

British Banks Licensed in Hong Kong

Barclays Bank PLC
United Centre
95 Queensway, Central
5-215111

Standard Chartered Bank
4-4A Des Voeux Rd
Central
5-224011

Registered and Licensed Deposit-taking Company Affiliates of American Financial Institutions

Shearson Lehman/
American Express Finance Ltd
7/F St George's Bldg
2 Ice House St Central
5-257261

Asia Pacific Capital
Corporation Ltd
(Affiliate of Citicorp)
26/F Citicorp Centre
18 Whitfield Rd Causeway Bay
5-8308620

BA Asia Ltd
20/F Bank of America Tower
12 Harcourt Rd Central
5-2676666

BA Finance (HK) Ltd
3/F Bank of America Bldg
1 Kowloon Park Dr Kowloon
3-7342233

Beneficial Financial (HK) Ltd
1502 World-Wide House
19 Des Voeux Rd Central
5-250056

BT Finance Ltd
(Affiliate of Bankers Trust)
30/F Admiralty Centre
Tower 1
18 Harcourt Rd Central
5-281211

Canton Pacific Finance Ltd
(Affiliate of Security
Pacific National Bank)
6 Des Voeux Rd Central
5-8411811

Chase Manhattan Asia Ltd
28th Floor
Bank of America Tower
12 Harcourt Rd Central
5-8431234

Manufacturers
Hanover Asia Ltd
43/F Edinburgh Tower
15 Queen's Rd Central
5-8416900

Rainier Intl Finance Co Ltd
United Centre, 'A' 32/F
95 Queensway, Central
5-294461

Security Pacific
Credit (HK) Ltd
15/F Bank of East Asia Bldg
10 Des Voeux Rd Central
5-253021

Washington International Ltd
1101 New World Tower
16 Queen's Rd Central
5-266351

American Brokerage Firms

Bache Halsey Stuart (HK) Ltd
9/F Shell House
24 Queen's Rd Central
5-229051

Dean Witter Reynolds
(HK) Ltd
1501 Gloucester Tower
11 Pedder St
Central
5-213322

Drexel Burnham Lambert Inc
2708 New World Tower
16-18 Queen's Rd Central
5-265163

Kidder Peabody & Co Ltd
Room 1707-09
Connaught Centre
Connaught Place,
Central
5-249291

Chemical Asia Ltd
43/F Gloucester Tower
5-2673555

Crocker National (HK) Ltd
Midland Bank Group
24/F Prince's Bldg
10 Chater Rd
Central
5-265821

Dow MBF Ltd
18th Floor
Bank of America Tower
12 Harcourt Rd Central
5-211105

First Chicago
Hong Kong Ltd
13/F Connaught Centre
1 Connaught Place,
Central
5-8449222

First National Boston
(Asia) Ltd
8/F Connaught Centre
1 Connaught Place,
Central
5-260171

FNCB Financial Ltd
36/F Hopewell Centre
183 Queen's Rd East
5-273021

Hawaii Financial Corp
(HK) Ltd
(Subsidiary of Bank of Hawaii)
4/F St George's Bldg
2 Ice House St
Central
5-210107

Canadian Brokerage Firms

Dominion Securities Pitfield
(Asia) Ltd
Rm 2208 22/F
16-20 Chater Rd Central
5-266731

Richardson Greenshields
of Canada (Pacific) Ltd
18/F China Bldg
29 Queen's Rd Central
5-258211

Merrill Lynch, Pierce,
Fenner & Smith
Hong Kong Ltd
15/F St George's Bldg
2 Ice House St Central
5-2678678

British Brokerage Firms

Astaire & Co Far East
901 Hutchison House, Central
5-230160

James Capel (Far East) Ltd
39/F Exchange Square II,
Central
5-237156

W I Carr Sons & Co
8/F St George's Bldg
2 Ice House St Central
5-255361

Cazenove & Co (Overseas)
808 Hutchison House
10 Harcourt Rd
5-264211

Hoare & Govett (Far East)
3001 Edinburgh Tower
15 Queen's Rd Central
5-256291

Rowe & Pitman
(Far East) Ltd
3210 Connaught Centre
1 Connaught Place,
Central
5-246113

Vickers Da Costa
& Co HK Ltd
43/F Exchange Square 1,
Central
5-8435777

Appendix VI

Professional and Trade Associations

Association of Cost
and Executive Accountants
in Hong Kong
G.P.O. Box 9210
Hong Kong
Tel: 5-8917648 (Chairman)

The Association
of International Accountants
G.P.O. Box 6778
Hong Kong
Tel: 5-451595 (President)

The Chartered Association
of Certified Accountants
G.P.O. Box 6324
Hong Kong
Tel: 5-261385 (Chairman)

Hong Kong Society of
Accountants
17/F Belgian House
77-79 Gloucester Road
Wanchai, Hong Kong
Tel: 5-299271

The Institute of Cost
and Management Accountants
G.P.O. Box 4059
Hong Kong
Tel: 5-8438238 (President)

The Hong Kong
Advertisers Association
Rm 303
The Red A Central Bldg.
37 Wellington Street
Hong Kong
Tel: 5-263637

The Association
of Accredited Advertising
Agents of Hong Kong
c/o M.C. Ng
& Company Ltd.
Rm 303
The Red A Central Bldg.
37 Wellington Street
Hong Kong
Tel: 5-263637

The Hong Kong
Chinese Commercial
Advertising Association Ltd
22/F Dominion Centre
43-59 Queen's Road East
Hong Kong
Tel: 5-271721

International Advertising
Association
10/F OTB Bldg
259-265 Des Voeux Road,
Central
Hong Kong
Tel: 5-412091

Association of Hong Kong
Air Freight Agents
G1, 70 Sung Wong Toi Road
Kowloon, Hong Kong
Tel: 3-628880

Society of IATA (International
Air Transport Association)
Passenger Agents
1403 Tung Ming Bldg.
40 Des Voeux Road, Central
Hong Kong
Tel: 5-230640

Hong Kong Aluminium
Manufacturers' Association
11/F 550 Nathan Road
Front Portion, Kowloon
Hong Kong
Tel: 3-852874

The Hong Kong Institute
of Architects
10/F 52 Wellington Street
Cheong Sun Bldg. Central
Hong Kong
Tel: 5-211459

Hong Kong National Group
of Asian Patent Attorneys
Association
c/o Mr Robert Bridge
15/F Unit C2 United Centre
95 Queensway
Hong Kong
Tel: 5-202531 (President)

The Institute
of Internal Auditors, Inc
c/o John Swire
& Sons (HK) Ltd.
Finance & Accounts Dept
G.P.O. Box 1
Hong Kong
Tel: 5-230011 Ext. 131

The Institute of Bankers
9/F Yardley Commercial Bldg.
1-6 Connaught Road West
Sheung Wan
Hong Kong
Tel: 5-8151552

The Chinese Banks'
Association Ltd
5th Floor
South China Commercial Bldg
1-3 Wyndham Street
Hong Kong
Tel: 5-226692, 5-224789

The Hong Kong
Association Of Banks
G.P.O. Box 11391
Hong Kong
Tel: 5-211288-9

The Beverage Manufacturers
Association of Hong Kong
KMG Byrne
41/F Hopewell Centre
183 Queen's Road East
Hong Kong Tel: 5-286570

Hong Kong
Biochemical Association
c/o Dept of Biochemistry
University of Hong Kong
Sassoon Road, Hong Kong
Tel: 5-8199240

Hong Kong Booksellers' &
Stationers' Association Co Ltd
2/F Ferry Point
8 Man Wui Street
Kowloon, Hong Kong
Tel: 3-882356

The Society of Builders
Rm 801-2 On Lok Yuen Bldg
25 Des Voeux Road
Central, Hong Kong
Tel: 5-232081-2

The Building Contractors'
Association Ltd
182 Hennessy Road
Hong Kong
Tel: 5-724414

The Chartered Institute
of Building
c/o Dept of Building
& Surveying
Hong Kong Polytechnic,
Kowloon
Hong Kong
Tel: 3-668304 (Chairman)

Cargo Supervisors Association
2/F Man Wah Bldg
14-16 Ferry Point
Yaumati, Kowloon
Hong Kong
Tel: 3-300381

Hong Kong Cargo-Vessel
Traders' Association Ltd
2/F Man Wai Bldg
21-23 Man Cheong Street
Ferry Point, Kowloon
Hong Kong
Tel: 3-855221

International
Cartographic Association
Survey Division
Lands Dept, Murray Bldg
Garden Road, Hong Kong
Tel: 5-26702267

The Clothing
& Footwear Institute
c/o Institute of Textiles
& Clothing
Hong Kong Polytechnic,
Kowloon
Hong Kong
Tel: 3-638344 Ext. 671-4

Hong Kong Computer Society
Rm 913,
Hunghom Commercial Centre
Tower B,
37 Ma Tau Wei Road
Kowloon, Hong Kong
Tel: 3-628333

The Concrete Society
(Hong Kong) Ltd
6/F Portland House
20 Hok Yuen Street East
Hunghom
Kowloon, Hong Kong
Tel: 3-7651211

Hong Kong and Namyang
Import & Export
Consignees' Mutual
Help Association Ltd
7/F Flat A,
71 Connaught Road West
Hong Kong
Tel: 5-498364

Hong Kong
Container Tractor Owners
Association Ltd
Flat 29 Profit Industrial Bldg
Kwai Fong Street
Kwai Chung,
New Territories
Hong Kong
Tel: 0-229122

The Cosmetic
and Perfumery Association
of Hong Kong Ltd
Rm. 1508
Rise Commercial Bldg
7-11 Granville Circuit
Tsimshatsui,
Kowloon
Hong Kong
Tel: 3-668801

The Federation of Hong Kong
Cotton Weavers
14/F Astoria Bldg
24-30 Ashley Road
Kowloon
Hong Kong
Tel: 3-672383

Hong Kong Cotton
Made Up Goods
Manufacturers Association
12/F Flat
D'739 Nathan Road
Kowloon,
Hong Kong
Tel: 5-943128

Victoria Cotton Yarn
& Piece Goods Merchants
Association
5/F
1-3 Mercer Street
Hong Kong
Tel: 5-441234

Credit Union League
of Hong Kong
6/F Flat 3
Jade Mansion
40 Waterloo Road
Kowloon,
Hong Kong
Tel: 3-856982

Hong Kong
& Kowloon Curios, Furniture,
Miscellaneous Utensils
& Hardware Merchants
& Employees Association
4/F
370 Queen's Road Central
Hong Kong
Tel: 5-451329

EDP (Electronic Data
Processing)
Management Club
c/o The Hong Kong
Management Association
14/F Fairmont House
8 Cotton Tree Drive
Hong Kong
Tel: 5-266516

Hong Kong
Designers Association
Rm. 407-411 Hankow Centre
5-15 Hankow Road
Tsimshatsui,
Kowloon
Hong Kong
Tel: 3-7230818

Institute of Patentees,
Inventors and Designers Ltd
P.O. Box 97423
Tsimshatsui, Kowloon
Hong Kong
3-7219773

The Diamond Importers
Association Ltd
Rm 401
Hong Kong Diamond
Exchange Bldg.
8-10 Duddell Street
Hong Kong
Tel: 5-235497

Hong Kong
Direct Selling Association
c/o Mrs Eva Cheng
Rm. 1617-1623 Star House
Tsimshatsui, Kowloon
Hong Kong
Tel: 5-665615 (President)

Chinese Distilleries Association
C/F 99 Queen's Road East
Hong Kong
Tel: 5-277509

Hong Kong Printers
& Dyers Association Ltd
11/F 557-559 Nathan Road
Kowloon, Hong Kong
Tel: 3-841363

Hong Kong
& Kowloon Spinning,
Weaving and Dyeing Trade
Workers General Union
4/F Victory Court
187 Castle Peak Road
Tsuen Wan, New Territories
Hong Kong
Tel: 0-467561-4

The Society of Dyers
and Colourists
c/o Institute of Textiles
& Clothing
Hong Kong Polytechnic,
Hunghom
Kowloon,
Hong Kong
Tel: 3-638344 Ext. 671-674

Hong Kong Dyestuffs
Merchants Association
3/F 248 Lai Chi Kok Road
Kowloon, Hong Kong
Tel: 3-961846

Hong Kong
Economic Association
G.P.O. Box 4004
Hong Kong
Tel: 5-8592183 (President)

Pacific Basin
Economic Council
c/o The Hong Kong General
Chamber of Commerce
22/F Unit A
United Centre
95 Queensway,
Hong Kong
Tel: 5-299229

The Hong Kong and Kowloon
Electric Trade Association
6/F Cheong Ip Bldg
350-354 Hennessy Road
Hong Kong
Tel: 5-737005

Hong Kong & Kowloon
Electrical Appliance Merchants
Association Ltd
4/F 732 Nathan Road
Kowloon,
Hong Kong
Tel: 3-942135

Hong Kong & Kowloon
Electrical Contractors'
Association Ltd
8/F 195-197 Johnston Road
Wanchai,
Hong Kong
Tel: 5-720483

Hong Kong & Kowloon
Electro-Plating Trade
Merchants Association Ltd
G/F 5 Fuk Wing Street
Kowloon, Hong Kong
Tel: 3-7768282-5

Hong Kong & Kowloon
Oxyacetyl Electro
Welding Trades
Association
6/F 985 Canton Road
Kowloon, Hong Kong
Tel: 3-847970

The Hong Kong
Electronics Association Ltd
c/o 9/F
First Commercial Bldg
33-35 Leighton Road
Causeway Bay,
Hong Kong
Tel: 5-554881

Hong Kong Embroidery
Merchants Association Ltd
4/F 1-4 On Hing Terrace
Hong Kong
Tel: 5-246496

Hong Kong & Kowloon
Embroidery, Bedding
& Cotton Quilt
Merchants Association Ltd
4/F Block C
241 Portland Street
Kowloon, Hong Kong
Tel: 3-852491

Employers Federation
of Hong Kong
1001 East Town Bldg
41 Lockhart Road
Hong Kong
Tel: 5-280536

The Hong Kong & Kowloon
Engineering Employers
Association Ltd
2/F 43 Bute Street
Mongkok,
Kowloon
Hong Kong
Tel: 3-948360

Hong Kong
Enamelware Manufacturers'
Association
11/F Front Portion
550 Nathan Road
Kowloon
Hong Kong
Tel: 3-852874

The Association of Consulting
Engineers of Hong Kong
14/F Bank of America Bldg.
1 Kowloon Park Drive
Hong Kong
Tel: 3-7211125

The Chartered Institution
of Building Services
P.O. Box 20342
Hennessy Road Post Office
Hong Kong
Tel: 3-7512454 (Chairman)

Chinese Engineers Institute
20/F Flat C Continental Bldg
294 King's Road
North Point,
Hong Kong
5-710037

Hong Kong Association
of Energy Engineers
Rm 1602
Tung Wah Mansion
199 Hennessy Road
Wanchai
Hong Kong
Tel: 5-720802

The Hong Kong Institution
of Engineers
9/F Island Centre
1 Great George Street
Causeway Bay,
Hong Kong
Tel: 5-7954446

Institute of Electrical
& Electronics Engineers, Inc
c/o Dept of
Electrical Engineering
University of Hong Kong
Pokfulam Road
Hong Kong
Tel: 0-4987411 (Chairman)

Institute
of Industrial Engineers
c/o Mr Chris Wong
Industrial Centre
Hong Kong Polytechnic,
Hunghom
Kowloon,
Hong Kong
Tel: 3-638344
Ext. 383 (President)

The Institution
of Structural Engineers
c/o Mr. S.H. Ng
The Buildings
Ordinance Office
8/F Murray Bldg
Garden Road
Hong Kong
Tel: 5-26702323

Society of Manufacturing
Engineers
c/o Hong Kong
Productivity Centre
2/F Unit E
Freder Centre
68 Sung Wong Toi Road
Tokwawan
Kowloon, Hong Kong
Tel: 3-624351 (Chairman)

Hong Kong Equipment
Leasing Association
c/o Mrs Catherine H Bacon
601 Swire House
Hong Kong
Tel: 5-216688

The Hong Kong
Chinese Importers'
& Exporters' Association
8/F Champion Bld
287-29 Des Voeux Road
Central
Hong Kong
Tel: 5-448474

The Hong Kong
Exporters Association
Rm 825 Star House
3 Salisbury Road
Kowloon, Hong Kong
Tel: 3-699851

The Wah On Exporters
& Importers Association
1/F 46 Bonham Strand East
Hong Kong
Tel: 5-433111

Hong Kong Factory Owners
Association Ltd
11/F 557-559 Nathan Road
Kowloon, Hong Kong
Tel: 3-843889

Hong Kong
Fashion Designer Association
Unit 104
Tai Kok Tsui Centre
11 Kok Cheung Street
Kowloon, Hong Kong
Tel: 3-954243

Hong Kong Institute
of Fishery Ltd
2/F Caltex House
258 Hennessy Road
Hong Kong
Tel: 5-720330

Hong Kong & Kowloon
Footwear Manufacturers
Association
5th Floor
191 Shanghai Street
Yaumati, Kowloon
Hong Kong
Tel: 3-843004

Hong Kong Rubber
& Footwear Manufacturers'
Association Ltd
2/F Block A
185 Prince Edward Road
Kowloon, Hong Kong
Tel: 3-812297-9

Hong Kong Forex Club
12/F Bank of East Asia Bldg
10 Des Voeux Road
Central
Hong Kong
Tel: 5-218168

Hong Kong Fresh Fruits
Importers Association Ltd
202 Peter Building
62 Queen's Road
Central
Hong Kong
Tel: 5-211228

Federation of
Fur Manufacturers & Dealers
(Hong Kong) Ltd
Rm 1204
Chatham Commercial Centre
45-51 Chatham Road
Tsimshatsui
Kowloon,
Hong Kong
Tel: 3-674646

The Federation
of Hong Kong Garment
Manufacturers
4/F 25 Kimberley Road
Tsimshatsui,
Kowloon
Hong Kong
Tel: 3-7211383

Hong Kong Garment
Manufacturers Association
Rm 708
Universal Commercial Bldg
69 Peking Road
Kowloon
Hong Kong
Tel: 3-673392

Hong Kong & Kowloon
Machine Sewing
and Garment-Making
Trade Workers' General Union
5/F 8 Choi Hung Road
Sampokong,
Kowloon
Hong Kong
Tel: 3-280951

Hong Kong & Kowloon
Glass Merchants & Mirror
Manufacturers'Association
3/F 6 Burrows Street
Wanchai,
Hong Kong
Tel: 5-8912219

The Association
of Hong Kong Gloves
Manufacturers Ltd
c/o Action Secretarial Ltd
16/F Block A
Hang Tat Bldg
161 Lockhart Road
Wanchai,
Hong Kong
Tel: 5-728224

The Chinese Gold
& Silver Exchange Society
1/F 12-18 Mercer Street
Hong Kong
Tel: 5-441945

Hong Kong Christian
Industrial Committee
14/F Rm 1404
57 Peking Road Kowloon
Hong Kong
Tel: 3-665860

Hong Kong
Industrial Design Council
Rm 407-411 Hankow Centre
5-15 Hankow Road
Tsimshatsui, Kowloon
Hong Kong
Tel: 5-611647

The Federation
of Hong Kong Industries
Rm 407-411 Hankow Centre
5-15 Hankow Road
Tsimshatsui, Kowloon
Hong Kong
Tel: 3-7230818

The Insurance Council
of Hong Kong
705 D'Aguilar Place
D'Aguilar Street
Hong Kong
Tel: 5-253095

Hong Kong
Jade & Stone
Manufacturers Association
16/F Hang Lung House
184-192 Queen's Road
Central
Hong Kong
Tel: 5-430543

Hong Kong
Jewellers' & Goldsmiths'
Association Ltd
13/F Hong Kong Jewel Bldg
178-180 Queen's Road
Central
Hong Kong
Tel: 5-439633

Hong Kong Jewellery
& Industrial Product
Merchants Association
3/F
16-20 Bonham Strand East
Hong Kong
Tel: 5-448858

Hong Kong
Jewellery Management
& Development Association
901 Bank of Canton Bldg
6 Des Voeux Road
Central
Hong Kong
Tel: 5-255295

Hong Kong
Woollen & Synthetic
Knitting Manufacturers'
Association Ltd
5/F Rm 507A-B
Harbour Crystal Centre
100 Granville Road
Tsimshatsui East,
Kowloon
Hong Kong
Tel: 3-682091

Hong Kong Knitwear
Exporters & Manufacturers
Association Ltd
12/F Rm 1201
Hang Pont Commercial Bldg
31 Tonkin Street
Shamshuipo,
Kowloon
Hong Kong
Tel: 3-7290111

The Hong Kong
Association of
Certification Laboratories Ltd
3/F CMA Building
64-66 Connaught Road
Central
Hong Kong
Tel: 5-456166

The Mail Order Association
of Hong Kong Ltd
P.O. Box 91074
Tsimshatsui,
Kowloon
Hong Kong
Tel: 3-695565 (Chairman)

The Hong Kong
Management Association
14/F Fairmont House
8 Cotton Tree Drive
Central
Hong Kong
Tel: 5-266516

Hong Kong Medical
& Health Departments,
Medical Technicians
& Technologists Association
c/o Histopathology
Clinical Pathology Unit
Princess Margaret Hospital
Kowloon, Hong Kong
Tel: 3-7427111
Ext. 244 (Chairman)

Nam Pak Hong Association
(Chinese Merchants Association)
135 Bonham Strand East
Hong Kong
Tel: 5-441967

Hong Kong Metal Merchants
Association
6A Hankow Apartment
43-49 Hankow Road
Kowloon, Hong Kong
Tel: 3-7227485

Movie Producers
& Distributors Association
of Hong Kong-Kowloon Ltd
6/F Front Block
236 Nathan Road Kowloon
Hong Kong
Tel: 3-682164

The Newspaper Society
of Hong Kong
G.P.O. Box 47 Hong Kong
Tel: 5-620161

China Vegetable Oil
Exporters Association
11/F Wing Shun Bldg
64-64A Bonham Strand West
Hong Kong
Tel: 5-485801

Hong Kong General
Association of Edible Oils
Importers and Exporters Ltd
4/F Hang Seng Bank Bldg
77 Des Voeux Road Central
Hong Kong
Tel: 5-261111

Hong Kong Oil Merchants
Association Ltd
11/F Block J Sun On Bldg
484-496 Queen's Road West
Hong Kong
Tel: 5-474334

Hong Kong Optical
Manufacturers Association Ltd
2/F 11 Fa Yuen Street
Kowloon, Hong Kong
Tel: 3-326505

Hong Kong
Packaging Council
4/F Rm 407-411
Hankow Centre
5-15 Hankow Road
Tsimshatsui
Kowloon, Hong Kong
Tel: 3-7230818

Hong Kong
Paints & Pigments
Merchants Association Ltd
4/F Luen Tak Bldg
44 Jordan Road
Kowloon
Hong Kong
Tel: 3-673503

Chinese Paper Merchants
Association
4/F 132-136
Des Voeux Road West
Hong Kong
Tel: 5-481969

The Hong Kong
Corrugated Paper
Manufacturers' Association Ltd
15/F Flat B
568 Nathan Road
Hong Kong
Tel: 3-856894

South China Paper Merchants
Association
Rm 901
Hong Kong House
17-19 Wellington Street
Hong Kong
Tel: 5-244604

The Hong Kong
Pharmaceutical Manufacturers
Association Ltd
c/o Neochem Pharmaceutical
Laboratories Ltd
5/F 30 Factory Street
Shaukiwan,
Hong Kong
Tel: 5-696227-8

The Hong Kong & Kowloon
Photographic Merchants
Association Ltd
Rm 304
Beverley Commercial Centre
87-105 Chatham Road
Kowloon, Hong Kong
Tel: 3-669997

The Hong Kong Piece-Goods
Merchants' Association
4D Wing Cheong
Commercial Bldg
25-27 Jervois Street
Hong Kong
Tel: 5-441143

Hong Kong & Kowloon
Plastic Products Merchants
United Association Ltd
13/F 491 Nathan Road
Kowloon, Hong Kong
Tel: 3-840171

Hong Kong Plastics
Manufacturers Association Ltd
Rm 302 Red A Central Bldg
37 Wellington Street
Hong Kong
Tel: 5-232229

The Hong Kong Wine Society
c/o Hong Kong Polytechnic
Library
Hunghom, Kowloon
Hong Kong
Tel: 3-640694 (Chairman)

Hong Kong & Kowloon
Provisions/Wine
& Spirit Dealers' Association
3/F Yuen Yick Bldg
27-29 Wellington Street
Hong Kong
Tel: 5-238668

International Public Relations
Association
G.P.O. Box 2565 Hong Kong

The American Chamber
of Commerce in Hong Kong
1030 Swire House
Connaught Road Central
Hong Kong
Tel: 5-260165

Canadian Chamber
of Commerce in Hong Kong
G.P.O. Box 1587
Hong Kong
Tel: 5-225081

The Chinese General Chamber
of Commerce, Hong Kong
7/F 24-25 Connaught Road
Central
Hong Kong
Tel: 5-256385

The Hong Kong General
Chamber of Commerce
22/F Unit A,
United Centre
95 Queensway,
Hong Kong
Tel: 5-299229

Hong Kong Industry
and General Commerce
Association Ltd
Rm 1002A Everest Bldg
241-243 Nathan Road
Kowloon, Hong Kong
Tel: 3-677871

The Hong Kong
Japanese Chamber
of Commerce & Industry
38/F Hennessy Centre
500 Hennessy Road
Causeway Bay, Hong Kong
Tel: 5-776129

Hong Kong Junior Chamber
of Commerce
15/F Block C,
272 Queen's Road Central
Hong Kong
Tel: 5-444174

The Indian Chamber
of Commerce, Hong Kong
2/F Hosinee House
69 Wyndham Street
Hong Kong
Tel: 5-233877

ICC (International Chamber
of Commerce) Services
Asia Pacific Ltd
14/F Aubin House
171-172 Gloucester Road
Hong Kong
Tel: 5-726387-8

The Korean
Society of Commerce
in Hong Kong Ltd
Rm 503 Korean Centre Bldg
119-121 Connaught Road,
Central
Hong Kong
Tel: 5-439387

Kowloon Chamber
of Commerce
3/F KCC Bldg,
2 Liberty Avenue
Homantin,
Kowloon
Hong Kong
Tel: 3-7600393-6

New Territories General
Chamber of Commerce
25th Floor
Far East Bank Mongkok Bldg
Block A
11 Nelson Street
Kowloon,
Hong Kong
Tel: 3-961845

Appendix VII

Representative Offices Of Chinese Trade Organizations In Hong Kong

General

China Everbest Machinery
Enterprises Co Ltd
Rm 903, Tower 2,
South Sea Ctr
Tsim Sha Tsui East
Kowloon
Tel: 3-7239228

China Insurance Co Ltd
15/F International Bldg
141 Des Voeux Road,
Central
Hong Kong
Tel: 5-45077

China International Trust
& Investment Corp
Rm 2908-2910,
29/F China Resources Bldg
26 Harbour Road
Hong Kong
Tel: 5-8934391

China Merchants Steam
Navigation (Holdings)
Co Ltd & its
Hong Kong subsidiaries
China Merchants Bldg, 20/F
152-155 Connaught Road,
Central
Tel: 5-434444

China National Aviation
Corp
Rm 602 Gloucester Tower
Central
Hong Kong
Tel: 5-216416

China Overseas Building
Development Co Ltd
21/F China Resources Bldg
26 Harbour Road
Wanchai
Hong Kong
Tel: 5-8938339

China Products Co (HK) Ltd
Lok Sing Centre
31 Yee Wo Street
Hong Kong
Tel: 5-7908321

China Reinsurance Co Ltd
Rm 1201 Nanyang
Commercial (HK) Bank Bldg
151 Des Voeux Road Central
Hong Kong
Tel: 5-411031

China Resources (Holdings)
Co Ltd & its 26 subsidiaries
49/F China Resources Bldg
Harbour Road
Wanchai
Hong Kong
Tel: 5-8317111

China Travel Service
Holding (HK) Ltd
China Travel Bldg
77 Queen's Road C
Hong Kong
Tel: 5-259121

The Chinese Merchandise
Emporium Ltd
Chiao Shang Bldg
94-104 Queen's Road
Central
Hong Kong
Tel: 5-241051

Chu Kong Shipping Co Ltd
7/F Wayson Commercial Bldg
28 Connaught Road West
Hong Kong
Tel: 5-489428

China Everbright Holdings
Co Ltd & its 16 subsidiaries
39/F Far East Finance Centre
Harcourt Road
Hong Kong
Tel: 5-299350

Far East Marine Surveyors Ltd
7/F China Merchants Bldg
152-155 Connaught Road
Central
Hong Kong
Tel: 5-457652

The Ming An Insurance
Co (HK) Ltd
14/F International Bldg
141 Des Voeux Road
Central
Hong Kong
Tel: 5-446101

Ocean Tramping Co Ltd
9-12/F Ocean Building
167 Connaught Road West
Hong Kong
Tel: 5-403421

The Tai Ping Insurance
Co Ltd
24/F International Bldg
141 Des Voeux Road
Central
Hong Kong
Tel: 5-433261

Yick Fung Shipping &
Enterprises Co Ltd
7/F Ocean Bldg
167 Connaught Road West
Hong Kong
Tel: 5-468141

Yiu Lian Dockyard Ltd
855 Lai Chi Kok Road
Kowloon
Tel: 3-7418036

China International Travel
Services (HK)
Rm 606
Tower II
South Seas Centre
75 Mody Road
Kowloon
Tel: 3-7215317

Provinces

Chun Shing Trading Co
(Jilin)
Rm 1606
Arion Commercial Centre
2-12 Queen's Road West
Hong Kong
Tel: 5-451021
Tlx: 74905 CHUSH HX

Chung Liou Trading Co
(Liaoning)
18/F Nan Dao Commercial
Bldg
359-361 Queen's Road Central
Hong Kong
Tel: 5-440711
Tlx: 71941 CHULI HX

Fu Chung Co (Zhejiang)
Rm 314-318 3/F
Causeway Centre
28 Harbour Road
Wanchai, Hong Kong
Tel. 5-7569211

Fujian Enterprises (Holdings)
Co & its Hong Kong
subsidiaries (Fujian)
115-119 Queen's Road West
Tel: 5-404021
Tlx: 73986 FUJEN HX

Guangdong Enterprises
(Holdings) & its
subsidiaries (Guangdong)
10-13/F
152-155 Connaught Road
Central, Hong Kong
Tel: 5-451939
Tlx: 62103 GDEL HX

Gui Jiang Enterprises Co
(Guangxi)
Flat A, 1/F
Seaview Commercial Bldg
21-24 Connaught Road West
Hong Kong
Tel: 5-495622
Tlx: 71886 KWD HX

Henan Hong Kong Enterprise
(Henan)
19/F Far East Consortium Bldg
121 Des Voeux Road Central
Tel: 5-418808, 5-418939
Tlx: 84755 HTTRG HX

Heng Shan Trading Co
(Shanxi)
Rm 2710 27/F
China Resource Bldg
26 Harbour Road
Wanchai, Hong Kong
Tel: 5-8330928
Tlx: 89053 HSHTC HX

Hebei Enterprises (Hebei)
5/F Rm 503 Pensinsula Centre
67 Mody Road
Tsim Sha Tsui East
Kowloon
Tel: 3-7226530
Tlx: 41179 HBETP HX

Hing Yuen Trading Co
(Inner Mongolia)
802 Seaview Commercial Bldg
21-24 Connaught Road West
Hong Kong
Tel: 5-486101

Hong Kong Lishan Co
(Shaanxi)
Rm 1801
Tung Wai Comm Bldg
109-112 Gloucester Road
Hong Kong
Tel: 5-733709
Tlx: 83628 SWCOL HX

Hua Gan Enterprises Co
(Jiangxi)
64 Connaught Road C
Hong Kong
Tel: 5-432662
Tlx: 80215 HGECL HX

Hunan Trading Co (Hunan)
9/F Tien Chu Commercial Bldg
173-174 Gloucester Road
Hong Kong
Tel: 5-8920789, 5-8920209
Tlx: 89072 HNX HX

HLJ Loong Fung Co
(Heilongjiang)
Rm 701 World-Wide House
19 Des Voeux Road C
Hong Kong
Tel: 5-212425
Tlx: 65347 LFHLJ HX

Jialing (HK) Co
(Sichuan)
Rm 507-509
Prince's Bldg
Hong Kong
Tel: 5-259357
Tlx: 65871 JIALG HX

Nin Xia Enterprises
(Ningxia)
Room 901
Jubilee Commercial Bldg
Hong Kong
Tel: 5-273327
Tlx: 72475 BIRK HX

Yi Feng Trading Co
(Hubei)
Rm 510
Peninsula Centre
67 Mody Road
Tsim Sha Tsui East
Kowloon
Tel: 3-692415, 3-7221586
Tlx: 41189 YIFEN HX

Zhong Shan Co
(Jiangsu)
45/F China Resources Bldg
26 Harbour Road
Wanchai
Hong Kong
Tel: 5-8329968
Tlx: 89699 ZHOSA HX

China Shandong Co
(Shandong)
17/F 340 Queen's Road C
Hong Kong
Tel: 5-417125
Tlx: 77243 WELDN HX

Can High International
Trading (Anhui)
Rm 3906-3909 39/F
Hong Kong Plaza
186-191
Connaught Road West
Hong Kong
Tel: 5-407155
Tlx: 70246 CHITL HX

Hong Kong Gui Hai Co
(Guizhou)
7/F
15-16 Connaught Road West
Hong Kong
Tel: 5-8153218
Tlx: 65193 HTMMS HX

OHL Trading Co (Qinghai)
Unit 905
Tower 2, South Sea Centre
75 Mody Road
Tsim Sha Tsui
Kowloon
Tel: 3-681211
Tlx: 50937 MGHOT HX

Municipality/City

Scriven Trading
(Peking)
Rm 2004
Arion Commercial Centre
2-12 Queen's Road West
Hong Kong
Tel: 5-422017
Tlx: 71852 CBST HX

Shanghai Industrial
Investment Co (Shanghai)
2/F Tien Chu
Commercial Bldg
173-174 Gloucester Road
Hong Kong
Tel: 5-8916313
Tlx: 71777 SHANG HX

Tsin Lien Trading Co (Tianjin)
Unit 401-406 4/F Tower 2
South Sea Centre
75 Mody Road
Tsimshatsui
Kowloon
Tel: 3-7232072
Tlx: 37476 TSINS HX

Dalian International Co
(Dalian)
6/F
Hing Yip Commercial Centre
272-284 Des Voeux Road C
Hong Kong
Tel: 5-8153318
Tlx: 83700 CKS HX

Foshan Development Co
(Foshan)
21/F
Hing Yip Commercial Bldg
272-284 Des Voeux Road C
Hong Kong
Tel: 5-8152112 (6)
Tlx: 83616 WSGRC HX

Guang Shao Development Co
(Shaoguan)
15/F Yardley Commercial Bldg
1-6 Connaught Road West
Hong Kong
Tel: 5-8153331
Tlx: 89256 GSDCL HX

Hua Rong Co
(Fuzhou)
Rm 1701-1702 Island Centre
1 Great George Street
Causeway Bay,
Hong Kong
Tel: 5-7901716
Tlx: 77434 RONG HX

Ning Shing Development
Co (Ningbo)
Rm 903-904
General Comm Bldg
164 Des Voeux Road C
Hong Kong
Tel: 5-8151581

Yue Xiu Enterprises
(Guangzhou)
13/F
Yardley Commercial Bldg
3 Connaught Road West
Hong Kong
Tel: 5-8151221
Tlx: 89554 YXEL HX

Zhum Heng Development
(Zhanjiang)
5/F
Yardley Commercial Bldg
3 Connaught Road West
Hong Kong
Tel: 5-8151167
Tlx: 77412 ZHUHE HX

Special Economic Zones

Guangdong East Development
(Shantou)
Suite 2105-6
Far East Consortium
Bldg 121 Des Voeux Road C
Hong Kong
Tel: 5-8152303, 5-8152496
Tlx: 89880 EBEDL HX

Shum Yip Holdings Co
(Shenzhen)
1/F East Ocean Centre
98 Granville Road
Tsim Sha Tsui
Kowloon
Tel: 3-692886
Tlx: 41454 SYTCO HX

Xing Xia Co (Xiamen)
1701-1705 Wing On House
71 Des Voeux Road C
Hong Kong
Tel: 5-215491
Tlx: 83625 XIMEN HX

Zhuhai Trading Co
(Zhuhai)
14/F Yardley Bldg
1-6 Connaught Road West
Hong Kong
Tel: 5-8150201

Banks

Bank of China, Hong Kong
Bank of China Bldg.
2A Des Voeux Road C
Hong Kong
Tel: 5-212626

Bank of Communications,
Hong Kong
3A Des Voeux Road
Central
Hong Kong
Tel: 5-259261

The China & South Sea
Bank Ltd
77 Queen's Road C
Hong Kong
Tel: 5-256041

The China State Bank Ltd
39-41 Des Voeux Road
Central
China State Bank Bldg
Hong Kong
Tel: 5-263235

Chiyu Banking Corp Ltd
78 Des Voeux Road
Central
Hong Kong
Tel: 5-8430111

Hua Chiao Commercial
Bank Ltd
98 Des Voeux Road C
Hong Kong
Tel: 5-429888

Kincheng Banking Corp
Bank Ltd
51-57 Des Voeux Road C
Hong Kong
Tel: 5-222076

The Kwangtung Provincial
Bank, HK Branch
13-14 Connaught Road C
Euro Trade Centre
Hong Kong
Tel: 5-8410410

The National Commercial
Bank Ltd
1-3 Wyndham Street
Hong Kong
Tel: 5-217261

Po Sang Bank Ltd
71 Des Voeux Road C
Hong Kong
Tel: 5-434761

Nanyang Commercial
Bank Ltd
151 Des Voeux Road C
Nanyang Commercial
Bank Bldg
Hong Kong Tel: 5-421111

Sin Hua Trust, Savings &
Commercial Bank Ltd
2-8 Wellington Street, G/F
Central
Hong Kong
Tel: 5-8420668

Yien Yieh Commercial Bank
242 Des Voeux Road C
Hong Kong
Tel: 5-411601

Source: Hong Kong Trade Development Council

Appendix VIII

Hong Kong Representation Overseas

Government Offices

Hong Kong Government Office,
6 Grafton Street,
London W1X 3LB, England.
Tel: (01)499-9821 Cable: HONGAID LONDON
Telex: 05218404 HKGOVT G

United Kingdom Mission (Hong Kong Government Office)
37-39 rue de Vermont, 1211 Geneva 20, Switzerland.
Tel: (02)34-43-51
Cable: PRODROME GENEVA
Telex: 04528880 HKGV CH

British Embassy, Hong Kong Government Office,
Avenue Louise, 228, (Bte 2), 1050 Brussels, Belgium.
Tel:(02)648-38-33 Cable: HONREP BRUSSELS
Telex: 04661750 HONREP B

Office of the Commissioner for Hong Kong Commercial Affairs,
British Consulate General,
Tower 56, 17/F, 126 East 56 Street, New York,
NY 10022, U.S.A.
Tel:(212)355-4060
Telex: 025 961075 NYHKO HK

British Embassy (Hong Kong Office),
3100 Massachusetts Avenue, N.W.,
Washington D.C. 20008, U.S.A.
Tel: (202)462-0139
Cable: PRODROME WASHINGTON
Telex: 023440484 HK WSH UI

Industrial Promotion Offices

Industrial Promotion Office (Japan),
No. 32 Kowa Building, 5-2-32 Minami Azabu, Minato-ku, Tokyo,
Japan.
Tel: (03)446-8111
Telex: 0720 2425122 HKGIPO J

Industrial Promotion Office (London),
Hong Kong Government Office, 6 Grafton Street,
London W1X 3LB, England.
Tel: (01)499-9821 Cable: HONGAID LONDON
Telex: 051 28404 HKGOVT G

Industrial Promotion Office (Stuttgart)
Koenigstr 43B,
7000 Stuttgart 1, F.R.Germany.
Tel: (0711)22 13 25
Telex: 041 721435 HKIP D

Industrial Promotion Office (San Francisco),
McKesson Plaza, Suite 2130, 1 Post Street,
San Francisco, CA 94104, U.S.A.
Tel: (415)956-4560
Telex: 023 340192 HK IND SFO

Industrial Promotion Office (New York),
Hong Kong Government Industrial Promotion Office
Tel: 1-212-752-3650
Telex: 025420086 NYHKO
Tower 56, 17/F, 126 East 56 Street, New York,
NY 10022, U.S.A.

Other Organisations

Hong Kong Trade Development Council

Rotenturmestrasse 1-3/8/24, A-1010 Vienna, Austria.
Tel: (0222)639818 Cable: CONOTRADREP WIEN
Telex: 115079 HKTDCA

Prinsengracht 771-773 g/f, 1017 JZ Amsterdam, Netherlands.
Tel: (020)253865 Cable:
CONOTRAD AMSTERDAM
Telex: 15081 HKTDC NL

Ulmenstrasse 49, D-6000 Frankfurt/Main, Federal
Republic of Germany.
Tel: (069)721655 Cable: CONOTRAD FRANKFURT
Telex: 414705 COFRAD

Hansastrasse 1, D-2000 Hamburg 13, Federal Republic of
Germany.
Tel: (040)417422 Cable: CONOTRAD HAMBURG
Telex: 214352 CONHAD

8 St. James's Square,
London SW1Y 4JZ, England.
Tel: (01)930-7955 Cable: CONOTRAD LONDON SW1
Telex: 916923 CONLON G

4 St. James's Square, Manchester M2 6DN, England.
Tel: (061)834-6164 Cable: CONOTRAD MANCHESTER
Telex: 669767 HKTDCM G

2 Piazzetta Pattari, 20122 Milan, Italy.
Tel: (02)865405 Cable: KONGTRAD MILAN
Telex: 333508 HKTDC I

18 rue d'Aguesseau, 75008 Paris, France.
Tel: (1)47 42 41 50
Telex: 641098 HKTDC

Brahegatan 30, 114 37 Stockholm, Sweden.
Tel: (08)610072 Cable: CONOTRAD STOCKHOLM
Telex: 58550 CONZH CH

Bellerivestrasse 3, 8008 Zurich, Switzerland.
Tel: (01)251-01-85 Cable: CONOTRAD JURICH
Telex: 58550 CONZH CH

548 Fifth Avenue, 6th Floor, New York, N.Y.
10036, U.S.A.
Tel: (212)730 0777
Telex: 710 581 6302 HKTDC NYK

333 North Michigan Avenue, Suite 2028, Chicago,
Illinois 60601, U.S.A.
Tel: (312)726-4515 Cable: CONOTRAD CHICAGO
Telex: 728335 HONG KONG CGO

154-2 World Trade Centre, 2050 Stemmons Freeway,
Dallas, Texas 75258, U.S.A.
Tel: (312)726-4515 Cable: HONGTRADS DALLAS
Telex: 791719 HKTDC DAL

350 South Figueroa Street, Suite 520, Los Angeles,
California 90071, U.S.A.
Tel: (213)-622-3194 Cable: CONOTRAD LOS ANGELES
Telex: 194288 HKTDC LA LSA

Suite 1100, National Building,
347 Bay Street, Toronto, Ont. M5H 2R7, Canada.
Tel: (416) 366-3594 Cable: CONOTRAD TORONTO
Telex: 06218056 HKTDC TOR

Suite 1996, One Biscayne Tower,
19/F, 2 Biscayne Boulevard, Miami, Florida 33131,
U.S.A.
Tel: (305) 374-3876/8
Telex: 803044 HK TDC MIA

Condominio Plaza Internacional, Primer Alto, Ofician
No. 27, Edificio del Banco Nacional de Panama, Via
Espanay Calle 55, Panama, Republic of Panama.
Tel: 695894 Telex: 2989 HKTDCP PG (From U.S.A. 3682989;
from other countries 3792989)

Osaka Ekimae No. 3 Building, 6/F, 1-1-3 Umeda,
Kita-ku, Osaka 530, Japan.
Tel:(06) 344-5211/4 Cable: CONNOTRADD OSAKA
Telex: J26917 HKTDCT

Toho Twin Tower Building, 4/F, 1-5-2 Yurakucho,
Chiyoda-ku, Tokyo 100, Japan.
Tel: (03) 502-3251/5 Cable: CONNOTRADD TOKYO
Telex: J26917 HKTDCT

71 York Street, Sydney, N.S.W. 2000, Australia.
Tel: (02) 298343/6 Cable: HONGKONREP SYDNEY
Telex: AA21313 CONSYD

Hong Kong Trade Development Council — Consultants

Hong Kong Trade Development Council,
Vekiarelli 19 & Ag. Filothei 2, Filothei,
152 37 Athens, Greece.
Tel: (1) 682-9701 Cable: KLONTRAD ATHENS
Telex: 219908 GHK GR

Balmes, 184,. Barcelona-6, Spain.
Tel: (3) 217-6250 Cable: PUBLICRELATIONS BARCELONA
6 (Spain)
Telex: 97862 SARPE

c/o Lintas Middle East,
Dubai Pearl Building, 14/F, Dubai, U.A.E.
Tel: 284236 Telex: 47200 LME EM

Hong Kong Trade Development Council,
16 Northside Drive, Northside Plaza, Kingston 6.
Jamaica, W.I.
Tel: 927-6486 Cable: CARMIL
Telex: 2214 JAMCARP JA

Hong Kong Tourist Association

Suite 200, 421 Powell Street, San Francisco,
California 94102-1568, U.S.A.
Tel: (415) 781-4582
Telex: 023 470247 LUYU UI

548 Fifth Avenue, New York,
N.Y. 10036-5092, U.S.A.
Tel: (212) 869-5008/9
Telex: 023 425817 LUYU UI

333 N. Michigan Avenue, Suite 2422, Chicago,
Illinois 60601, U.S.A.
Tel: (312) 782-3872 Telex: 023 4330404 DITTRENDDDCGO

125 Pall Mall, London SW1Y 5EA, England.
Tel: 01-930 4775
Telex: 051 8950160 LUYULOG

c/o Sergat Italia, s.r.l., Piazza Dei Cenci 7/A,
00186 Roma, Italy.
Tel: 656-91-12

38 Avenue George V, (53 rue Francois ler, 7/F),
75008 Paris, France.
Tel: 720-39-54 Telex: 042 650055 ANIF

Wieenau 1, D-6000 Frankfurt 1, West Germany.
Tel: Frankfurt 722841, 722842
Telex: 041 412402 HKTAFD

4th Fl., Toho Twin Tower Building, 1-5-2 Yurakucho,
Chiyoda-ku, Tokyo 100, Japan.
Tel: (03) 503-0731
Telex: 0720 2225678 LUYUTO J

Kintetsu Honmachi Building, 4-28-1 Honmachi,
Higashi-ku, Osaka 541, Japan.
Tel: (06)-282-1250

10 Collyer Quay 13-08 Ocean Building,
Singapore 0104, Republic of Singapore.
Tel: 5323668 Telex: RS28515 LUYU SN

National Australia Bank House, 20th fl, 255 George St.,
Sydney N.S.W. 2000, Australia.
Tel: 251-2855 Telex: 24668 HKTA SYD

Appendix IX

United States Tax Aspects

Unlike most jurisdictions, American citizens and residents (including greencard holders) living abroad and US corporations operating abroad are subject to US taxation on their worldwide income. However, many US tax benefits are available to expatriate Americans and the foreign operations of US business. These benefits can be enhanced by locating in a low tax jurisdiction such as Hong Kong.

Individuals

Although American citizens and residents living abroad are subject to US taxation, they can minimize the US tax impact if they meet the requirements of either of two qualifying tests. Qualifying individuals can elect to exclude from US taxable income up to US$70,000 of foreign earned income plus an additional exclusion measured by foreign housing costs. Self employed persons are permitted a foreign housing cost deduction.

Qualifying for the Exclusions

To qualify for the foreign earned income and housing cost exclusions, an individual must have foreign earned income, his tax home must be in a foreign country, and he must meet either of two tests:

1. The bona fide residence test, which requires that the individual be a bona fide resident of a foreign country or countries for a period that includes a full tax year; or

2. The physical presence test, which requires the individual to be present in a foreign country or countries at least 330 days during a period of 12 consecutive months. A US citizen may qualify under either the bona fide residence or physical presence test. A US resident alien working abroad can qualify under the physical presence test, and in certain limited cases, tax treaty non-discrimination rules may permit qualification under the bona fide residence rule.

The Foreign Housing Cost Amount Exclusion

In addition to the foreign earned income exclusion, qualified individuals may generally elect to exclude from US taxable income any reasonable foreign housing expenses that exceed a base housing amount. Housing expenses eligible for the exclusion are the reasonable expenses paid during the year by, or on behalf of, an individual and spouse and the dependents who live with them. Housing expenses include rent, utilities (other than telephone charges), insurance, certain occupancy taxes, non-refundable fees paid for securing a leasehold, rental of furniture and accessories, non-capital household repairs, and automobile parking costs. Capital expenditures and the cost of purchasing furniture and domestic labor do not qualify as housing expenses; nor do items such as mortgage interest and taxes that are otherwise deductible.

Eligible housing costs do not include those that are 'lavish or extravagant under the circumstances'. The excludable housing cost amount is the individual's actual foreign housing expenses that exceed a base housing amount of 16 percent of the annual salary of a federal employee at grade GS-14, step 1. The base housing amount for 1986 was US$7,109.

Foreign Tax Credit

All or a portion of an expatriate's income may be subject to tax in a foreign jurisdiction as a result of either the individual's residence or presence in the foreign country. Since US citizens and residents are subject to US tax on their worldwide income, the expatriate may be subject to tax both in the foreign country and in the United States. The foreign tax credit provisions of the US tax law are designed to eliminate the double taxation of foreign source income by allowing a credit against US tax for qualifying foreign taxes. This credit is generally limited to the US tax on the individual's foreign source income, and it cannot exceed the actual foreign tax paid or accrued. The US tax law does not permit an expatriate to take a foreign tax credit for any foreign taxes related to income excluded from US taxable income.

Tax Returns

US expatriates are not relieved of their US tax return filing requirements. The ordinary due date (April 15) for US income tax returns of individuals applies to expatriate taxpayers as well. However, a special two-month automatic extension of time for filing (to June 15) is provided to US citizens and resident aliens who, on the normal due date of the return, are either residing abroad or physically travelling outside the United States. It should be emphasized that the automatic extension of time for filing does not extend the time for payment of tax. Interest will be charged by the Internal Revenue Service on any unpaid balance of tax from the normal due date (April 15) until the date the return is filed, even if the due date is extended. US expatriates should avoid non-compliance with the tax law. A delinquent return may result in the disallowance of the foreign earned income and foreign housing cost amount exclusions.

Employer Tax Reimbursement Policies

Most US multinational employers have expatriate compensation policies designed to ensure that American employees on overseas assignments receive total compensation that is comparable to that which they would have earned if living in the United States, taking into account additional costs of living overseas, including income taxes. Generally, the policy is designed to ensure that the individual will not suffer combined taxes on income (US and foreign income and social security taxes) in excess of that which would have been paid if the individual were living in the United States.

A full explanation of tax reimbursement policies is beyond the scope of this chapter. Nevertheless, it is important that an expatriate fully understand the provisions of the employer's policy. In many cases the impact of a tax reimbursement policy may be greater than the impact of the income tax laws.

The Tax Benefit

American expatriates and their employers may find Hong Kong appealing from a tax point of view. A combination of low Hong Kong Salaries Tax and a limited US tax exclusion for foreign earned income and housing costs may provide a tax benefit to the expatriate. If a tax reimbursement plan exists, the employer may benefit by minimizing reimbursement of excess taxes to the expatriate.

Hong Kong Corporations Owned by US Persons

Many US citizens, residents and US corporations form Hong Kong corporations to generate income which may be deferred from current US taxation while incurring relatively low Hong Kong taxation.

The United States tax law has complex provisions for taxing the US shareholders on the undistributed income of a foreign corporation (incorporated outside the United States) if the corporation is considered a controlled foreign corporation ("CFC"). A CFC is a foreign corporation that is owned (by value or by vote) more than 50 percent by US shareholders directly or indirectly. A US shareholder is defined as a US person who owns 10 percent or more of the shares of the CFC. Nevertheless, certain types of income earned by a CFC may escape US taxation until the income is paid as a dividend or otherwise repatriated. A complete summary of the US taxation of a foreign corporation and its shareholders is beyond the scope of this section. However, to illustrate the benefits, the following is a summary of a few of the types of income which, if earned through a Hong Kong corporation, may avoid current taxation to its US shareholders:

1. Income derived from the sale of property manufactured, produced, constructed, grown or extracted within Hong Kong;

2. Income derived in connection with the sale of personal property for use consumption or disposition within Hong Kong;

3. Income derived in connection with the sale of personal property manufactured or produced by the Hong Kong corporation;

4. Income derived in connection with the performance of services (excluding personal service contracts) if the services are not provided for a related entity outside Hong Kong;

5. Income derived from the purchase and sale of personal property if both the purchase and sale are not from or to related entities.

Other US tax provisions eliminate the benefit of a US tax deferral to US persons who own shares in a foreign personal holding company or passive foreign investment company. US persons considering an equity interest in a foreign corporation should consult with their US tax advisor in order to be fully advised of the tax and compliance ramifications. Doing business in today's Hong Kong is enhanced by low taxation and an uncomplicated tax system which caters to international business. Nevertheless the reader is advised to consult with a tax advisor before starting a business or employment in Hong Kong, to be informed of the application of the tax law to the intricacies of modern life and business.

Appendix X

Example of Salaries Tax Liabilities

Facts

The taxpayer is a married man with two children.

His annual salary is HK$500,000

He also receives the following annual benefits and allowances.

Cost of living allowance ('COLA')	HK$ 60,000
Bonus	HK$100,000
Education allowance	HK$ 20,000
Leave passage allowance	HK$ 50,000

Full time maid employed by the company at a cost of HK$40,000

Use of a company car with all costs contracted for by the company. Total annual cost to company is HK$40,000

The company provides a flat at a monthly cost of HK$30,000. The taxpayer contributes HK$2,500 per month towards the cost of the flat. The company contracts for and pays utilities totalling HK$30,000 per annum.

Find. Currency exchange rate?

Analysis of cost and Salaries Tax liability for 1987/88

	Cost to Company HK$	Salaries Tax Liability HK$	
Salary	500,000	500,000	
COLA	60,000	60,000	
Bonus	100,000	100,000	
Education Allowance	20,000	20,000	Note 1
Leave Passage Allowance	50,000	—	Note 2
Full Time Maid	40,000	—	Note 3
Company Car	40,000	—	
Utilities	30,000	—	
	840,000	680,000	
Housing Cost 360,000 – 30,000	330,000		
Housing Benefit			
(10% × 680,000) – 30,000		38,000	Note 4
	1,170,000	718,000	
	Note 5		
Salaries Tax at 16.5%		118,470	Note 6

Notes: 1. If the employer contracted for and paid for the children's education, this amount would not be taxable.
2. Provided the allowance is fully expended on the holiday, it is not taxable.
3. Not taxable as the maid is under contract to and is paid for by the employer.
4. Housing benefit is 10% of assessable income less any housing contribution.
5. The cost to the employer is fully deductible for Hong Kong Profits Tax purposes.
6. Taxed at 16.5% as it is above the break-even level.

Appendix XI

Average, Median, and Quartiles of Monthly Salary Rates as at June 1986, Analysed by Major Economic Sector by Occupation*

Sector/Occupation‡	Average* HK$	Lower* Quartile HK$	Median* HK$	Upper* Quartile HK$
Manufacturing/Electricity, Gas and Steam				
Administration Manager/ Company Secretary/ Office Manager	11,200	7,600	8,800	13,400
Financial Manager/Chief Accountant/Accounting Manager	14,900	10,000	14,000	21,200
Production Manager	11,400	8,900	10,200	13,300
Marketing/Sales Manager	13,900	8,700	9,300	15,500
Plant/Mills Manager	10,600	7,400	9,100	13,500
Product Design Manager	14,600	9,900	14,700	19,000
Personnel Officer/Staff Relations Officer	7,100	5,100	5,400	7,900
Administrative Officer/ Executive Officer	6,500	5,400	5,900	7,200
Accountant	11,200	7,300	9,100	15,400
Electrical Engineer	21,000	15,800	19,000	26,700
Mechanical Engineer	9,200	5,200	7,900	10,400
Electronics Engineer	5,800	3,900	5,200	6,100
Production/Industrial Engineer	7,000	4,500	6,100	7,300
Building, Construction and Related Trades				
Administration Manager/ Company Secretary/ Office Manager	13,600	9,300	12,100	16,400
Financial Manager/Chief Accountant/Accounting Manager	15,700	8,500	12,800	23,500

Sector/Occupation‡	Average* HK$	Lower* Quartile HK$	Median* HK$	Upper* Quartile HK$
Administrative Officer/ Executive Officer	7,800	5,900	7,100	7,800
Accountant	10,100	7,300	10,400	12,500
Electrical Engineer	14,000	7,500	9,000	17,000
Mechanical Engineer	10,700	7,700	9,400	11,800
Safety Officer	6,700	6,500	6,800	7,600
Project Manager	17,100	11,700	16,500	22,200
Architect	22,900	15,400	20,700	28,600
Quantity Surveyor	11,900	8,200	10,200	14,500
Building Services Engineer	9,600	7,800	9,200	11,200
Civil Engineer	12,000	8,400	10,400	14,900
Structural Engineer	16,600	10,400	13,600	19,700
Wholesale/Retail and Import/Export Trades				
Personnel Manager/Staff Relations Manager	17,300	10,700	18,200	22,600

Administration Manager/
  Company Secretary/
  Office Manager
	14,400	11,300	13,000	16,400

Financial Manager/Chief
  Accountant/Accounting
  Manager
	16,400	12,300	14,600	19,800

Marketing Manager	15,800	12,400	14,800	18,000
Data Processing Manager/ E.D.P. Manager	15,200	12,600	14,200	17,100
Personnel Officer/Staff Relations Officer	7,900	6,900	7,500	8,000
Administrative Officer/ Executive Officer	7,500	6,500	7,400	9,100
Accountant	11,100	9,900	11,200	11,800
Merchandising Manager	19,400	12,800	18,400	19,800
Store Manager	9,800	5,700	7,400	14,400
Department Manager	10,300	5,100	7,800	15,300
Import/Export Shipping Manager	16,100	11,200	14,600	20,600
Merchandising Officer	11,400	5,700	6,800	18,700
Sales Manager	20,100	15,700	20,400	21,900

Sector/Occupation‡	Average* HK$	Lower* Quartile HK$	Median* HK$	Upper* Quartile HK$
Transport, Storage and Communications				
Personnel Manager/Staff Relations Manager	17,300	7,600	15,900	25,300
Administration Manager/ Company Secretary/ Office Manager	12,800	7,700	10,700	16,000
Personnel Officer/Staff Relations Officer	10,400	7,200	11,200	13,200
Administrative Officer/ Executive Officer	8,900	7,600	8,800	10,400
Financial Manager/ Chief Accountant/ Accounting Manager	14,000	8,200	11,400	18,100
Marketing Manager	13,200	9,200	12,100	16,100
Data Processing Manager/ E.D.P. Manager	17,900	10,800	14,400	24,300
Mechanical Engineer	9,400	3,900	5,500	8,000
Accountant	12,400	9,100	11,300	13,000
Electronics Engineer	15,900	12,400	17,300	17,700
Operations/Traffic Manager	14,200	9,300	13,000	17,000
Engineering Manager/ Chief Engineer	23,600	14,500	26,500	30,700
Aeronautic/Marine Engineer	15,900	8,900	12,900	22,800
Passenger Traffic Manager/ Customer Services Manager	9,500	5,500	7,700	9,600
Maintenance Manager	18,900	12,700	14,400	25,900
Financial Institutions and Insurance				
Personnel Manager/Staff Relations Manager	12,900	9,400	10,700	14,700
Administration Manager/ Company Secretary/ Office Manager	17,200	10,000	16,200	22,200
Financial Manager/Chief Accountant/Accounting				

Sector/Occupation‡	Average* HK$	Lower* Quartile HK$	Median* HK$	Upper* Quartile HK$
Manager	15,700	10,300	14,500	20,000
Marketing Manager	17,500	10,400	16,300	22,000
Data Processing Manager/ E.D.P. Manager	18,300	14,000	19,700	21,400
Training Officer	14,000	9,200	11,200	17,800
Personnel Officer/Staff Relations Officer	8,600	5,800	7,200	10,600
Administrative Officer/ Executive Officer	8,900	6,100	8,100	9,800
Marketing Research Executive	6,100	4,700	5,600	6,700
Accountant	11,900	10,800	12,000	13,200
Internal Auditor	16,200	9,300	14,700	19,000
Credit Manager	15,200	8,500	14,600	19,800
Cash Control Manager/ Chief Cashier	11,700	8,900	10,400	11,800
Bills Manager	12,400	8,300	10,500	14,300
Investment Manager	19,400	10,100	14,500	22,800
Branch (Full Services) Manager	10,300	7,900	9,200	10,800
Foreign Exchange Manager/ Chief Dealer	18,400	9,200	16,600	27,400
Investment Analyst	9,300	7,100	8,700	11,000

* The averages, medians and quartiles of monthly salary rates are calculated to the nearest hundred HK dollars.

‡ In each economic sector, averages, medians and quartiles of monthly salary rates of some occupations covered are not published due to confidentiality reasons.

Notes: 1. Apart from basic salary, salary rate is defined to include also cost-of-living allowance, guaranteed year-end bonus, commission and tips and other regular and guaranteed bonuses and allowances.
2. The monthly salary rates are derived by dividing the annual salary rates by twelve.
3. The lower quartile, median and upper quartile divide the range of salary rates into four equal parts. Such that 75%, 50% and 25% of employees receive salary rates equal to or more than the lower quartile, median and upper quartile respectively.

Appendix XII

Transport

Hong Kong has a land area of 1,070 square kilometers, of which only 17 percent is built-up, making its urban residential densities the highest in the world. Also among the highest in the world are the territory's vehicle densities. There are about 200 licensed vehicles for every kilometer of road, and Hong Kong's limited topography makes it increasingly difficult to provide additional road capacity in heavily built-up areas.

In terms of public transportation, however, the territory offers a variety of systems which are among the most varied and cheapest anywhere.

Every day, more than nine million passenger journeys are made on public transport facilities that include two high-capacity railways, buses, trams, minibuses, taxis and ferries.

Buses and Minibuses

Kowloon Motor Bus Company (1933) Ltd operates 200 regular daytime services in Kowloon and the mainland New Territories, and carries three million passengers daily. On urban routes, flat fares range from 80 cents to $2.00, while on rural services fares range from $1.00 to $4.40, according to route length. The buses are one-man operated, using an "exact fare" system.

With a fleet of more than 2,700 buses, the company is one of the largest road passenger transport operators in Southeast Asia. *China Motor Bus Company Ltd* operates 82 regular routes on Hong Kong Island, carrying 683,000 passengers daily. Fares range from $1.00 to $4.80, according to distance and category. The fleet is more than 1,000-strong, buses being one-man operated and almost entirely double-deck.

The two companies operate an extensive network of 13 daytime and two all-night services through the Cross-Harbor Tunnel under a pooled mileage scheme, while the Kowloon Motor Bus Company runs three cross-harbor routes of its own.

New Lantao Bus Company (1973) Ltd, operates six regular and two recreational routes on Lantau Island, which carry an average of 8,300 passengers daily. The greatest traffic occurs on summer and fall Sundays, when the normal fares of 80 cents to $5.70 are raised to between $1.60 and $9.00. The fleet comprises 11 double-deck and 43 single-deck vehicles.

Public Light Buses (PLBs) are 14-seat minibuses; their number has been fixed at a maximum of 4,350 vehicles, most of which are individually owned. Some PLBs are used on scheduled services (green minibuses) and others on non-schedules servces (red PLBs). The latter are free to operate anywhere, except where special prohibitions apply, without control over routes or fares. Currently they operate on 118 identifiable routes, often in competition with bus and tram services.

Green minibuses operate on fixed routes at fixed fares, which are generally somewhat higher than those of franchised buses. There are 41 green minibus routes on Hong Kong Island, 43 in urban Kowloon and 78 in the New Territories. Red PLBs carry almost a million passengers a day, whilst the green minibuses carry almost 520,000 daily.

Trams

Hongkong Tramways Ltd operates six services along the urban north shore of Hong Kong Island, between Shau Kei Wan and Kennedy Town, and around Happy Valley. The adult fare is a flat rate of 60 cents. The trams are all double-deck, and carry 335,000 passengers daily.

Peak Tramways Company Ltd operates a funicular railway from Central (Garden Road) to the Peak (Victoria Gap), and serves four intermediate stops en route. This cable-hauled line is 1.4 kilometers long and climbs 373 meters; it is the second steepest funicular in the world. The service began in 1888, and the fare is now $5.00.

Ferries

Star Ferry Company Ltd operates two passenger services linking Central District on Hong Kong Island with Tsim Sha Tsui and Hung Hom in Kowloon. Fares on the seven-minute crossing from Central to Tsim Sha Tsui are 70 cents on the upper deck and 50 cents on the lower deck, while a flat fare of 70 cents is charged on the Hung Hom crossing.

Hongkong and Yaumati Ferry Company Ltd provides a comprehensive network of ferry services across the harbor, and links Hong Kong Island with outlying districts and islands. The company operates 26 regular services. Passenger fares range from $1.00 to $11.00 for regular services, while the charge for vehicles on the cross-harbor services range from $3.00 for motorcycles and $6.00 for private cars, to $85.00 for vehicles over 11 meters long.

HYT's fleet comprises double and triple-deck ferries, water buses and hoverferries. Carrying an average of 210,000 passengers daily, the company is one of the world's largest ferry operators.

Railways

The Mass Transit Railway (MTR) is a metropolitian underground/elevated railway network comprising three lines with a combined length of 38.6 kilometers, and having 37 stations. Cars and stations are air conditioned, and fares range from $2.00 to $5.00 according to the distance traveled. There is at present one harbor crossing, between Admiralty and Tsim Sha Tsui, but a second combined road and rail link is currently under construction between Quarry Bay and Kwun Tong, and due to open early 1990.

Kowloon-Canton Railway Corporation operates a 34-kilometer line which connects Hung Hom in Kowloon with Lo Wu, at the border with China. There are 10 intermediate stations, including one on a loop line at Sha Tin racecourse, which is used for race-day traffic only.

Fares range from $1.50 to $14.50 (second class) according to the distance traveled. In addition, there are four daily through trains each way to and from Guangzhou at a fare of $125. Freight traffic is also handled on the railway.

A light-rail transit system is being built in the northwest New Territories, and due to be in operation by August 1988. The first phase will link Tuen Mun with Yuen Long. Kowloon-Canton Railway Corporation will operate the system, and initially 70 single-deck cars will be used. The company has ordered a number of double-deck buses to provide feeder services to the light railway.

Taxis

There are some 14,000 urban taxis, 2,640 New Territories taxis and 40 Lantau taxis, between them carrying an estimated 1.2 million passengers daily. The urban taxis operate throughout the territory, while the latter two categories are largely confined to the rural areas of the New Territories and Launtau Island respectively.

Fares are charged by metered tariff. Urban taxis charge $5.5 for the first two kilometers and 70 cents for every 0.25 kilometer thereafter. For New Territories and Lantau taxis, the flagfall is $4.00 for the first two kilometers, with a charge of 80 cents for every subsequent 0.4 kilometer.

Appendix XIII

Hotels
Hong Kong Island
Central
Furama
Tel. 5-255111;
Tx. 73081 FURAM HX

Hilton
Tel. 5-233111;
Tx. 73355 HILTL HX

Mandarin
Tel. 5-220111;
Tx. HX73653

Kowloon
Tsim Sha Tsui
Holiday Inn Golden Mile
Tel. 3-693111;
Tx. HX56332

Holiday Inn Harbour View
Tel. 3-7215161;
Tx. HX 38670

Hongkong Hotel
Tel. 3-676011;
Tx. 43838 HONHO HX

Hyatt Regency
Tel. 3-662321;
Tx. HX 43127

Marco Polo
Tel. 3-7215111;
Tx. 40077 MPHK HX

New World
Tel. 3-694111;
Tx. 35860 NWHTL HX

Causeway Bay
Excelsior
Tel. 5-767365;
Tx. HX 74550

Lee Gardens
Tel. 5-767211;
Tx. 75601 LEGAR HX

Park Lane
Tel. 5-7901021;
Tx. 75343 PLH HX

Peninsula
Tel. 3-666251;
Tx. 43821 PEN HX

Prince
Tel. 3-7237788;
Tx. 50950 PRN HX

Regal Meridien
Tel. 3-7221818;
Tx. 40955 HX HOMRO

Regent
Tel. 3-7211211;
Tx. 37134 REG HX

Royal Garden
Tel. 3-7215215;
Tx. 39539 RGHTL HX

Shangri-La
Tel. 3-7212111;
Tx. 36718 SHALA HX

Sheraton
Tel. 3-691111;
Tx. 45813 HKSHR HX

Appendix XIV

Private Clubs (With Sporting Facilities)

Aberdeen Boat Club
20 Shum Wan Road
Aberdeen
5-533032

Aberdeen Marina Club
8 Shum Wan Road
Aberdeen
5-558321

American Club
48/F Two Exchange Square
Central
5-8427414

Clearwater Bay Golf
and Country Club
Lot 227 DD 241
Po Toi O
New Territories
3-7191595

Craigengower Cricket Club
Leighton Road
Happy Valley
5-778331

Discovery Bay Golf Club
Lantau Island
5-9877271

Gordon Hard Boat Club
181/2 Miles, Castle Peak Road
New Territories
0-807336

Hebe Haven Yacht Club
101/2 Miles,
Hiram's Highway
Pak Sha Wan, Sai Kung
New Territories
3-7199682

Hilltop Country Club
Hilltop Road
Lo Wai Tsuen Wan
New Territories
0-4984481

Hong Kong Country Club
Deep Water Bay Road
Hong Kong
5-524165

Hong Kong Cricket Club
137 Wong Nei Chung
Gap Road
Hong Kong
5-746266

Hong Kong Football Club
Sports Road
Happy Valley
5-762808

Hong Kong Marina
Hebe Haven
Sai Kung
3-2811436

Indian Recreation Club
Sookunpoo Happy
Valley
5-761673

Jewish Recreation Club
70 Robinson Road
Mid-Levels
5-594872

Kowloon Bowling
Green Club
123 Austin Road
Kowloon
3-687733

Kowloon Cricket Club
10 Cox's Road Kowloon
3-674141

Ladies Recreation Club
10 Old Peak Road
The Peak
5-220151

Prison Officers' Club
51 Tung Tau Wan Road
Stanley
5-931745

Royal Hong Kong
Golf Club

Royal Hong Kong
Jockey Club
A) 2 Sports Rd.
Happy Valley
5-837811

B) Bee's River Country Club
Fanling
New Territories
0-900125

C) Shatin

Royal Hong Kong Yacht Club
A) Kellet Island
Causeway Bay
5-8322817

B) Middle Island
Deep Water Bay
5-8120365

C) Shelter Cove
Sai Kung
3-2812744

Sea Ranch Resort Club
Yilong Wan
Lantau Island
5-9892111

Shek-O Country Club
5 Shek O
Hong Kong
5-8094458

United Services
Recreation Club
1 Gascoigne Road
Kowloon
3-670672

Appendix XV

Clothing Sizes
British, American and European

Women	British	American	European
Dresses, coats, and suits	10	8	38
	12	10	40
	14	12	42
	16	14	44
	18	16	46
	20	18	48
Cardigans, sweaters, and blouses	32	10	38
	34	10	40
	36	12	42
	38	14	44
	40	16	46
	42	18	48
		20	
Stockings	8	—	0
	8½	8½	1
	9	9	2
	9½	9½	3
	10	10	4
Shoes	3½	5	35½
	4	5½	36
	4½	6	36½
	5	6½	37
	5½	7	38
	6	7½	38½
	7	8½	40
	7½	9	40½
	8	9½	41
	8½	10	42

Men	British	American	European
Suits	34	34	34
	35	35	46
	36	36	48
	37	37	49½
	38	38	51
	39	39	52½
	40	40	54
	41	41	55½
	42	42	57
Shirts	12½	12½	32
	13	13	33
	13½	13½	34
	14	14	35-36
	14½	14½	37
	15	15	38
	15½	15½	39
	16	16	40-41
	16½	16½	42
	17	17	43
	17½	17½	44
	18	18	45
Socks	10	—	38-39
	10½	10½	40-41
	11	11	42-43
	11½	11½	44-45
	12	12	46
	13	13	47-48
Shoes	6	7	39½
	7	8	41
	8	9	42
	9	10	43
	10	11	44½
	11	12	46
	12	13	47
Hats	6¾	6⅞	55
	6⅞	7	56
	7	7¼	57
	7⅛	7⅛	58
	7¼	7⅜	59
	7⅜	7½	60

Appendix XVI

Weights and Measures

Conversions Metric/Imperial

Symbol	When You Know	Multiply By	To Find	Symbol
		LENGTH		
in	inches	2.5	centimeters	cm
ft	feet	30	centimeters	cm
yd	yards	0.9	meters	m
mi	miles	1.6	kilometers	km
		AREA		
in^2	square inches	6.5	square centimeters	cm^2
ft^2	square feet	0.09	square meters	m^2
yd^2	square yard	0.8	square meters	m^2
mi^2	square miles	2.6	square kilometers	km^2
	acres	0.4	hectares	ha
		MASS (weight)		
oz	ounces	28	grams	g
lb	pounds	0.45	kilograms	kg
	short tons (2,000 lb)	0.9	tonnes	t
		VOLUME		
tsp	teaspoons	5	milliliters	ml
tbsp	tablespoons	15	milliliters	ml
fl oz	fluid ounces	30	milliliters	ml
c	cups	0.24	liters	l
pt	pints	0.47	liters	l
qt	quarts	0.95	liters	l
gal	gallons	3.8	liters	l
ft^3	cubic feet	0.03	cubic meters	m^3
yd^3	cubic yards	0.76	cubic meters	m^3
		LENGTH		
mm	millimeters	0.04	inches	in
cm	centimeters	0.4	inches	in
m	meters	3.3	feet	ft
m	meters	1.1	yards	yd
km	kilometers	0.6	miles	mi

AREA

cm²	square centimeters	0.16	square inches	in²
m²	square meters	1.2	square yards	yd²
km²	square kilometers	0.4	square miles	mi²
ha	hectares(10,000m²)	2.5	acres	

MASS(weight)

g	grams	0.035	ounces	oz
kg	kilograms	2.2	pounds	lb
t	tonnes (1000 kg)	1.1		

VOLUME

ml	milliliters	0.03	fluid ounces	fl oz
l	liters	2.1	pints	pt
l	liters	1.06	quarts	qt
l	liters	0.27	gallons	gal
m³	cubic meters	35	cubic feet	ft³
m³	cubic meters	1.3	cubic yards	yd³

TEMPERATURE

C	Celsius	9/5 Fahrenheit (then add 32)	F

Chinese Measurements

Chinese Length
 10 fan   = 1 tsun (Chinese inch)
   = 1.4625 inches
   = 37.1475 millimeters
 10 tsun = 1 chek (Chinese foot)
   = 1.21875 feet
 2.4 chek = 1 yard

Chinese Mass
 10 fan   = 1 tsin (mace)
   = 58.3333 grains
   = 3.77994 grams
 10 tsin = 1 leung (tael)
   = 1.3333 ounces
   = 37.7994 grams
 12 leung = 1 pound
 16 leung = 1 kan (catty)
   = 1.3333 pounds
   = 0.604790 kilograms
 100 gan = 1 tam (picul)
   = 1.19048 cwt (hundred weight) = 60.4790 kilograms

Index